METAPHOR AND MODERNIST

The Polarization of Alfred Loisy and His Neo-Thomist Critics

C.J.T. Talar

UNIVERSITY
PRESS OF
AMERICA

Copyright © 1987 by

University Press of America,® Inc.

4720 Boston Way
Lanham, MD 20706

Grateful acknowledgement for permission to use copyrighted material is made to the following publishers: Cambridge University Press (Imre Lakatos and Alan Musgrave, *Criticism and the Growth of Knowledge,* 1970; Maude Petre, *Alfred Loisy: His Religious Significance,* 1944); Casterman S.A. Editeurs (Emile Poulat, *Histoire, dogme et critique dans la crise moderniste,* 1979); E.P. Dutton & Co. (Alfred Loisy, *My Duel with the Vatican,* 1924); The Johns Hopkins University Press (Hayden White, *Metahistory,* 1973; Hayden White, *Tropics of Discourse,* 1978); Oxford University Press (Gabriel Daly, *Transcendence and Immanence,* 1980); Scholars' Press (T. Howland Sanks, *Authority in the Church: A Study in Changing Paradigms,* 1974); University of California Press (Stephen Pepper, *World Hypotheses,* 1970); *Irony,* 1974; Thomas S. Kuhn, The Structure of Scientific Revolutions, 1962 and 1970; Thomas S. Kuhn, *The Essential Tension,* 1977).

Library of Congress Cataloging-in-Publication Data

Talar, C. J. T., 1947-
Metaphor and modernist : the polarization of Alfred Loisy and his
neo-Thomist critics / C.J.T. Talar.
p.   cm.
Bibliography: p.
Includes index.
ISBN 0-8191-6654-5 (alk. paper)
1. Loisy, Alfred Firmin, 1857-   . 2. Modernism—Catholic Church—
History. 3. Thomists—History—19th century. 4. Catholic Church—
Doctrines—History—19th century.   I. Title.
BX4705.L7T34   1988
273'.9—dc19   87-21773
CIP

All University Press of America books are produced on acid-free
paper which exceeds the minimum standards set by the National
Historical Publication and Records Commission.

To My Parents

    -- Who wondered a lot what I was
doing in school all those years.

Acknowledgements

Just how collective an effort a book is becomes really apparent in the process of doing one. Chief among the many people who have made this one possible are Ron Chochol, Jim Finley, Gene Burke, Raymond Potvin, John McCarthy, John Ford, Stephen Happel, Robert Leavitt, Osborne Wiggins, Chris Kauffman, Francis Fiorenza, Roger Statnick, Thomas Donaghy, and Francesca van Duren (in roughly chronological order).

The roots of this do go back a long way now. It's sobering to see how comparatively little of it all this particular fruit in fact represents. But I suppose that's a comparatively common sentiment at this point.

v

Table of Contents

Abbreviations

APL -- Alfred Loisy, Autour d'un petit livre. Paris: Alphonse
    Picard et fils, 1903.

BLE -- Bulletin de litterature ecclésiastique.

Duel -- Alfred Loisy, Choses passées (1913). ET: My Duel with
    the Vatican. Translated by Richard W. Boynton. New York:
    Greenwood Press, Publishers, 1968.

EThL -- Ephemerides theologiae lovanienses.

GC -- Alfred Loisy, L'Evangile et l'eglise. ET: The Gospel and
    the Church. Translated by Christopher Home. Philadelphia:
    Fortress Press, 1976.

CP -- Alfred Loisy, Choses passées. Paris: Emile Nourry, 1913.

La crise moderniste -- Emile Poulat, Histoire, dogme et
    critique dans la crise moderniste. Tournai: Casterman, 1979.

Lettre 1901 -- E. Le Camus, Lettre de Monseigneur l'Evêque de
    la Rochelle et Saintes réglant la réorganisation des études
    ecclésiastiques dans son grand séminaire de la Rochelle. La
    Rochelle: Imprimerie Rochelaise, 1901.

Lettre 1902 -- E. Le Camus, Lettre sur la formation
    ecclésiastique de ses séminaristes. Paris: H. Oudin, 1902.

Mémoires -- Alfred Loisy, Mémoires pour servir à l'histoire
    religieuse de notre temps, 3 vols. Paris: Emile Nourry,
    1930-1931.

Movement -- Alec Vidler, The Modernist Movement in the Roman
    Church. Cambridge: Cambride University Press, 1934.

Q bib. XX -- Albert Houtin, La Question biblique au XXe
    siècle. Paris: Emile Nourry, 1906.

RCF -- Revue du clergé français.

Rule -- Paul Ricoeur, The Rule of Metaphor. Translated by
    Robert Czerny et al. Toronto: University of Toronto Press,
    1979.

Simples réflexions -- Alfred Loisy, Simples réflexions sur le
    decret "Lamentabili sane exitu" et sur l'encyclique "Pascendi
    dominici gregis". 2nd ed. Ceffonds: chez l'auteur, 1908.

SSR -- Thomas S. Kuhn, The Structure of Scientific Revolutions.
Chicago: University of Chicago Press, 1962.

Tropics -- Hayden White, Tropics of Discourse. Baltimore: The
Johns Hopkins University Press, 1978.

Variety -- Alec Vidler, A Variety of Catholic Modernists.
Cambridge: Cambridge University Press, 1970.

Introduction

> For scholastic philosophy and theology they have only
> ridicule and contempt . . . . the passion for novelty
> is always united in them with hatred of
> scholasticism, and there is no surer sign that a man
> is on the way to modernism than when he begins to
> show his dislike for this system.
>
> Pascendi Dominici Gregis[1]

> If Catholicism is to live, the school-theology must
> go.
>
> George Tyrrell[2]

In the latter decades of the 19th century Alfred Loisy
(1857-1940) arrived at the same conclusion as his fellow
modernist, Tyrrell, though via a somewhat different route.
Loisy's exposure to the reigning scholasticism during his
seminary years was, as he later described it, "an excruciatingly
harrowing experience . . . four years of mental and moral
torture."[3] Apparently the heavily intellectualist bent of that
theology succeeded in disturbing the young seminarian's hitherto
unquestioning acceptance of the truths of the Catholic faith.
Having confided his state of mind to his spiritual director, he
was urged that a religion which had satisfied geniuses such as
St. Augustine, St. Thomas Aquinas, Pascal, Bossuet, and Fénelon
was surely not unworthy of his own adherence. In his
autobiography he later reflected, "I did not then dream of
answering him that these men had not lived in the Nineteenth
Century, and that no one could tell what might have been the turn
of mind of a Blaise Pascal who had been born a contemporary of
Ernest Renan."[4] Loisy was able to regain some peace of mind
through the largely independent study of Hebrew. But if
linguistic studies provided in the short run a distraction from
unsettling doubts, their longer range effect was to raise
questions of even greater consequence regarding adherence to
scholastic orthodoxy.

After ordination to priesthood, while a student at the
Institut catholique at Paris, Loisy's exposure to Tischendorf's

1

edition of the New Testament led him to compare the various gospel narratives, bringing into relief the contradictions in the texts. At this stage, if Loisy did not find the gospel accounts reliable, nonetheless he still adhered to the events to which the texts bore witness. If he did not find the accounts of the virgin birth or of the resurrection to be free from problems, nevertheless, he continued to hold that Jesus was born of a virgin and he rose again after his death. "It was an insecure position, but I was not, and could not then be, aware of it."[5] And if, in mid-1883, he could write, "I was still too little convinced of my critical results to employ them as conclusive arguments against the substantial truth of [the Church's] dogmas"[6], that lack of confidence would erode gradually before the increasing mastery of critical biblical exegesis. And if confidence in the results of scientific exegesis increased, adherence to Catholic dogma could only undergo significant change. Already by 1886 Loisy can write in some personal notes, "that the literal sense of the theological formulas becomes constantly less credible . . . I see more and more distinctly . . ."[7]

Thus from the 1880s Loisy had the impression of assisting at what Emile Poulat calls "the end of the mental universe consecrated by the Council of Trent."[8] He was keenly aware of the challenge to that thought world posed by critical scholars such as Renan, and still more impressed by the insufficiency of Catholic apologists to meet that challenge. Of Abbé Fulcran Vigouroux, S.S., "the leading French Catholic apologist for the Bible", Loisy observes: "his instruction and his writings did more to turn me away from orthodox opinions in this regard than all the rationalists together, Renan included."[9] From the early 1890s, then, the exegete began to evolve a plan by which a transition from that Tridentine universe to the one shaped by modern science could be effected. Occupying the second chair of Scripture at the Institut catholique (Vigouroux occupied the first), Loisy had a forum for his exegetical endeavors, a forum which he extended through publication of his lectures in a small periodical which he founded, L'Enseignment biblique. Seemingly cut short by his dismissal from the Institut catholique in 1893 due to his views on biblical inspiration, and his assignment to the non-academic post of chaplain to a convent school at Neuilly, in reality his designs merely underwent modification. Cut off from the bibliographical resources for critical exegetical work, and obliged to teach catechism as part of his regular duties as chaplain, his attention turned to wider religious questions. His exegetical research had challenged his understanding of the traditional dogmas; further, it undermined the apologetic which sought to make them credible. Loisy's effort to reformulate the traditional teaching so as to adapt it to minds formed by the contemporary intellectual climate inevitably encompassed attempts at a new apologetic. Thus it was during the course of the years

2

spent at Neuilly, 1893-1900, that the scholar formulated the ideas which, upon publication, would mark him as a threat to orthodoxy, would become the object of ecclesiastical condemnation, and would lead to his eventual excommunication in 1908.

The ideas that constituted his revisionist apologetic gained written expression over the course of July 1898 through May 1899, in the form of a long work which never saw publication integrally. Drawn from it were the substance of six articles which appeared in the Revue du clergé français (beginning in Dec. 1898 through Oct. 1900) under the pseudonym "A. Firmin"; much of the material that formed L'Evangile et l'Eglise (1902) -- the book which precipitated the modernist crisis; and something of the work of clarification which followed, Autour d'un petit livre (1903).[10] Drawn from the same larger work, the positions taken in these several publications are rather consistent throughout. Nonetheless, opposition to them mounted comparatively slowly at first; only with the publication of Autour d'un petit livre did growing uneasiness transform into massive resistance.

Not that orthodox uneasiness with Loisy had to wait upon his apologetical efforts for its arousal. Attacks upon his more strictly historical and exegetical work had commenced with the publication of his first book, Histoire du canon de l'Ancien Testament (1890), while an article published that same year likely was delated to Rome.[11] Two years later the students of Saint Sulpice were forbidden to attend Loisy's lectures at the Institut catholique. Despite these earlier incidents -- to which must be added the circumstances surrounding his dismissal from the Institut -- the initial Firmin articles passed unremarked. W. J. Wernz adduces a number of factors contributory to this: their place of publication, a liberal journal with a limited readership; their publication under a pseudonym; the brevity of the statement made in them, together with their treatment more on the level of principle than on concrete example.[12] Only with the sixth Firmin article did Loisy incur the censure of Cardinal Richard, Archbishop of Paris. The series was interdicted, and the exegete's collaboration with the review in question ceased.[13]

More elaborate rejoinders really only commenced with the publication of L'Evangile et l'Eglise. Under the form of a refutation of the German liberal Protestant exegete, Adolf von Harnack, the book advanced Loisy's aim of a renovated apologetic for Catholicism. Partly because a portion of the readership was impressed by the tenor of the critique of Harnack they tended to overlook the deeper implications of the position on which that critique was founded. The suspicions of others were not lulled so readily; the book provoked a mounting tide of opposition.

Its critics included among their ranks ecclesiastical polemicists such as the Abbé Hyppolite Gayraud, a former Dominican noteworthy for his political activity. His articles appeared in L'Univers[14] and had their counterpart in another publication of the same conservative tenor, La Vérité française, these authored by Abbé Charles Maignen[15] who had lately written against Americanism.[16] Gayraud's articles have been judged "as violent as uncomprehending"[17], an understandable evaluation since it is evident from the argumentation that their author has read Loisy hastily and Harnack not at all. Still, even if he be faulted on his account of Loisy's position, Gayraud remains representative of a line of approach taken by a certain style of criticism. His engagement with Loisy's apologetic will be considered at greater length in the second chapter.

L'Evangile et l'Eglise generated opposition from among the episcopacy as well. Cardinal Perraud faulted the book for its "vague, insidious propositions, bordering on double meaning, which, accompanied by 'perhaps' and question marks, slip furtively into the mind and carry with them, if not deliberate and consented doubt, at least hesitation and a sort of vertigo."[18] Mgr. Emile-Paul Le Camus, bishop of La Rochelle, replied in a brochure, Vraie et fausse exégèse (1903). If Perraud could fault Loisy with being difficult to understand, Le Camus could be faulted for not having understood the exegete, or at least with having failed to come to grips with the heart of his position. Mgr. Mignot, an archbishop of liberal tenor and supportive of Loisy, wrote to the latter: "Evidently, Mgr. Le Camus has responded beside the point and has not refuted your thesis."[19] Cardinal Richard once again resorted to condemnation, declaring the book of "a nature gravely to trouble the faith of believers in the fundamental dogmas of the Catholic teaching."[20] Seven other bishops, including Cardinal Perraud, gave their adherence to the ordinance of condemnation. One of this number, Mgr. Sonnois, archbishop of Cambrai, in a pastoral letter counterposed to Loisy's developmental apologetic: "Truth is one and does not change."[21]

While the arguments of a polemicist such as Gayraud, or of a member of the episcopacy such as Perraud were certainly grounded in theology, nonetheless, professional theologians constituted a third source of critical evaluation. Among their ranks were those such as Pére Joseph Brucker, S.J., whose input to Cardinal Richard was instrumental in the latter's condemnation of L'Evangile et l'Eglise.[22] Brucker's fellow Jesuit, Pére Léonce de Grandmaison, took a more moderate tone toward Loisy than his confrere. In marked contrast to Gayraud, who had not read Harnack, de Grandmaison had devoted a long critique to the German exegete.[23] This provided a basis for a rather informed study of L'Evangile et l'Eglise.[24] (Interestingly, Loisy never did engage moderates such as Grandmaison, but consistently chose as his

4

opponents the more conservative.)

This sampling of sources of critical rejoinder is hardly complete with regard to individual names. It also glosses over the extent of the internal diversity among the critics themselves[25], and ignores those who were supportive of the exegete in print in face of orthodox objectors.[26] Nonetheless it does provide a sense of the reaction engendered by Loisy's program, the net effect of which has been summarized by Albert Houtin:

> The orthodox campaign was begun and managed by Abbé Gayraud. The bishops' intervention stirred up the refuters more yet, and rendered the defenders more circumspect. The initial effect of these polemics and anathemas was to sell out the famous book promptly. The last copies fetched an elevated price.[27]

Urged by supporters to clarify sections of his book that critics had found ambiguous, or had misunderstood, Loisy chose to write another, rather than to revise the work which had occasioned the controversy. _Autour d'un petit livre_ took the form of a series of seven "letters" addressed to various people. The second, "Letter to a Cardinal, on the Biblical Question" was directed to Cardinal Perraud; while the third, "Letter to a Bishop, on the Criticism of the Gospels and Especially on the Gospel of Saint John" had Mgr. Le Camus in view. Thus there emerges a conversation of sorts between the exegete and at least some of his critics.

In this work of clarification Loisy's neo-Catholicism stood out more starkly, presented without the shading afforded by the critique of Harnack present in its predecessor. Unsurprisingly, it provoked a renewed response, from each of the three principal sources noted earlier, and in some cases from the same individuals. Gayraud once again took pen in hand[28], although this time exhibiting signs that he had done his homework more carefully. Nevertheless, if he read Loisy more attentively, his line of criticism remained the same. These articles which again appeared in _L'Univers_ apparently enjoyed considerable success -- according to Poulat, "often reproduced, cited, commented on in provincial periodicals and translated widely."[29] If Gayraud had succeeded in gaining greater influence for his opinions, according to another Loisy sympathizer, George Fonsegrive, the former Dominican had not succeeded in gaining the requisite understanding of his object of attack. In a letter Fonsegrive commented, "Our theologians understand next to nothing of what is happening. Abbé Gayraud is a very remarkable example."[30] Maignen also renewed his polemics, once again in two series of articles.[31]

From the episcopal camp Le Camus responded with another brochure, Fausse exégèse, mauvaise théologie (1904). Discussion of Le Camus' work likewise will be deferred to the second chapter. Perraud's instruction to the clergy of his diocese appeared in L'Univers[32], and was later published as a brochure, Les erreurs de M. Loisy condemnées par le Saint-Siège. Other bishops also contributed to a growing corpus of anti-Loisy literature.[33]

Among the theologians, only one response will be noted here: that of Pierre Bouvier, S.J. In L'exégèse de M. Loisy (1903; 2nd edition 1904) he characterized the exegete's method as one of conserving the terms of the traditional teaching while modifying their meaning, under the pretext of harmonizing Catholic thought with the modern spirit.[34] Bouvier is singled out here, however, not so much for his antiloisyste brochure, but for his contribution to a work which, while not designed for publication, was destined to have greater effect on the official reaction to Loisy. In mid-September 1903, together with the Sulpician Georges Letourneau, Bouvier began researching the most suspect pages of L'Evangile et l'Eglise. From this book they extracted 18 propositions which, after the appearance of Autour d'un livre, they expanded to 41, then condensed to 38. These were communicated to Cardinal Richard, who in turn transmitted them to the Holy Office augmented by his own authority. Although the Holy Office decided to condemn the two "little red books" as such, rather than focus on specific propositions extracted from them[35], in 1907 it did issue a Syllabus of condemned propositions, Lamentabili Sane Exitu. The point of departure for the Roman measure was the Paris Syllabus drawn up by Letourneau and Bouvier, with the collaboration of the Roman neo-Thomist Louis Billot, S.J., under the patronage of Cardinal Perraud and transmitted to Rome through the offices of Cardinal Richard.[36]

Lamentabili, issued in July 1907, was soon followed by an antimodernist encyclical, Pascendi Dominici Gregis, which appeared the following September. The apparent diversity which characterized the movement which by then had escalated from "loisysme" to "modernism", an international effort on the part of theological innovators and reforming Catholics to adapt the Church to the modern spirit, was viewed as a tactic. According the the encyclical, "the Modernists . . . employ a very subtle artifice, namely to present their doctrines without order and systematic arrangement into one whole, scattered and disjointed from one another, so as to appear to be in doubt and uncertainty, while they are in reality firm and steadfast . . ."[37] Underlying surface diversity, then, there could be discerned a deeper unity. Pascendi proceeded to link theological conclusions and critical method to a philosophical base[38], reconstructing a system from the scattered fragments. Thus "every Modernist sustains and comprises within himself many personalities, a believer, a theologian, an historian, a critic, an apologist, a reformer."[39] Impressive credentials which produced a system impressive in its perniciousness: "a synthesis of all heresies". In the assessment by Friedrich von Hügel, also an active partisan of the modernist movement,

> the vehemently scholastic redactor's determination to piece together a strictly coherent, complete a priori system of 'modernism' and his self-imposed restriction to medieval categories of thought as the vehicles for describing essentially modern discoveries and requirements of mind, make the identification of precise authors and passages very difficult.[40]

With that Loisy would likely have agreed.[41] But, prescinding from precise passages and their precise authors, to the exegete's mind the task of ascertaining who was struck by the encyclical was not at all difficult. In reemphasizing scholasticism once more as the orthodox standard, Pascendi undercut in principle any alternative formulations. For this reason he said, "The true is found attacked in the false."[42]

Even in this brief overview the polarization of positions that increasingly came to mark Loisy and his critics, that divided "loisystes" and neo-scholastics, and that found the most extreme formulation in the opposition of modernists and integralists, is readily apparent. In the foregoing it finds symptomatic expression in the reiterated comments that the critics have really failed to understand Loisy's thought -- as reflected in statements by Mgr. Mignot and George Fonsegrive. Complaints were not all one-sided. Repeatedly, Loisy's theological opponents make reference to the ambiguity of the exegete's expression -- often represented as a studied ambiguity. So Perraud. According to critics, one especially noteworthy form of equivocation resided in the tendency to use orthodox terminology but with a very different meaning than that supplied by the orthodox tradition. In this connection Bouvier has been cited; similar observations could be multiplied.

Seemingly at issue is something which runs deeper than a studied ambiguity of language, or innovation in theological vocabulary. The portrait of modernism presented by the encyclical and von Hügel's evaluation of that points to a divergence that runs deeper than terminology and broader than Loisy. It is not simply a translation problem, a rendering of "modern discoveries" into "medieval categories". It reaches down to the level of foundations, of fundamental assumptions. Loisy had said that the encyclical had attacked the truth by intermingling it with falsity. At issue was something of the

7

nature of truth itself -- unchanging and unchangeable for a scholastic such as Mgr. Sonnois. For Loisy, under the influence of historical studies, truth had to be something rather different. Once again, von Hügel witnesses to something of the depth of divergence. Referring to Loisy, he wrote in 1900, "as Duchesne says of him -- he worries his antagonists, his whole attitude of mind and treatment of subjects being so different from theirs, that they slip about the premises, trying to find a common starting-point and measure, and failing utterly."[43]

Certainly there were substantive issues which divided Loisy and his critics. The ordinance promulgated by the Cardinal Archbishop of Paris in January 1903 targeted several areas in L'Evangile et l'Eglise which merited reproval, describing the book as "of a nature to trouble the faith of believers in the fundamental dogmas of the Catholic teaching, notably on the authority of the Scriptures and of the tradition, on the divinity of Jesus Christ, on his infallible knowledge, on the Redemption brought about by his death, on the Eucharist, on the divine initiation of the Sovereign Pontificate and the Episcopate."[44] The propositions extracted from Loisy's book by Bouvier and Letourneau, and soon supplemented by a greater number taken from Autour d'un petit livre, rendered the areas of difficulty more precise. And an examination of other critics and other condemnations would yield still further differences of substance.

Nonetheless, the foregoing survey of Loisy's apologetical efforts and critical response suggests that other factors are at work. The recurring references to theological vocabulary, conceptualization, to the meaning of words indicate that it is not only a question of what is said but also of how it is said. Language is not a mere clothing of content, a transparent medium through which content comes to light. Language is itself constitutive of content; it sets limits and creates possibilities regarding what can come to expression, what cannot be said. The recurring references to language suggest that something of the polarization which occurred between Loisy and his scholastic critics can be accounted for by examining their respective linguistic structures, especially their characteristic metaphors. Further, just as the foregoing survey pointed to very profound differences between positions, foundational differences engaging "premises", reflecting divergent world views, so it will be argued that linguistic divergence has deep roots reaching to that level. To state this rather abstractly, it will be argued that theological problems (and their solutions) have to be treated in the context of the discourse in which they arise, since what counts as a problem (or solution) in a discourse depends on factors internal to that discourse which must be conceptualized and assessed as such. Somewhat more precisely, it will be maintained that the dominant metaphors used by Loisy and his theological opponents inform their understanding of what is

8

problematic; that the links among these metaphors -- their respective "metaphorical networks" inform their mutual understanding (or misunderstanding); that such metaphorical networks are reflective of "root metaphors" which are foundational for thought, and which may enhance or inhibit the ability to communicate, depending on the form they assume.

The conceptualization of factors internal to discourse will be somewhat complex. The first stage of that will depend upon certain concepts fundamental to Thomas S. Kuhn's assessment of scientific growth and the adaptation of those to the theological positions of interest here. The task of the first chapter, then, will be to provide a summary exposition of Kuhn's model of scientific development, arguing for the utility of its application to theology. The broad lines of such application will be indicated with respect to neo-Thomism and modernism, to delineate the theological contexts from which theological discourse emerged. Since the polarization of Loisy and critics is under scrutiny here, Kuhn's concept of "incommensurability" will assume prominence. Partisans of rival paradigms often evidence tendencies to talk past one another, to fail to make contact with the other's viewpoint. Kuhn's conceptualization will provide some direction for investigating this phenomenon, obviously present in neo-Thomist - modernist exchanges.

Kuhn's framework points to the phenomenon of polarization, and indicates that language plays an important role in its occurrence. Since the intent here is not only to note the presence of "incommensurability" or to simply comment on its extent, but to investigate its dynamics, the second chapter will proceed to an analysis of metaphor. Both Loisy's work and that of representative critics will be examined with a view toward eliciting the characteristic metaphors and the networks in which they are embedded. Then the work of Max Black and Paul Ricoeur will be summarized to provide a framework to approach the dynamics of metaphorical interaction, of mutual (mis)understanding.

Incommensurability engages foundational levels of thought. For Kuhn this extends to the world views underlying rival positions. As a way of linking the analysis of language pursued in chapter 2 with this further aspect, Hayden White's analysis of historical narrative will be utilized. For White, world views are themselves linguistically constituted, and this provides an avenue toward understanding the dynamics of the interaction of works reflecting differing historiographies. Since the issue of historicity is central to the exchanges between Loisy and his critics, and since his exegetical and apologetical work falls within the range of historical narrative and philosophy of history considered by White, a theological application of that conceptualization will be attempted in the third chapter -- again

9

with a view toward understanding polarization of position from the standpoint of what was <u>said</u>.

A third aspect of incommensurability targeted by Kuhn returns to a less encompassing level. Failure to make contact occurs because partisans of rival positions do not experience the same things as problematic (and in consequence also differ on what will be considered an acceptable solution), diverge in their methodological commitments, and in what they deem as appropriate data. To examine this more concrete level, more concrete issues will be pursued. Accordingly, the fourth chapter will focus on their respective approaches to eucharist, viewed against a backdrop of understandings of sacrament and Church.

A concluding chapter will draw the three operative frameworks together somewhat -- Kuhn's on incommensurability, Black's and Ricoeur's on metaphor, White's on linguistic analysis of historical narrative -- and provide some assessment of their utility for understanding theologies.

Notes to Introduction

[1]The Encyclical of His Holiness Pius X on the Doctrines of the Modernists. Translated by Thomas E. Judge. (n.p.), p. 89.

[2]George Tyrrell to Wilfred Ward, 4 Jan. 1904. Quoted in Maisie Ward, Insurrection verses Resurrection, (New York: Sheed & Ward, 1937), p. 167.

[3]Alfred Loisy, Choses passées (1913). ET: My Duel with the Vatican. Translated by Richard W. Boynton. (New York: Greenwood Press, Publishers, 1968), p. 67.

[4]Duel, p. 74. Ernest Renan (1823-1892). A treatment of Renan's impact upon French Catholicism may be found in Vytas V. Gaigalas, Ernest Renan and His French Catholic Critics. North Quincy, Mass.: The Christopher Publishing House, 1972.

[5]Ibid., p. 87.

[6]Ibid., p. 96.

[7]Ibid., p. 101.

[8]I am unable to retrieve the source of this quote from my notes.

[9]Duel, p. 88. In an oft-quoted passage, Loisy has characterized the tenor of Vigourouox's approach: "One found it easy, for example, to abandon all belief in the flood of Genesis after hearing the professor explain gravely that the passages attributed to the Yahwist writer (after the source in which God is given the name Yahwe) are a description of what was going on in the Eternal mind, while the passages called Elohist (after the source which employs as the divine name the collective noun Elohim) have regard to the revelation of these thoughts to Noah, and their practical execution; that, the flood covering only the then inhabited portion of the earth, the ark was plenty large enough to contain all the animal species known to Noah; that a calculation had been made, and the ark shown to be capable of enclosing six thousand, six hundred and sixty-six species, allowing so much cubic space to each couple -- and much more of the same sort!" p. 89.

[10]The contributions of the livre inédit to these publications are discussed in William J. Wernz, The "Modernist" Writings of Alfred Loisy: An Analysis. Unpublished Ph.D. Dissertation: University of Iowa, 1971.

[11]Duel, pp. 120-125. The article in question was "Les Proverbs de Salomon", Revue des Religions (1890): 28-44; 97-115; 217-240.

[12]Wernz, pp. 72, 119n.

[13]The censured article, "La Religion d'Israël", was the first of the Firmin articles concretely to treat biblical matters at length. The article was to have been in three parts, only the first of which actually appeared. Loisy had the study published integrally as a brochure (1901) which he retained for private circulation only. A greatly expanded version was published in 1906 which formed the basis of an English translation. See Emile Poulat, ed., Alfred Loisy, sa vie son oeuvre, (Paris: Editions du centre national de la rechreche scientifique, 1960), pp. 305, 306, 310. Valentine Moran has noted that while this article was the one to receive censure, the entire series was implicitly in view: "The ban on Loisy's writing in the RCF was not due only to his final article, on the religion of Israel. This certainly revived the fears that had led to exclusion from the Institut. . . . There can be little doubt that Loisy's treatment of miracles and prophecy as proofs of revelation and the extent to which he was prepared to use the notion of development were as much factors in his condemnation as was the article." Valentine Moran, S.J., "Loisy's Theological Development", Theological Studies 40 (1979): 426-427.

[14]1, 2, 4, 9 and 10 Jan. 1903.

[15]18, 19, 22 Jan., 4-9 Feb. 1903; second series: 2, 4, 6, 7, 12, 14, 21 March 1903. La Vérité française had its origins in a schism of L'Univers in 1893.

[16]Etudes sur l'Americanisme: Le Père Hecker, est-il un saint? (1898). On Americanism see James Hennesey, S.J., American Catholics, (New York: Oxford University Press, 1981), ch. XV. On Maignen's role see Thomas T. McAvoy, C.S.C., The Great Crisis in American Catholic History, 1895-1900, (Chicago: Henry Regnery Company, 1957), especially chapter 5.

[17]The judgment is René Marlé's. Cited by Emile Poulat, Histoire, dogme et critique dans la crise moderniste, (Tournai: Casterman, 1979), p. 127.

[18]Semaine religieuse d'Autun 7 Feb. 1903; also in L'Univers 6 Feb. 1903. Extracts cited in Albert Houtin, La Question biblique au XXe siècle, (Paris: Librairie E. Nourry, 1906), pp. 91-92.

[19]Mignot to Loisy, 3 Feb. 1903. Alfred Loisy, Mémoires pour servir à l'histoire religieuse de notre temps, 3 vols. (Paris: Emile Nourry, éditeur, 1930-1931), II: p. 213.

[20]Duel, p. 230. Signed 7 Jan. 1903 and promulgated a few days later.

[21]Pastoral letter dated 11 Jan. 1903. Poulat, La crise moderniste, p. 137n.

[22]Joseph Brucker, S.J., "La condemnation du livre L'Evangile et l'Eglise", Etudes 94 (1903): 495–511.

[23]Etudes 20 March 1902.

[24]Etudes 20 Jan. 1903: 145–174. In Choses passées Loisy characterized this study as "quite sensible and moderate, in no way flattering, but written in a dignified manner by a man with whom I could have entered into a discussion . . . ." Duel, pp. 229–230. C.P., p. 249.

[25]Poulat notes, for example, that among the responses to Gayraud's series were those which took him to task for going too far, while others for not going far enough. La crise moderniste, pp. 128–129.

[26]Poulat cites Abbé Naudet writing in La Justice sociale, Abbé Dabry in L'Observateur français, and Abbé Bricout (under a pseudonym) in the Revue du clergé français. Ibid., pp. 157–160. In his article Bricout also noted the moderation and equitable nature of Grandmaison's study.

[27]Houtin, Q bib. XX, p. 88.

[28]24 Oct., 16 and 30 Nov., 2, 14, 28 Dec. 1903.

[29]Poulat, La crise moderniste, p. 191.

[30]Fonsegrive to Paul Sabatier, 24 Dec. 1903. Ibid., pp. 201–202n.

[31]La Vérité française 24, 25, 28, 29, 30 Oct. 1903; 11, 12, 13, 17, 23, 26 Nov. and 2, 6, 12, 16, 23 Dec. 1903.

[32]17–18, 20 Feb. 1904.

[33]See Houtin, Q bib. XX, ch. VII.

[34]Poulat, La crise moderniste, p. 213. Cf. Gayraud's judgment that, with regard to dogmatic formulae, Loisy's language is perfectly Catholic, "but I would desire the substance [chose] with the word . . . . Let us be Catholic not only in language but let us be such also in thought and in sentiment." "L'Interprétation du loisysme", RCF, 15 Dec. 1903, p. 197.

13

[35]On 16 Dec. 1903 the Holy Office condemned, together with L'Evangile et l'Eglise and Autour d'un petit livre, three additional works by Loisy: La Religion d'Israël, Etudes évangéliques, and Le Quatrième évangile.

[36]A comparison of the two documents is given in Paul Dudon, "Origines françaises du décret Lamentabili (1903-1907)", BLE 32 (1931): pp. 94-95. The principal documentation from which Dudon reconstructed the story of Bouvier's and Letourneau's contribution has been published in Roger Aubert, "Aux origines de la réaction antimoderniste: deux documents inédits", EThL 37 (1961): 557-578.

[37]Pascendi Domenici Gregis. Judge, p. 51.

[38]In doing so the encyclical was only applying to the movement a logic which had already surfaced in relation to L'Evangile et l'Eglise. In Nov. 1903 Vigouroux had observed to his fellow Sulpician Letourneau: "The most serious and most competent men who have read the book repeat that it is not a work of exegesis, nor of criticism, but the pure and simple application of a Kantian and evolutionist system of philosophy." Quoted in Dudon, p. 89.

[39]Pascendi. Judge, p. 51.

[40]Friedrich von Hügel, "Loisy", The Encyclopedia Britannica, 11th ed., vol. 16, (New York: Encyclopedia Britannica, Inc., 1911), p. 927. By one of his contemporaries von Hügel was called "the lay bishop of the modernists". Paul Sabatier, Modernism. Translated by C.A. Miles. (London: T. Fisher Unwin, 1908), p. 42. The comment pays tribute to von Hügel's organizational efforts in introducing the work of critical scholars to one another, generating support for threatened positions and persons, and generally encouraging them in the work of theological renewal of Roman Catholicism. More recently, Sabatier's characterization of von Hügel was reaffirmed in Alec Vidler's less ecclesiastical metaphor, designating the Baron, "the chief engineer of the modernist movement". Alec Vidler, A variety of Catholic Modernists, (Cambridge: Cambridge University Press, 1970), p. 113. On von Hügel see Michael de la Bedoyere, The Life of Baron von Hügel. London: J.M. Dent & Sons Ltd., 1951. John J. Heaney, The Modernist Crisis: von Hügel. Washington: Corpus Books, 1968. Lawrence Barmann, Baron Friedrich von Hügel and the Modernist Crisis in England. Cambridge: Cambridge University Press, 1972. Thomas M. Loome, Liberal Catholicism, Reform Catholicism, Modernism. Mainz: Matthias-Grünwald-Verlag, 1979.

14

[41]Loisy did attempt, however, to trace the origins of the propositions given in _Lamentabili_. He judged the majority to have their source in his own works, principally in the two most notorious of his "little red books", _L'Evangile et l'Eglise_ and _Autour d'un petit livre_. Alfred Loisy, _Simples réflexions sur le décret du saint-office "Lamentabili sane exitu" et sur l'encyclique "Pascendi dominici gregis"_. 2nd ed. Ceffonds: chez l'auteur, 1908. Cf. Poulat, _La crise moderniste_, ch. V.

[42]Loisy, _Mémoires_ II: 580.

[43]Von Hügel to Tyrrell, 4 March 1900. Quoted in Barmann, p. 146.

[44]Quoted in Houtin, _Q bib. XX_, p. 87.

Chapter 1

Polarization and Paradigm:
The Incommensurability of Theological Positions

Fundamental conceptual change . . . presupposes
new world views and new languages capable of
expressing them. Now, building a new world view,
and a corresponding new language, is a process
that takes considerable time . . . . The terms of
the new language become clear only when the
process is fairly well advanced, so that each
single word is the centre of numerous lines
connecting it with other words, sentences, bits of
reasoning, gestures which sound absurd at first
but which become perfectly reasonable once the
connections are made.[1]

The clash of the modernists with Rome represents a
classic example of the confrontation of
conflicting world views. Conversation was doomed
from the beginning, not because of any intrinsic
dogmatic differences, but because the basis of
conversation was missing, i.e., a shared horizon
of common meaning. The mind-set of the Roman
authorities was that of traditional Catholicism .
. . [which] Bernard Lonergan has described . . .
as 'classicist' . . . . The modernists, on the
other hand, represented the emerging mind-set of
historical consciousness.[2]

In The Structure of Scientific Revolutions (1962) Thomas Kuhn
challenged the textbook portrayal of scientific development as
one of cumulative growth. His model of scientific growth through
"revolutions" -- of replacement of a received view of science (or
"paradigm") by another, relatively discontinuous paradigm --
created something of a "revolution" within the philosophy of
science.

To summarize Kuhn's central argument: science is able to
progress because scientists share agreement regarding the
fundamentals of their discipline. Not that such consensus always
reaches explicit thematization: in learning the classical and
contemporary problems that characterize a science, together with

the approved methods/ procedures it recognizes, a scientist learns some basic assumptions "tacitly"[3]. Informing what is considered to be an appropriate problem and what is held to be an acceptable solution, together with the kinds of allowable procedures, are some very basic convictions regarding the nature of the discipline, and even more profoundly the nature of the world which that discipline seeks to explain. In Kuhn's terminology such rather complex ensembles are designated "paradigms": "universally recognized scientific achievements that for a time provide model problems and solutions to a community of practitioners", achievements that are acknowledged "as supplying the foundation for its further practice."[4] This makes Kuhn's concept a rather encompassing one, which contributes to its utility. Unfortunately, it also engenders a corresponding vagueness; the term, then, must undergo further refinement before it can be utilized in analyzing specific cases. Keeping to Kuhn for the moment, when such agreement is present within a science, "normal-scientific" activity is rendered possible. This refers to the puzzle-solving activity that constitutes most of what science does most of the time. The shared consensus which the paradigm provides inhibits the kind of debate over fundamentals exemplified in the metaphysical debates which characterize competing schools which do not share a common paradigm. Thus the paradigm permits practitioners to concentrate on a relatively restricted set of problems, which can be presumed to be amenable to solution, and designates some classes of data as relevant while excluding others from consideration. "By focusing attention upon a small range of relatively esoteric problems, the paradigm forces scientists to investigate some part of nature in a detail and depth that would otherwise be unimaginable."[5]

This characteristic of normal science -- its ability to focus on specific problems and their solutions -- is productive of what Kuhn terms "anomaly". This refers to the violation of paradigm-induced expectations by the observed data. Since normal science is able to provide increasingly specified expectations regarding its subject matter, it becomes increasingly sensitive to any deviations from those expectations.[6] Anomalies may be handled in a number of ways: faith in their eventual solution may lead scientists to work at them without calling their conception of their field into question. Or such anomalies may simply be shelved, left for a subsequent generation of scientists with more refined methods, or equipment. In such cases anomalies continue to be defined as "puzzles" rather than as counterinstances. If persistent, however, and if considered sufficiently crucial to the ongoing credibility of the received scientific tradition, such deviation from the expected norm may provoke a period of "crisis" within a science. Repeated attempts at solution may involve ad hoc modifications to the paradigm. This can lead to a proliferation of competing versions of a paradigm, eroding clarity, loosening the rules of normal-scientific puzzle-solving,

18

"blurring" the contours of the discipline -- and perhaps of the world as conceived by the paradigm. At this stage the kinds of "metaphysical" argumentation occasioned by no longer agreed-upon fundamentals may re-emerge.[7]

Even when a discipline is in such a state of "crisis", however, there is no guarantee that a "scientific revolution" will occur. For this to become a possibility, not only must there be persistent and crucial anomaly (or anomalies), but also at least one other candidate for paradigmatic status. While proliferating versions of the received paradigm lead to a loosening of the rules of normal science in ways that permit new paradigms to emerge, scientific revolution is contingent on the actual emergence of a candidate. Should the rival paradigm provide attractive solutions to anomalies, and should it show promise in generating its own set of puzzles to constitute a normal-scientific research traditiion based on it, it may succeed in attracting a sufficient number of practitioners and emerge as dominant. If that occurs, the scientific revolution has been successful. Thus Kuhn's model of scientific growth allows for cumulative development <u>within</u> normal science. The transition to a new paradigm, capable of generating its own research tradition is non-cumulative. Revolutionary episodes in science introduce discontinuity into scientific change:

> The transition from a paradigm in crisis to a new one from which a new tradition of normal science can emerge is far from a cumulative process, one achieved by an articulation or extension of the old paradigm. Rather it is a reconstruction of the field from new fundamentals, a reconstruction that changes some of the field's most elementary theoretical generalizations as well as many of its paradigm methods and applications. . . . When the transition is complete, the profession will have changed its view of the field, its methods, and its goals.[8]

Kuhn's views on the nature of scientific development evoked controversy within the philosophy of science[9], and led to applications beyond the scope of his initial formulation. (Most of Kuhn's illustrations were drawn from physics and chemistry, and occasionally biology.) His paradigm analysis has been adapted to the social sciences[10], and the humanities[11]. Kuhn's framework was extensively utilized in a theological dissertation by T. Howland Sanks[12], and has found resonances in other theological works as well. These extensions of Kuhn's analysis to areas outside of the realm of the hard sciences stand contrary to his stated intentions in his original work. There he identified a discipline as having reached "scientific" status by its being governed by a dominant paradigm. Since he saw little evidence for this in the social sciences, and even less in the humanities, he did not extend his analysis to them. There is an interesting set of observations on one other discipline in that original work, however. Kuhn explicitly draws on theology as a discipline that parallels in significant respects the characteristics of "normal science".[13] Nonetheless, the nature of "progress" in theology sets it apart from scientific progress in the hard sciences, and in the company of the kind of development characteristic of art, political theory, or philosophy.[14]

Kuhn adduces several reasons for the difference in types of progress. First, there is the hegemony established by a dominant paradigm in science -- in contrast to the competing schools that characterize social science and the humanities. "Scientific progress is not different in kind from progress in other fields, but the absence at most times of competing schools that question each other's aims and standards makes the progress of a normal-scientific community far easier to see."[15] In addition, the scientific community enjoys an insulation from society that permits the practitioners of science to concentrate on problems because they appear amenable to solution rather than because they are of social concern. "Unlike the engineer, and many doctors, and most theologians, the scientist need not choose problems because they urgently need solution and without regard for the tools available to solve them."[16] Related to this is a third factor: the nature of the educational initiation. For the scientist this proceeds via textbooks until very far in the student career. In other disciplines, even where textbooks are employed in basic courses, the "classics" have an important role in student formation. In the latter case, therefore, the student "has constantly before him a number of competing and incommensurable solutions to these problems, solutions that he must ultimately evaluate for himself."[17]

Related to these differences in the kinds of progress characteristic of science as compared to other disciplines is a divergence which is bound up with the nature of science itself. Kuhn observes,

> If authority alone, and particularly if non-professional authority, were the arbiter of paradigm debates, the outcome of those debates might still be revolution, but it would not be <u>scientific</u> revolution. The very existence of science depends upon vesting the power to choose between paradigms in the members of a special kind of community.[18]

Despite Kuhn's disclaimers I shall argue that his framework is a useful one within which to consider theology --

specifically, to analyze Roman Catholic theology during the modernist crisis at century's turn. In part, Kuhn's objections can be met due to the limited objectives of this work. The intent is not to generate a model of theological progress in general, but rather to draw upon a framework to illuminate the dynamics of a particular theological controversy -- as those dynamics surfaced in the interaction of Alfred Loisy with critics representative of the official theology. Put another way, some of the disclaimers noted previously will appear to lose their force for historically contingent reasons. To explore some of those reasons a summary description of the dominant theology is necessary. With that in hand it will be possible to reconsider Kuhn's objections to the application of his conceptualization beyond hard science, and to indicate the broad lines of such an application to the theologies of interest here.

At the beginning of the 19th century scholasticism no longer was a significant force within Catholic theology. What little influence it maintained was rather restricted in scope. Theologians were attracted to post-Cartesian philosophies in their attempts to provide foundations for theology. Wolffian rationalism, Hegelian idealism, eclectic combinations of modern and contemporary authors -- these and others were pressed into service to provide what was felt to be a more adequate basis for theology, one better adapted to the exegencies of modern thought. Yet at century's end scholasticism in its neo-Thomist form had established itself as the dominant theology in the Church.[19] Neo-Thomism enjoyed pontifical patronage: through a number of papal measures -- the most important being Aeterni Patris (1878) -- the thought of St. Thomas Aquinas was granted a prominent position. In proclaiming the Church's official option for the Aristotelian method of St. Thomas in philosophical and theological instruction, the encyclical in fact legitimated an interpretation of the nature of theology and philosophy particular to neo-Thomism. Not only had the neo-Thomist reading of Thomas received official sanction; prior to the encyclical the evaluation of non-scholastic theologies by Roman authorities had proceeded along the lines set by prominent neo-Thomist theologians. The post-Cartesian philosophies were charged with being incapable of providing the proper relation of faith and reason that would preserve the orthodoxy of theology.[20] If by mid-century the neo-Thomist movement had succeeded in attracting a dedicated core of proponents, by the final quarter of the 19th century it had largely accomplished the elimination of alternative theologies through Roman condemnation. After Aeterni Patris it was able to consolidate its position through the further appointment of neo-Thomists to faculties at Rome and elsewhere, through the diffusion of its teaching internationally in Latin manuals, and through a number of newly-founded journals.[21] Not that neo-Thomism achieved complete dominance, even with its formidible ecclesiastical advantages. In itself it remained marked by tensions between those who interpreted the doctrine of the Angelic Doctor more strictly and those who were more flexible.[22] Also it did not succeed in entirely eliminating the influence of other great scholastic figures of the past such as Duns Scotus, St. Bonaventure -- although it mitigated their effect via a tendency to reduce any differences among scholastics to disagreement in secondary matters, while asserting unity in fundamentals.[23] Thus by the time Loisy came to publish piecemeal his innovating apologetic, neo-Thomism had established theological hegemony -- most solidly at Rome, strongly in France.[24] That apologetic hit the received theology at its most vulnerable point: its inability to deal with history. This weakness was inherent in this theology's conception of the very nature of that discipline, and was the product of underlying metaphysical and epistemological commitments.

Neo-Thomism derived its first principles from Scripture and tradition. Its first principles, then, were revealed and as such required faith on the part of the theologian to apprehend them. The assent of faith could be made only by a mind elevated by grace; hence theology's character as a supernatural science, as "the science of divine things, known by the light of revealed principles."[25] Philosophy, which derived its first principles from the natural light of reason (hence its character as a natural science), was to provide the organizing structure through which the various parts of theology were unified into a single, interrelated body of knowledge. Put another way, philosophy furnished the principles with which to organize revelation's diverse and scattered data -- in short, to endow theology with the character of a genuine science. This conception of theology as the science which derives its doctrines from faith with the aid of reason tended to emphasize the speculative side of that discipline. As Gerald McCool summarizes it,

> The syllogisms of an Aristotelian deductive science move from its self-evident first principles to its derived conclusions. In an Aristotelain 'science of faith' the Catholic theologian can proceed from his revealed first principles through his naturally known minor premises to his theologically certain conclusions. This is not the only function of an Aristotelian science of faith but . . . in the post-Vatican I Church speculative theologians devoted most of their attention to its development. Catholic speculative theology became a 'conclusion theology', whose aim was to derive an increasing number of theologically certain conclusions from its revealed first principles.[26]

Together with this speculative emphasis, the conception of theology as a science of the supernatural helped to determine its normative relation to other disciplines. For theology's first principles, being revealed, possessed a higher certitude, serving to distinguish scientific theology from every other science, and to establish a principle of theological control over them.

Therefore Gayraud could characterize Catholic theology as "precisely the synthesis of scholastic philosophy and of Christian faith" while being careful to note their unequal status in that synthesis. "Thus in comparison with sacred theology, philosophy does not have the place of a sister or an associate of the same rank and equal dignity, but rather the position of vassal, bound to service and the charge of a hired servant: ancilla theologiae."[27] In other words, philosophy, drawing as it does its evidence from the natural light of human reason, has its limits. In this sense, philosphy -- while intimately bound up with the very nature of theology, is subordinate to revealed truth and normed by it.[28]

History too is subordinated to theology. Against the tendency "to set history up as judge, to consider it the first element in the formation of judgments and the basis of opinions, outside of and anterior to all doctrinal authority", censured as "unfortunate and false" by one scholastic writer[29], there was counterposed:

> . . . it is always true that theology is the science of the principles of which history studies the application and the facts; but, these principles are infallible insofar as they are revealed; and if history takes them as the norm of its judgments, it has every guarantee against error.[30]

If history is tied to theology, ecclesiastical history is the more so, specifically to doctrine. Indeed, J.-B. Aubry stresses that this form of historical study is less a study of facts than a study of doctrines; its task is to discern the application of principles in the facts. In doing this it takes as a priori the two principles of the substantial unity of dogma and the accidental transformations (as opposed to transformations in essence) of the Church's teaching. It is only in this role that it may fulfill its proper function as the "servant of theology".[31]

If from the side of theology history occupied a subordinate status, that subordination was further determined by philosophical infrastructure. Ontologically, things have their specific natures, which make them necessarily what they are, and which are immutable. Epistemologically, objective knowledge is

23

had when the concepts of the external object existing in the mind of the knower accurately represent the concepts (essences) of objects existing in the extra-mental world. In other words, truth results from the correspondence of the mind's judgment with the object -- much like matching diagrams or congruent triangles. And since objects were immutable in their natures, truth likewise was immutable. While error could be introduced into the knowing process in a variety of ways, if the object grasped in its essence was properly represented in the mind of the knower, true knowledge would result; knowledge that like its object, was not subject to essential change but at most further clarity and explicitness. If this conception of the essential irrelevance of historical context and environing condition could hold for natural knowledge, one can gather how much the more so it would apply to revealed truth.[32] The truths which were revealed were immutable, and though subsisting in the flux of history remained untouched by its particularities.

In the course of criticizing this theological attitude, George Tyrrell gave what I judge to be basically a fair representation of its logic:

> If God's word vouches for any one science that science must be the rule and criterion of all the rest. To be under its control is not slavery but liberty -- liberty from error. Nay, it must be a cause of rapid and fruitful progression. While an unaided astronomy or geology or history is delayed and weakened by uncertainties; that which derives were it only three or four fixed and infallible truths, from Scripture or Tradition, has a solid foundation to build upon, and builds itself up rapidly and securely.[33]

With this summary in hand, it is now possible to return to Kuhn's disclaimers restricting the scope of his original analysis. After providing some response to those, in favor of the the application of a paradigm analysis to theology, I shall proceed to outline how that application can be effected, considering first neo-Thomism and then modernism.

Looking first at the issue of progress, one can qualify Kuhn's first disclaimer -- his contrast between paradigmatic hegemony in science versus competing schools elsewhere -- by drawing on his observation regarding the authority structure of disciplines. Precisely because of its authority structure, Roman Catholcism was able to establish a relatively high degree of uniformity in theology. Neo-Thomism had succeeded in eliminating possible rivals in the form of post-Kantian modern theologies.

Within scholasticism, a large measure of internal unity was secured through a synthesis which reflected neo-Thomism's ahistorical stance. Its fundamental tenet that there existed a uniformity among scholastic systems on basic issues relegated any differences to a secondary status. Different schools could be admitted, but based on a Baroque notion of scholastic synthesis (which owed more to Suarez than to Aquinas), these were not admitted as "competing".[34] Kuhn's second disclaimer regarding the insulation of communities of disciplinary practitioners from society, with consequences for their selection of problems, can be qualified for historically contingent reasons as well. Sanks makes reference to "the insulation of the . . . cultural milieu of . . . ecclesiastical Romanitas"[35] and comments with regard to theologians of the "Roman School" that they had the answers -- only no one was asking those questions! A third factor raised by Kuhn engages the educational initiation of the scientist via textbooks. But it is precisely the initiation of students into this theology via manuals that constituted a salient characteristic of it. Further, the standardization of ecclesiastical language in Latin facilitated an international audience for the manuals of an authoritative theological paradigm. The manuals both reflected the cultural insulation of Roman theology, and helped to reinforce and propagate it.[36]

There remains yet a more fundamental objection: that of the authority structure characteristic of science and theology respectively. According to Kuhn's analysis, paradigms have their locus in a community of practitioners -- the latter set the fundamental standard of judgment regarding them. With respect to Roman neo-Thomism one must deal, of course, not only with theological practitioners but also with ecclesiastical hierarchy -- in some cases overlapping, in others not so much. Nonetheless, let me first observe that Kuhn's analysis in this regard is perhaps conditioned by the historical examples in science which he chooses. If one were to take account of the movement of contemporary science with research grants, government funding, and the like, the insulation of the scientific community and its non-entanglement with extra-scientific authority could not stand unqualified. To deal with the contemporary structure of science, Kuhn's framework would, in all likelihood, have to be supplemented. In any event, in considering Roman Catholic theology that framework most certainly has to be supplemented.[37] When applied to theology, Kuhn's conceptualization must be used somewhat analogously, as Sanks has argued.[38] Since the focus of this project is not on applying the overall dynamics of Kuhn's model to the interaction of two theological tendencies -- neo-Thomism and modernism -- the salience of this issue is diminished considerably.[39] The intent rather is to examine -- and then elaborate -- a portion of the Kuhnian analysis, to focus on the polarization of position that can occur between adherents of rival paradigms.

25

It is also important to note that the conceptualization will be used heuristically. There is a real temptation to reify paradigms.[40] If, however, the latter are taken less as analogous to Durkheimian social facts and more as descriptions of the way practitioners go about their craft -- their application to a discipline such as theology is facilitated. Once again, the aim is to illuminate the dynamics of a particular theological controversy, not to develop a general model of theological development.

Keeping these qualifications in mind, it is now possible to reconsider neo-Thomism, this time as a theological paradigm. This will facilitate application of Kuhn's conceptualization to modernism in its turn. For, as an emergent rival, modernism can be expected to be less well defined by comparison. Just as modernists historically defined themselves by contrast to the dominant theology, conceptualization of their theological orientation may profit from the same practice. To begin, then, with neo-Thomism:

> The major issue between the neo-Thomists and the post-Kantian modern theologians was the ability of their respective theological methods to handle adequately the Catholic teaching on faith and reason, grace and nature. To settle that issue the neo-Thomists and their rivals had to define the relation between revelation and philosophy, apologetics, and positive and speculative theology in their theological methods. And, since theological method had inevitable epistemological and metaphysical presuppositions, the neo-Thomists and their rivals also had to define the philosophy of knowledge, man, and being which their theological methodology implied.[41]

McCool here is speaking of neo-Thomism and the theological rivals it had prevailed over earlier in the 19th century -- Güntherism, ontologism, and others. If McCool's interpretation is correct, then the elements he distinguishes must be taken into account in formulating a paradigm analysis of neo-Thomism and its late 19th-century rival, modernism. First, however, Kuhn's concept of "paradigm" must be considered in its own right: the vagueness of that pivotal term is notorious. A sympathetic critic has noted that in the original presentation Kuhn used "paradigm" "in not less than twenty-one different senses . . . possibly more, not less."[42] Some measure of order is reintroduced by the further assertion that these multiple senses can be grouped according to three major classifications.[43] Even so, that presents a rather complex concept to utilize for analysis. This complexity is

26

amplified in Kuhn's attempts to respond to his critics and refine the concept.[44] Since the interest here is not in explicating Kuhn but in explicating theologies, a long detour through this critical literature can be avoided. George Ritzer has proffered a definition of paradigm that represents a synthesis of the threefold typology referenced earlier, and elaborates this concept in ways that are particularly helpful for purposes here. For Ritzer,

> A paradigm is a fundamental image of the subject matter within a science. It serves to define what should be studied, what questions should be asked, how they should be asked, and what rules should be followed in interpreting the answers obtained. The paradigm is the broadest unit of consensus within a science and serves to differentiate one scientific community (or subcommunity) from another. It subsumes, defines, and interrelates the exemplars, theories, and methods and instruments that exist within it.[45]

Neo-Thomism's recognized achievement was its claim to have secured an understanding of the proper relationship between faith and reason -- a fundamental requirement for faithful preservation of the Catholic tradition in its view, as its objections to the post-Kantian theologies attest. That understanding of faith and reason found expression in a conception of theology as a unified Aristotelian science comprising philosophy and theology: the latter as an Aristotelian science of faith to which an Aristotelian science of philosophy was subordinated. That understanding of faith and reason was founded upon an Aristotelian metaphysics and epistemology.

Expanding upon this, the faith-reason relationship achieved by neo-Thomism was expressed in a conception of theology that was "paradigmatic". The Aristotelian notion of science as a deductive enterprise informed the character of theology as an Aristotelain science of faith.[46] Revealed first principles were organized into a coherent system, and elaborated by the natural light of reason. This set theology, with its dogmatic, speculative emphasis, in a normative relation not only to philosophy; but also with regard to the theological subdisciplines of Scripture, positive theology, apologetics, ecclesiastical history; and finally to the profane sciences as well. While philosphy and history have already received brief attention as illustrative of this tendency, a further suggestion of this theology's priorities with regard to Scripture is not out of place here, given the eventual concern with Loisy. The ahistorical stance of neo-Thomism permitted the utilization of

Scripture as a simple repertoire of proof-texts -- a source where one could retrieve without regard for historical period or literary context, the revealed arguments to establish theological theses. As J.-B. Aubry nicely it, "The program of every professor of Sacred Scripture must be rigorously that of St. Thomas: the investigation of the dogmatic meaning -- nothing else! Once this meaning is grasped, he possesses all, for dogma is the germ of all that is good, above all of the mystical life."[47]

At this point it is convenient to raise and deal with criticism of Kuhn's paradigm concept as that bears on the nature of scientific change. One of the grounds on which Stephen Toulmin challenges Kuhn's schema is its alleged assumption that an entire science necessarily forms a single, coherent intellectual system. "If the component elements of an entire . . . science . . . are as tightly interrelated as this view implies, there will be no way of modifying them piecemeal or one at a time: the only chance of radical change will lie in rejecting the entire 'system' as a whole, and starting afresh."[48] Neo-Thomism approaches this ideal type to an extent greater than that of the hard science examples cited by Toulmin in his discussion of Kuhn. And thus any major reconceptualization of a theological subdiscipline would have significant repercussions for this theology. Modernism levelled its challenge on several fronts: ecclesiastical history, Scripture, apologetics. And it was not only the broad sweep of the challenge but the point of attack that put the entire system on notice. Precisely because modernism raised the issue of historicity it struck at the very heart of an essentialist neo-Thomism whose very notion of scholastic synthesis rested on an ahistorical rendering of the major scholastic systems and their proponents. Just as neo-Thomist theologians could juxtapose Scriptural texts varying widely in historical composition and context, so they did with medieval and Baroque scholastic texts and commentaries. The very nature of the neo-Thomist synthesis as that was architected by Joseph Kleutgen, S.J., derived more from the great post-Reformation scholastics than from Thomas, though that went unrecognized at the time. Thus modernism's challenge, explicitly formulated on the terrain of specific theological subdisciplines, contained an implicit challenge which engaged the very foundations of the neo-Thomistic theology in its Aristotelain metaphysics and epistemology.

The neo-Thomist determination of the faith/ reason relation and the Thomistic theology of grace and nature, both demanded an Aristotelain metaphysics of substance and accident, faculty, habit and act.[49] This in turn required an Aristotelian theory of knowledge to ground it. Georges van Riet in his analysis of Thomistic epistemology has remarked on the relatively unchanging character of its formulation, and its general insulation form

contemporary thought -- particularly that oriented to a modern
conception of science.[50] The nature of that epistemology and
concomitant metaphysics has been sketched previously. Here it
worth connecting their orientation to a larger world view, termed
by Bernard Lonergan, "classical culture":

> It stressed not facts but values. It could
> not but claim to be universalist. Its
> classics were immortal works of art, its
> philosophy was the perennial philosophy, its
> laws and structures were the deposit of the
> wisdom and the prudence of mankind.
> Classicist education was a matter of models
> to be imitated, of ideal characters to be
> emulated, of eternal verities and universally
> valid laws.[51]

Given modernism as representative of an emerging mind-set of
historical consciousness, it is little wonder that Bernard Scott
could describe the "crisis" in Catholic theology at century's
turn as "the confrontation of conflicting world views."[52]

Having determined the relation of faith and reason, the
notion of theology predicated upon that, and theology's realtion
to other disciplines as paradigmatic -- as "the broadest unit of
consensus within a science", I will give some attention to
elements of that science itself: its data ("what should be
studied"), its problems ("what questions should be asked"), and
its methods ("what rules should be followed").[53] These latter
three aspects of paradigms Kuhn refers to as their "normative"
aspect -- as distinguished from "cognitive" aspect, e.g., notion
of truth.

In brief, the two data sources for the dominant theology were
Scripture and tradition. This is as important for what it
excludes as for what it encompasses. Data from other scientific
or humane disciplines were not considered data for theological
reflection, save for a possible propaedutic role. Similarly,
personal experience, the sense of the contemporary Christian
community, or the problems of the larger society did not function
as theological data.[54] The characteristic problems formulated by
this theology tended to be those of conceptual clarification and
refinement and the solution was the manipulation of immutably
fixed concepts. In this Sanks has detected a source of "anomaly"
that emerged from a "normal-scientific" theology: toward the end
of the 19th century,

> . . . the theological problems were all
> clearly defined and the possible opinions
> neatly laid out. The anomaly came from the
> fact that no one but the theologians had

29

these problems, and whatever option a theologian chose, it made little or no difference in the life of the Christian community.[55]

The nature of the accompanying theological method has been suggested by Aubry's portrayal of its function with respect to Scripture. Broadening that to include tradition, methodologically, key words and central statements could be culled from the Scriptures, from the Fathers, conciliar statements, liturgical texts, histories of individual churches or of the Church as a whole -- without regard for contextual location of the text or for the intention of the ancient author. Texts so recovered were used as the basis for deductive reasoning or as proof texts for already held dogmatic positions. And thus, "scholasticism is not a theology, it is the theology; it is not a method, it is the method!"[56]

To recapitulate: paradigmatic for neo-Thomism is a conception of the nature of theology, a conception which is reflective of underlying metaphysical and epistemological commitments. Collectively, these determine "a fundamental image of the subject matter within a science" -- in this case, theology as an Aristotelian science of faith. The nature of such a theological science is in turn regulative of what is admissable as data, what are taken to be appropriate problems for theologians to consider, and what methods regulate how those problems are approached and what constitutes acceptable solutions. These elements will reappear in the paradigmatic conceptualization of modernism, which may now be taken up.

The neo-Thomist theological synthesis constitutes an impressive unity. This has greatly facilitated its being rendered into a paradigm conceptualization. Since modernists differed in their philosophical positions, since their primary intellectual loyalties were in a variety of areas -- with consequences for their respective approaches to theology -- and since they did not always agree on what were the outstanding problems, and still less on what constituted an acceptable solution, this set of tendencies will of necessity be less amenable to any "tight" conceptualization. As an emergent rival to a theology "in possession" as it were, modernism will inevitably be more diffuse, more difficult to clarify paradigmatically. Nonetheless, if there is apparent diversity[57], there is also central tendency.[58] If there is not identity among positions, there is often affinity. At this point only a very general picture of the major contours of modernism will be given, drawing from a number of its representatives. How Loisy's thought embodied those tendencies, the more precise forms those contours assumed in his work, will emerge in following chapters.

30

Loisy wrote, "Since the Middle Ages, Catholic doctrine has taken on the form of a logical system. It is a coherent structure, of mutually sustaining parts; a splendid cathedral whose essential weakness, as Renan detected, lies in the flimsiness of its foundations."[59] Apparently the differences with scholasticism ran deep. They surfaced in the form of controversy concerning the legitimacy of historical critical method in its application to sacred texts. But methods were reflective of notions regarding the nature of science. Loisy's advocacy of critical method reflected an attack upon the deductive Aristotelian science espoused by neo-Thomism. And that assault in turn engaged the Aristotelian metaphysics and theory of knowledge that informed that conception of science, and conferred upon the official theology its ahistorical character. To pick up modernist-neo-Thomist differences at the issue of method, then, is to pick up a thread, one that winds around problems and data, leads farther on to the nature of theology and the nature of science, to the faith/ reason relationship that regulates their interrelation, and threads its way to foundational matters: truth, the nature of things.[60]

By 1890 an historically critical approach to the Bible was having clear impact on Catholic exegesis, which until that time had continued largely in the severely traditional climate of preceding periods. Contrary to the approach that dominated neo-Thomism, this orientation was marked by a return to the original languages, by an attempt to situate texts within their contexts through reconstruction of the author's life, ideas, environment, etc. Supplemented by philology, archaeology, geography, this sought to discern the facts, knowable in themselves and independent of other possibilities: empirical results arrived at through application of empirical methods.

Revolutionary methods generated a significant shift in problem perception. One can contrast the difference in horizons by comparing an 1867 address on "The Rights and Duties of Criticism with regard to the Bible" given by Abbé Vollot, with words spoken by Loisy a quarter of a century later. In 1867 the newly appointed Professor of Sacred Scripture at the Sorbonne took the occasion to disparage Richard Simon, the great pioneer of French biblical criticism, and said, "Everything has been said, wrote La Bruyère two hundred years ago -- well, on the Bible everything has been said now." By contrast, Loisy as Professor of Sacred Scripture at the Institut catholique took occasion in a seasonal address to speak of Richard Simon with respect, and observed: "The field of exegesis is immense, varied, and even in one sense and on many points almost unexplored."[61] The difference in outlooks could hardly be greater.

Kuhn remarks that a new paradigm may use the same data as the old one it challenges, but will understand them in a new way. In the case of modernism, a critical understanding transformed Scripture from a divinely authoritative repository of proof-statements, into an historically conditioned document, subject to the rules of composition and amenable to the same methods of interpretation of other historical documents. The data of the tradition were likewise treated historically. Modernism also recognized as data phenomena excluded by the traditional paradigm: e.g., the experience of the individual believer, and data from other scientific or humane disciplines.

Critical methods on the terrain of history (which have their analogues in the critical philosophy practiced by Blondel and Laberthonnière) are tied to a science that is conceived empirically rather than deductively, and which claims a measure of autonomy vis-à-vis theology. Precisely to be scientific, exegesis could not derive its first principles a priori, from the revealed truths articulated by theology, nor be subject to the latter's control, but rather arrive at its own conclusions through its own proper methods, and be subject to criticism through conclusions established through these same methods. Criticism, then, enjoys autonomy in its own domain. As expressed by Mgr. Mignot: "Theology has its domain as criticism has its own. Unfortunately it is like countries whose ill-defined boundaries are the occasion of interminible conflicts between rival peoples. Each one pretends to be on its own territory when it is on its neighbors . . ."[62]

In short, the theological innovators were content to pursue their various specialties, establish their conclusions according to the appropriate methodologies, and only then examine the consequences for theology.[63] And their conceptions of the theology that had to come to terms with those conclusions differed significantly from that of the dominant paradigm. In general, attempting to correct a perceived reduction of revelation into a verbal, conceptual presentation of objective principles about the divine, they stressed an experiential component. Revelation is a part of the complex religious experience which includes the heart and will as well as the mind. Theology attempts to formulate that experience in intellectual terms; as such its formulations will always be symbolic to a degree, and inadequate to the revelation it seeks to articulate. Accordingly, subject to different times and places, theological formulae -- expressed dogmatically -- can undergo change, indeed must undergo change in order to retain intelligibility, to adapt to changed circumstances, while retaining essential continuity with earlier formulations. Thus change can occur that is more than simply clarification of concepts -- but at the same time, while admitting of fundamental change, there is not discontinuity.

This approach to theology was undergirded by its own set of

metaphysical and epistemological presuppositions. The extent to
which these also diverged from neo-Thomist positions has been
encapsulated by von Hügel in his comment to Blondel that, "if
scholasticism ruins philosophy for me, it is also my implacable
enemy on the terrain of history and the Bible. There is no real
knowledge of the past stages of human thought . . . without the
three elements of <u>relativity</u>, <u>development</u>, and <u>interiority</u>
('moralisme') . . . The day when scholasticism would accept
these, it would cease to be."[64] Modernists drew upon various
philosophical tendencies to express these three elements, but the
elements themselves were more or less present among the
principals of the movement, in contradiction to the absoluteness,
immutability and objectivity which neo-Thomism drew from its
Aristotelian epistemological and metaphysical underpinnings.[65]

Put differently, modernists were the products of a world view
different from the classicist mentality reflected in neo-Thomism.
Described by Lonergan as pluralist, empirical in outlook, it is a
mentality informed by history both in principle and in fact --
its assumptions are based upon change, development, diversity.
The divergences between the two cultures are profound, and
possess important consequences for mutual understanding:

> The differences between the two are enormous,
> for they differ in their apprehension of men,
> in their account of the good, and in the role
> they ascribe to the Church in the world. But
> these differences are not immediately
> theological. They are differences in
> horizon, in total mentality. For either side
> really to understand the other is a major
> achievement and, when such understanding is
> lacking, the interpretation of Scripture or
> of other theological sources is most likely
> to be at cross-purposes.[66]

The long detour through a paradigmatic conceptualization of
theological tendencies has led back to Kuhn, indeed to that
aspect of Kuhn's analysis most of interest: the
"incommensurability" of competing paradigms. Since this notion
will provide a springboard to subsequent chapters -- to the
analysis of metaphor in the following chapter; to consideration
of historical narrative in chapter three; and to examination of
Church, sacrament, and eucharist in the fourth chapter, an
extended treatment of it is necessary at this point.

According to Kuhn, a characteristic development of periods of
revolutionary transition from a dominant paradigm to a rival one
is the inability of proponents of an innovative scientific
paradigm to communicate with representatives of the established
mode of viewing and doing science. This tendency to "talk past

one another" he termed "incommensurability". It turns out to be a complex phenomenon[67], as it engages several levels or aspects of paradigms:

1. Incommensurability of data/ methods/ problems: what are considered appropriate problems for feasible solution, how they are to be solved, and what data are to be employed in that process may differ considerably. Put more simply, the definitions of science are not the same.[68] Loisy's historical-critical exegesis and neo-Thomism's search for the "dogmatic" sense of Scripture reflected very different standards and indeed very different definitions of their discipline.

2. Incommensurability of language: since new paradigms are in part dependent on older ones, ordinarily they incorporate much of the vocabulary and apparatus that the traditional paradigm had previously employed. But new wine is often poured into new bottles: the borrowed elements are seldom employed in quite the traditional way. "Within the new paradigm, old terms, concepts, and experiments fall into new relationships one with the other. The inevitable result is what we may call, though the term is not quite right, a misunderstanding between the two competing schools."[69] Loisy is rather continually faulted by critics for a studied ambiguity of language, of expressing unorthodox ideas in seemingly orthodox language. From the modernist point of view, the linguistic problem resides in the attempt on the part of the official theology to strait jacket theological discussion into scholastic categories -- insufficient for grappling with modern discoveries. Blondel well-summarized it: "More and more I see myself forced to conclude that today there are two intellectual worlds present, which, while they use the same words, do not speak the same language, and remain incomprehensible to one another."[70]

3. Incommensurability of world view: since paradigms are rooted in ontological and epistemological assumptions about the way the world is, partisans of rival paradigms are said to practice their trades in different worlds.[71] Underlying differences in world view between modernists and their scholastic critics are alluded to by modernists themselves, as Blondel's remark just quoted attests. Von Hügel's observation, noted earlier, with reference to "Loisy's whole attitude of mind" being so different than that of his adversaries, their lack of "a common starting point", points in the same direction. The tenor of these and similar evaluations has been translated by commentators into more analytical terms, such as those of Lonergan's "classicist" and "empirical" cultures utilized by Bernard Scott.[72]

Engaging as it does the conception of the nature of a discipline, and reaching to the level of a discipline's foundations, incommensurability would appear to be a rather "totalizing" concept. As understood by Derek Phillips it implies that "the individual is epistemologically locked into the milieu in which he lives and the paradigm under which he practices science."[73] On this reading paradigms would not only represent frameworks within which the world comes to view, but formidible barriers to viewing it in any other way: "The scientist is trapped in the web of his own meanings."[74] The metaphors which Kuhn employs in his descriptions of paradigm shifts are capable of being read in this way: "Just because it is a transition between incommensurables, the transition between competing paradigms cannot be made a step at a time, forced by logic and neutral experience. Like the gestalt switch, it must occur all at once (though not necessarily in an instant) or not at all."[75] The implication of Kuhn's metaphor is that one sees a gestalt figure either in one way or another. And as long as it is seen in a particular way, it cannot be seen in another. In subsequent work Kuhn has tried to clarify his presentation of incommensurability, stressing that partial understanding across paradigms is indeed possible. This is exemplified in a shift of metaphor: problems of paradigm incommensurability are likened to translation problems.

> Proponents of different theories (or different paradigms, in the broader sense of the term) speak different languages -- languages expressing different cognitive commitments, suitable for different worlds. Their abilities to grasp each other's viewpoints are therefore inevitably limited by the imperfections of the processes of translation and of reference determination.[76]

Despite such attempts at more adequate formulation, Kuhn has not been able to satisfy his critics. In a sympathetic reading of Kuhn, Richard Bernstein has introduced some distinctions in an effort to further understanding, and has placed the discussion in a larger context.[77] A discussion of his work would involve an excursion into views controverted in the philosophy of science. Unlike the detour into theological terrain, this would not materially advance present interests. It will be sufficient to note that Bernstein closely connects incommensurability with meaning (in this he is closer to Feyerabend's preoccupations than to Kuhn's[78]), and that he argues that some translation of meaning across paradigms is possible in principle. In accepting the notion of incommensurability one is not thereby committed to what he calls the "Myth of the Framework" -- "where we are enclosed in the prison house of our own frameworks and forms of life."[79] Understanding a rival paradigm is likened to understanding an alien culture: one attempts to avoid extremes of ethnocentrism and cultural relativism. That is, one refrains from setting up one's own standards as sole criteria for judging the other; while avoiding the position that no judgments can be made regarding what is foreign, since everything must be judged solely within its own cultural framework.[80]

It would appear, then, _that_ incommensurability can occur between rival paradigms (although this is not inevitable[81]); _that_ when it does occur, it can do so at a number of levels or areas; _that_ given its occurrence, mutual understanding is not totally precluded (although successful translation is not guaranteed). Still, as Kuhn rightly notes, "reference to translation only isolates but does not resolve the problems which have led Feyerabend and me to talk of incommensurability."[82] A further problem is _how_ does incommensurability occur? How can one move beyond the "that" of its occurrence to some appreciation of its dynamics? The paradigm analysis of neo-Thomism/ modernism on the multiple levels of data/ methods/ problems, nature of theology/ science, and world view have suggested great divergences of content between the two. But is incommensurability simply a matter of what is thought and how divergent those thoughts are? Certainly the thought of modernists and neo-Thomists were contra-positional:

> In writing about the modernist controversy it is very difficult to avoid a Manichaean view of history; the players tended to view each other in black and white terms. The reactions of Church authorities were harsh and extreme. . . . When the definitive history of modernism is written, this Manichaean aspect will have to be explained.[83]

Scott's own contribution toward such an explanation is given in the form of Lonergan's "cultures": a clash of world views is at stake. A witness of the events of the modernist years, Maude Petre renders the proportions of that clash in these terms: "We must remember, in fairness to those who were not always fair, that the impact of historical criticism on the traditional teaching of the Church was terrifying; that it seemed a case of saving the very essence of the Christian faith from destruction. Not, perhaps, since the startling revolution of Copernicanism, had the shock been greater."[84]

Yet, is it solely a matter of a revolution in thought at issue? Or does the manner in which thought comes to expression also play a role? Is not language constitutive of thought, constituting rules of inclusion and exclusion, what can come to expression and what cannot be said? The survey of Loisy's career made in the introduction surfaced language as an issue between modernists and neo-Thomists. Is it not possible that _what_ was said (or written) is only part of what must bear examination?

36

That what was <u>said</u> (and written) must also come under analysis? That what was <u>said</u> by a modernist such as Loisy could not meaningfully be <u>said</u> by a neo-Thomist such as Billot?

Through yet another route we are led back to Kuhn. In attempting to explicate the sense of what occurs during paradigm shifts he had recourse to metaphors such as "translation" and "gestalt-switch". Margaret Masterman, in her efforts to render Kuhn's central concept more precise invokes metaphor as a metaphor of how a paradigm functions:

> I wish to say that a paradigm draws a 'crude analogy' . . . . The problem of saying something philosophical and yet exact about such a paradigm . . . is, I think, the same problem which Black tries to attack when he tries to discover the nature of an archetype, or when he asks himself how he is going to formalize the 'interaction view' of metaphor used in language. In my view, the new 'way of seeing' produced by Black's metaphoric 'interaction' is an alternative form of that produced by Kuhn's gestalt-switch.[85]

If comments by Loisy's contemporaries have put us on the trail of language, and if the central position of language in Kuhn's notion of incommensurability has indicated that it may be a trail well worth following, Masterman's suggestion has opened up a route to follow it up. In this chapter the utility of Kuhn's paradigm conceptualization for considering theology has been argued as a basis for employing incommensurability as a point of access to theological polarization. The elements of the paradigm application to theology -- epistemological and metaphysical commitments, operative notion of science and of the nature of theology, and problems/ data/ methods have specified points of contact with the various aspects of incommensurability advanced by Kuhn. In the next chapter, the "interaction view" of metaphor set forth by Max Black and others will be set out. It will provide a handle by which to grasp the language of Loisy and selected critics, and perhaps will also permit a grip on their mutual understanding -- given its connexion with the language aspect of the incommensurability thesis.

37

Notes to Chapter One

[1]Paul Feyerabend, Against Method, (London: Verso, 1980), p. 256.

[2]Bernard Scott's introduction to Alfred Loisy, The Gospel and the Church, (Philadelphia: Fortress Press, 1976), pp. xxviii, xxx.

[3]See Michael Polayni, The Tacit Dimension. Garden City, New York: Anchor Books, 1967. For an illustration of how such tacit knowledge functions in the communication of scientific research, see Michael Mulkay, Science and the Sociology of Knowledge, (London: George Allen and Unwin, 1979), pp. 74-75.

[4]Thomas S. Kuhn, The Structure of Scientific Revolutions, (Chicago: University of Chicago Press, 1962), pp. x, 10.

[5]Ibid., p. 24. For the kinds of problems characteristic of normal science, see pp. 25-33.

[6]"Anomaly appears only against the background provided by the paradigm. The more precise and far-reaching that paradigm is, the more sensitive as indicator it provides of anomaly and hence of an occasion for paradigm change." Ibid., p. 65.

[7]Ibid., ch. VII.

[8]Ibid., pp. 84-85.

[9]Imre Lakatos and Alan Musgrave, eds., Criticism and the Growth of Knowledge. Cambridge: Cambridge University Press, 1970. Stephen Toulmin, Human Understanding. Princeton: Princeton University Press, 1972. Frederick Suppe, The Structure of Scientific Theories. 2nd ed. Urbana: University of Illinois Press, 1979. John Krige, Science, Revolution and Discontinuity. New Jersey: Humanities Press, 1980. W.H. Newton-Smith, The Rationality of Science. London: RKP, 1981. Barry Barnes, T.S. Kuhn and Social Science. New York: Columbia University Press, 1982. Israel Scheffler, Science and Subjectivity. 2nd ed. Indianapolis: Hackett Publishing Company, 1982. Richard Bernstein, Beyond Objectivism and Relativism. Philadelphia: University of Pennsylvania, 1983. This list is far from exhaustive.

[10]George Ritzer, Sociology: A Multiple Paradigm Science. Boston: Allyn & Bacon, Inc., 1980.

[11]Gary Gutting, ed., Paradigms and Revolutions. Notre Dame: University of Notre Dame Press, 1980.

[12]T. Howland Sanks, _Authority in the Church: A Study in Changing Paradigms_. Missoula, Montana: Scholar's Press, 1974.

[13]Kuhn, SSR, pp. 165, 135.

[14]Ibid., ch. XIII.

[15]Ibid., p. 162.

[16]Ibid., p. 163.

[17]Ibid., p. 164.

[18]Ibid., p. 166.

[19]For a survey of neo-Thomism's rise to this stature see Thomas Hartley, _Thomism During the Modernist Era_. Toronto: University of St. Michael's College, 1971. For an analysis which centers more on the theological issues involved see Gerald McCool, _Catholic Theology in the Nineteenth Century_. New York: The Seabury Press, 1977.

[20]See McCool, ch. 6.

[21]J. Bellamy, _La théologie catholique au XIXe siècle_, (Paris: Gabriel Beauchesne et Cie, 1904), pp. 149-151.

[22]". . . unlike the neo-scholasticism at Rome, that at Louvain seeks honestly to reconcile itself with the results and the methods of science and to patch the new cloth of contemporary culture on to the old medieval garment . . ." George Tyrrell, _Medievalism_, (New York: Longmans, Green & Co., 1909), p. 25.

[23]For a survey of scholastic diversity within 19th century theology see Edgar Hocedez, S.J., _Histoire de la théologie au XIXe siècle_ t.3, (Paris: Desclée de Brouwer, 1947), ch. VII.

[24]"Italy apart, among the major countries it was in France that the [neo-Thomist] movement made the most headway and it was from France, thanks to the world-wide prestige of French books and periodicals, that its influence spread far afield." Roger Aubert et al., _The Church in a Secularized Society_, (New York: Paulist Press, 1978), p. 175.

[25]Grandmaison quoted in Jules Lebreton, _Le Père Léonce de Grandmaison_, (Paris: Gabriel Beauchesne et ses fils, 1932), p. 91. Cf. p. 92.

[26]McCool, p. 225.

[27]Abbé Gayraud, "L'Avenir de la philosophie scholastique", Questions du jour, (Paris: Bloud et Barral, libraires-éditeurs, 1897), pp. 359, 338.

[28]". . . faith is . . . the guard rail erected by God on the brink of the precipice to contain [reason's] intemperent and audacious impetuousity while indicating the abysses of error." Ibid., p. 339.

[29]J.-B. Aubry, Essai sur la méthode des études ecclésiastiques en France t.II, (Lille: Desclée, De Brouower et Cie, s.d.), p. 457. Gayraud in "A propos des études ecclésiastiques en France" discusses this book with general approval. Questions du jour, ch. X. The article originally appeared in Science catholique (1893) under the pseudonym of H. Delavet.

[30]Aubry, p. 452.

[31]Ibid., pp. 449-450, 464.

[32]Sanks, pp. 113-117. Cf. McCool, pp. 247-249.

[33]Tyrrell, Medievalism, p. 123.

[34]See McCool, pp. 213, 233, 243-244.

[35]Sanks, p. 125.

[36]"The existence, content, and form of the typical manual constitute a phenomenon of considerable theological, pedagogical, and sociological significance. . . . The fact that the most influential manuals were always written in Latin ensured that their influence would not be restricted to the native countries of their authors. Roman theology was ultramontaine not merely in its ecclesiology and church discipline but also in its cultural assumptions (a fact which is not always fully appreciated in accounting for the Italianization of the Roman Catholic Church in the late nineteenth and early twentieth centuries); and as it gradually permeated the seminaries of the world, it filtered out almost all regional variations." Gabriel Daly, O.S.A., Transcendence and Immanence, (Oxford: Clarendon Press, 1980), p. 12.

[37]Complicating the exercise of authority from without the paradigm would be the mode of legitimation available to ecclesiastical authorities (versus those available to scientists). Given the nature of theology's sources, and the possibility of appeal to extra-mundane authority, the risk of reification of theology's conceptual frameworks would be much greater than for science.

[38]Sanks, pp. 5-6, 138-139.

[39]In my dissertation, Paradigm and Structure in Theological Communities: A Sociological Reading of the Modernist Crisis. Unpublished Ph.D. Dissertation, Catholic University of America, 1979, considerable account had to to taken of the authoritative structures of social control exercised on modernism.

[40]Ritzer, p. 32.

[41]McCool, p. 14.

[42]Margaret Masterman, "The Nature of a Paradigm" in Lakatos and Musgrave, p. 61. Quotations from Kuhn's text in support of that numeration follow on pp. 61-65.

[43]Ibid., pp. 65ff.

[44]See "Postscript - 1969" in Thomas S. Kuhn, The Structure of Scientific Revolutions. 2nd ed. Chicago: University of Chicago Press, 1970. Stephen Toulmin has distinguished five phases in Kuhn's refinement of the term through SSR 1970. Toulmin, pp. 107-117. He comments: "Over the years, then, Kuhn's account of scientific revolutions has become not less ambiguous, but more so." p. 115.

[45]Ritzer, p. 7.

[46]"Aristotle thought that scientific truths are universal propositions which are deduced from indemonstrable premises, and which one justifies by resolving them into the first principles. Consequently, all the certitude of a factual truth is derived from a universal truth, and, ultimately, from the principle of contradiction, thus applied to a particular case. Finally -- and this last factor is a résumé rather than an addition -- the rationalistic idea of necessity tends to exclude from 'science' everything that is contingent." Georges Van Riet, Thomistic Epistemology vol. I. Translated by Gabriel Franks, O.S.B. (St. Louis: B. Herder Book Co., 1963), p. 117.

[47]Aubry, p. 382. Cf. Gayraud, "A propos des études ecclésiastiques en France", p. 290.

[48]Toulmin, p. 129.

[49]McCool, p. 8.

[50]"More profound knowledge of St. Thomas did not channel the epistemology of the nineteenth century into new directions. Problems and solutions both remained unchanged, and the general

41

atmosphere and preoccupations did not vary. The modifications introduced were only of secondary importance. When they draw on tradition for interesting themes, our authors insert what they borrowed into their tracts without comparing them first with currently popular ideas.

"Thus, for example, they make the traditional notion of science their own. . . .

"If one remembers that the development of the new sciences impelled Descartes and Kant to elaborate a 'critique' better adapted to the nature of scientific knowledge, . . . it will seem rather strange that before 1900 neo-Thomistic authors were content to interpret popular certitude in the light of Aristotelian science." Van Riet, I, p. 120.

[51]Bernard Lonergan, Method in Theology, (New York: Herder and Herder, 1972), p. 301.

[52]See note 2 supra.

[53]See note 45.

[54]Sanks, pp. 118-119.

[55]Ibid., p. 121. Cf. McCool, p. 225. Exemplary in this regard is the account provided in Joseph L. Dawson, Billot's Analysis of the Act of Faith. Unpublished S.T.L. Thesis, Baltimore: St. Mary's Seminary, 1951.

[56]Aubry, p. 208.

[57]A diversity noted by modernists themselves: Cf. Loisy, Simples réflexions, pp. 14-15; Mémoires III, p. 212; Tyrrell, Medievalism, p. 106; and commentators on the movement, e.g., Alec R. Vidler, 20th Century Defenders of the Faith, (London: SCM Press, Ltd., 1965), p. 35.

[58]Loisy also remarked, "The modernists are workers or isolated thinkers, whose general ideas are more or less convergent, because all follow, more or less, the modern methods of scientific investigation . . . ." Simples réflexions, pp. 269-270.

[59]Duel, p. 68.

[60]A paradigmatic analysis of modernism is carried out at some length in Paradigm and Structure in Theological Communities, pp. 78ff. What follows will merely summarize that treatment, highlighting material that pertains more specifically to the issues engaging Loisy.

[61]Cited in A. Leslie Lilley, Modernism: A Record and Review, (New York: Charles Scribner's Sons, 1908), pp. 51-52.

[62]E.I. Mignot, Lettres sur les études ecclésiastiques, (Paris: Librairie Victor Lecoffre, 1908), p. 160. For similar statements by Loisy, see Mémoires I, pp. 261, 265-266.

[63]Again, Mignot: "Theology, which was the point of departure for deductive science, can only be the point of arrival with analytical science." Quoted in Lilley, p. 40.

[64]von Hügel to Blondel, 26 May 1896. Quoted in Heaney, p. 243 n. 15.

[65]For expansion see Paradigm and Structure in Theological Communities, pp. 91-94.

[66]Bernard Lonergan, A Second Collection, (Philadelphia: The Westminster Press, 1974), p. 2.

[67]"As incommensurability depends on covert classifications and involves major conceptual changes it is hardly ever possible to give an explicit definition of it. . . . The phenomenon must be shown . . . ." Feyerabend, p. 225.

[68]Kuhn, SSR, p. 147.

[69]Ibid, p. 148.

[70]Blondel to Abbés Denis and Gayraud, 5 Oct. 1896. Lettres philosophiques, (Paris: Aubier, 1961), p. 110.

[71]Kuhn, SSR, p. 149.

[72]Cf. Thomas F. O'Dea, The Catholic Crisis, (Boston: Beacon Press, 1968), p. 75.

[73]Derek L. Phillips, Wittgenstein and Scientific Knowledge, (London: The Macmillan Press, 1977), p. 72.

[74]Scheffler, p. 46. "The thought that theories are incommensurable is the thought that theories simply cannot be compared and consequently there cannot be any rationally justifiable reason for thinking that one theory is better than another. Expressed in this bold universal form, the thesis that theories are incommensurable is extremely implausible." Newton-Smith, p. 148.

[75]Kuhn, SSR, p. 149.

[76]Thomas S. Kuhn, The Essential Tension, (Chicago: The University of Chicago Press, 1977), pp. xxii-xxiii.

[77]Bernstein, pp. 79-108.

[78]Ibid., pp. 85, 87-88.

[79]Ibid., p. 91.

[80]"In cultures that differ from ours, genres that also differ from ours may be available, embedded in social practices, and these genres may not lend themselves to translation in any simple or direct way into those with which we are familiar. The task of understanding an alien culture may require the imaginative elaboration of new genres, or the stretching of familiar genres, in order to compare what may be incommensurable." Ibid., p. 103. Cf. Newton-Smith's understanding of incommensurability, note 74 supra.

[81]Feyerabend, p. 274.

[82]Kuhn in Lakatos and Musgrave, p. 268.

[83]Scott's introduction to The Gospel and the Church, pp. xxvii, xxviii.

[84]Maude Petre, Alfred Loisy, His Religious Significance, (Cambridge: Cambridge University Press, 1944), p. 112.

[85]Lakatos and Musgrave, pp. 79-80.

Chapter 2

Metaphor and Modernist:

The Language of Development

> My efforts to reconcile Catholic orthodoxy
> with the sincere critical study of the Bible
> you compared, not without faint irony, to the
> exploits of a tight-rope walker who walks on
> a cord stretched in the air.
> Alfred Loisy[1]

> . . . to write theology is like dancing on
> the tight-rope, some hundred feet above the
> ground. It is hard to keep from falling, and
> the fall is great. The questions are so
> subtle, the distinctions so fine, and
> critical jealous eyes so many.
> John Henry Newman[2]

Loisy once characterized Newman as "le théologian le plus ouvert qui ait existé dans la sainte Eglise depuis Origène."[3] A decade later, the French exegete himself was regarded by an admirer as applying in his work "the best thought of Newman and especially of his theory of development to the whole history of religion in the light of and by the aid of modern criticism and the modern spirit."[4] The thought of both of these men stood outside the theological mainstream of the Catholicism of their times. One was excommunicated for his theological opinions, and in consequence his predecessor's work came to be regarded with suspicion for decades.

This chapter will center on Loisy's understanding of doctrinal development, as that found expression in the trio of "modernist" writings referenced previously: the series of Firmin articles in the Revue du clergé français, L'Evangile et l'Eglise, and Autour d'un petit livre. In eliciting that understanding, Loisy's use of Newman's work will of necessity be taken into account. Once the exegete's thought on the process of development has been delineated for the period in question, his engagement with selected critics will be taken up. The polarization of position between modernists and scholastics sketched in the introduction will re-emerge in this issue. Kuhn's notion of incommensurability has suggested that such polarization may fruitfully be examined on the level of language,

45

while Masterman's specifications have pointed more specifically in the direction of metaphor. Accordingly, by examining the metaphors and analogies characteristic of the exegete and selected orthodox critics, it is hoped that some light may be shed on this aspect of the modernist crisis. This chapter, then, will investigate the understanding of development expressed by Loisy, and the reactions of three important critics with a view toward determining their characteristic metaphors and analogies. Their interaction will then be analyzed, drawing principally on the work of Max Black and Paul Ricoeur.

i

> . . . the way in which we understand such 'formal' concepts as 'tradition' and 'dogma' affects the way in which we view each and every article of christian belief. It affects our approach to the whole problem of continuity and discontinuity in christian life, belief and understanding.[5]

After his dismissal from the Institut catholique, during the years spent at Neuilly, Loisy's attention turned from more narrowly exegetical concerns to those engaging apologetics. These he set forth in the livre inédit, an attempt to formulate an apologetic for Catholicism that would take account of developments in modern science -- especially that of historical criticism -- and thereby speak effectively to minds formed by modern culture. Undergirding this projected renewal was the reformulation of three postulates which Loisy set forth as forming the basis of the traditional demonstration of Catholic truth. The third of these, termed the ecclesiastical postulate, has a direct bearing on the topic under consideration. "The ecclesiastical postulate owns that the Church, with the essential stages of its hierarchy, its fundamental dogmas and the sacraments of its worship, has been directly instituted by Christ."[6] The adaptation of this position in a renewed apologetic would be obtained by the reformulation of a first postulate, the "theological" one, which held that "the fundamental religious ideas, beginning with the idea of God, have been essentially invariable, at least for a chosen portion of humanity, from the creation of the world down to the present time."[7] That adaptation/ reformulation would be predicated on the serious recognition of a process of historical development.

Loisy prudently refrained from publishing the initial portion of the livre inédit, as this apologetical manuscript came to be called. As noted, several of its more theoretical portions, dealing with the process of dogmatic development, and the nature of religion and revelation appeared under the name of "A. Firmin". Appropriately, the first of these articles advanced the

46

exegete's ideas in the context of a discussion of Newman's work. It was during the Neuilly years that Loisy made contact, via von Hügel, with the Cardinal's writings, including the Essay on the Development of Christian Doctrine. While the substance of Loisy's proposed reconciliation of Catholicism with criticism was already in his mind before he came under the influence of Newman, the latter's writings proved useful in its expression and commendation.[8]

Newman had written, "I believe _I_ was the _first_ writer who made _life_ _the_ mark of a true Church."[9] While Nicholas Lash has termed this emphasis on life, or holiness, "an uncharacteristically one-sided emphasis . . . as a test of sound doctrine" where Newman is concerned, it became rather characteristic indeed of the modernists in general, and of Loisy in particular.[10] Concerning development, the latter wrote in the initial Firmin article, "Fundamentally, there is something other and very much more than a movement of ideas; there is the entire life of the Church. Newman has seen and said this better than anyone before him."[11] Accordingly, Loisy draws upon the Cardinal's work to aid his own expression of the phenomenon of development. In doing so he used those aspects of Newman's thought which were most congenial to his own problematic. From the Essay, which contained in rudimentary form resources for constructing a number of theories (not all of them mutually compatible when in an elaborated form), the French exegete emphasized the biological ideas.[12] This appears rather prominently in the following:

> It is evident that according to the theory, and Newman would not have hesitated to add according to history, Christian development is not reduced to a simple perfecting of ecclesiastical language, to a work of logical deduction, to a multiplication of similar practices, but that development must be conceived as intimate, vital, real, as considerable in its order as that of animal life from birth until adult life, implying, consequently, the identity of being in all the transformations operating in it accordingly to the law of its institution, but excluding as a state of death the absolute immobility of the form once acquired.[13]

While employing Newman to help express his developmental solution to the problems raised by his exegetical efforts, Loisy was also conscious of extending the problematic. Primarily a Patristic scholar, Newman had attempted to account for the fact of development within Christian history. Loisy, aware of the problems posed by historical criticism of the Scriptures in the intervening period, expanded the range of development to encompass the Scriptures themselves. The exegete felt himself faced with the further issue of how revelation itself enters into a developmental process. That became the subject of subsequent Firmin articles.[14]

Before addressing the nature of revelation directly, however, Loisy inquired into the nature of religion.[15] Once again taking up the organic analogy, his concern was to emphasize the living character, the vitality of religion. A religious institution that is living cannot be immobile, for life involves movement, and movement entails change.[16] Further, there appears to be an automatic harmony between what will favor the Church's life, and what is authentically Christian. The necessities of life will dictate the forms of true religion and therefore of true Christianity; thus the very nature of religion comes to function as a criterion for judging development. Because it is "natural" for a religion to develop in a cognitive, ritual and institutional way, the growth of the Catholic Church, with its dogma, worship and institutional structure is vitally necessary and legitimate.

In consequence, Loisy distinguished between the reality which dogma seeks to express, and the formula in which it seeks to give expression to that reality:

> Dogma would be petrified in the Church and not living, if it were identified absolutely with its theological formula, and if the latter were declared entirely immutable. . . . But the Church does not teach and does not think that its dogmatic formulae are the adequate and absolutely perfect expression of the supernatural realities they represent . . . . The theological and dogmatic work, unceasing in the Church, is nothing else than a permanent effort for ever more and ever better adapting to the present and variable needs of humanity, the doctrinal formula of divine truth, which alone is perfect in itself and unchanging.[17]

This approach to dogma is predicated upon an approach to revelation which is concerned more with emphasizing the experiential dimension than with expounding upon the cognitive. In two further articles Firmin explored this key theological notion.[18] Again the stress falls upon the living character of the phenomenon. Revelation is a communication, in life, of divine truths to people living in a given era, one which receives continued explication in the living institution of the Church.[19]

Therefore, to appreciate revelation as a living reality, in a way more adequate to the data of history, scholastic intellectual habits must undergo some modification.

> When revelation is concerned, 'truth' must not be confused with 'doctrine'. Accustomed to regard faith objectively and theoretically, as a system of propositions rigorously formulated and divinely obligatory, we have difficulty in conceiving a religion without precise dogma, a revelation without official creed. The habits of mind that come to us from scholasticism are to be corrected on this point by history.[20]

Doctrines and dogmas are derivative upon the simple truths contained in the assertions of faith. It is the latter which constitute the "proper and direct object" of revelation, not the authoritative explications themselves. "The truths of revelation are alive in the assertions of faith before being analyzed in doctrinal speculations; their native form is a supernatural intuition and an affirmation of faith, not an abstract consideration and a systematic definition of their object."[21]

The truths contained in the assertions of faith are proportioned to the intellectual needs of the people to whom originally destined. Hence revelation as expressed in the formulas of human language cannot accomplish the adequate and imperfectible expression of religious truth. Human ideas in the religious order are always metaphors and symbols, and in relation to the reality which they represent, they are imperfect symbols. The human expression of divine truth, then, is secondary to the reality it would express; as such it is a living expression in principle changeable. As "imperfect symbols . . . their very imperfection would render them insufficient for intelligences more advanced than ours, and . . . even for us, because they are human in form, [they] are susceptible of explication, that is to say of modification and relative improvement."[22] As explications of revealed truths necessary to articulate those in relation to other areas of human knowledge, doctrine and dogma are also subject to the limitations of human language and human imagery. Hence doctrinal and dogmatic development is likewise necessary in principle, though secondary relative to "the permanent unity of [revelation's] spirit and the real continuity of its development."[23] Continuity in dogma, therefore, is not to be sought in immutability of external expression, but in unity of spirit, in general correspondance between developmental stages.[24]

For Loisy, then, "Revealed religion is a life, an active

organism, a fruitful institution before being a doctrine."[25]
"Firmin's" conceptions of revelation and religion therefore
legitimate the necessity of a developmental process as intrinsic
to Christianity. "Newman is above all an Anglican who became a
Catholic, a perfect Anglican who has become perfectly Catholic in
discovering that Catholic development was in the real logic of
Christianity, indispensible to its conservation, as divinely
legitimate as Christianity itself, from which, fundamentally, it
is not possible to distinguish it."[26]

The series of Firmin articles was interdicted with the
condemnation of the first installment of "La religion d'Israël"[27]
in 1900. As noted earlier[28], though only the latter article was
the one to receive censure, the conceptions running through the
entire series were implicitly in view. Loisy's subordination in
these articles of dogma to theology -- and, more fundamentally,
of both of these to the lived experience of faith -- would remain
at the very center of his conflicts with authorities. Several
characteristics of the exegete's style of presentation in the
Firmin series contributed to the forms that conflict assumed.

First, Loisy's vocabulary was very like the liberal
Protestants, such as Sabatier[29], whom he ostensibly criticized in
them, and correspondingly very unlike that of scholastic
theology. Moreover, there is little explicit attempt to relate
Firmin's positions to those of the official theology.

Second, there is notable ambiguity in some of the key
concepts of Loisy's theological vocabulary, which not only make
his position difficult to relate to both liberal Protestants and
scholastics, but not at all easy to understand in its own right.
In this vein W.J. Wernz has singled out the notion of "truths"
(vérités). Loisy's injunction not to confound "truth" and
"doctrine" is grounded in his emphasis on the truths contained in
the simple assertions of faith as primary and the systematic
elaboration of these truths via conceptual schemes of doctrine
and dogma as secondary. As "living" in the assertions of faith,
the "native" form of these truths is a "supernatural intuition";
their "exterior form" undergoes modification "through contact
with science", so as to remain in agreement with scientific
conceptions.[30] As living in the assertions of faith, then, these
"truths" would have an intellectual content, but cannot be
reductively translated into any conceptual formulation. They
remain primary, while the formulations that seek to establish
their harmony with other areas of knowledge are inevitably
limited by milieu and mode of expression.

As Wernz sums it up:

Several of the controversial points are
clear: contra Sabatier, theology and dogma

50

are necessarily associated with the primary religious experience, as its guardians and intellectual expressions. And contra traditional Roman Catholicism, there is a fair distance between dogmas and the primary material of revelation. The way for Loisy's conclusion is paved: revelation is neither a matter of mere feeling nor a once-for-all deposit of dogmas. With his concept of 'vérités' Loisy constructs something of an 'x' to perform the necessary mediating function between these extremes, without much elaboration of the content of this 'x.'[31]

The more theoretical portions of Loisy's apologetical treatise which appeared in the Revue du clergé français were not always replete with clarity. That lack of clarity was augmented by the separate publication of the more historical portions of the livre inédit. It was not until 1902 that they appeared in the form of a refutation of the liberal Protestant Adolf von Harnack's Das Wesen des Christentums. When the latter work was published in French translation, Loisy produced a rejoinder, attempting to insinuate his ideas for a renovation of Catholicism under the guise of a critique of liberal Protestantism. Popular in style, L'Evangile et l'Eglise reached a much larger audience and brought much larger repercussions.

As an extension of the work present (and occasionally implicit) in the Firmin articles, L'Evangile et l'Eglise represented an application of the underlying principles, of the reformulation of the above-mentioned triple postulates. As intimated previously, the alteration of the ecclesiastical postulate is predicated upon the reformulation of the theological postulate. Once development were shown in the realm of fundamental religious ideas, a way would be opened for the salvaging of official dogma, whose traditional interpretation it appeared, had been undercut by a scientific critical method.

In his attempt to distinguish the essence of Christianity Harnack had recourse to the image of a kernel within a husk, the husk representing what is traditional, the kernel what is essential in the teaching of Jesus. Loisy replied with a vegetative metaphor of his own, that of seed and full grown tree: "Why should the essence of a tree be held to be but a particle of the seed from which it has sprung, and why should it not be recognized as truly and fully in the complete tree as in the germ?"[32] Again, as in the Firmin articles, the underlying notion is that Christianity is a living reality, and growth and development are intrinsic to living things. Thus the very preservation of life mandates growth, change, adaptation. And whatever fosters that life, whatever fosters its increase, cannot

51

be written off as a deformation; on the contrary, it must be seen as legitimate for development.

> Are the processes of assimilation by which it
> grows to be regarded as an alteration of the
> essence present potentially in the seed, and
> are they not rather the indispensible
> conditions of its being, its preservation,
> its progress in a life always the same and
> incessantly renewed?[33]

As an historian, Loisy takes the parable of the mustard seed as his paradigm for the growth of Christianity. The new-born Christianity is compared to a little grain, out of which grows the spreading tree of the present-day Catholicism. Extending the analogy, "charity was its sap", and "its life impulse was in the hope of its triumph."[34] Like a real plant, Christianity is essentially identical "from the beginning of its evolution to the final limit and from the root to the summit of the stem."[35] The best apology for all that lives is thus life itself. And Christianity has not lived to preserve a kernel in the husk of a ripe (or overripe) fruit, but to preserve a living revelation, a living gospel through its very growth and development.

This vegetative language is quite naturally extended to dogma as well: "The ancient dogmas have their root in the preaching and ministry of Christ, and in the experiences of the Church, and their development in the history of Christianity and in theological thought . . ."[36] They "were not contained in primitive tradition, like a conclusion in the premises of a syllogism, but as a germ in a seed, a real and living element, which must become transformed as it grows, and be determined by discussion before its crystallization into a solemn formula."[37] As one surveys Loisy's works of this period, there appears to be an underlying equation between the fact of development and authentic development. The existence of the tree, as it were, legitimates the process of growth up to that point.[38] This raises the question of the relation between fact and faith, between history and belief -- an issue fundamental to an understanding of Loisy's positions in general, and his thought on dogma in particular.

That which the Church presents as her official dogmas are not "truths fallen from heaven", "preserved by religious tradition in the precise form in which they first appeared."[39] To the historian they are interpretations of religious facts, acquired over a period of time through a process of theological reflection, and necessarily expressed in human categories related to the contemporary state of human knowledge. "Though the dogmas may be Divine in origin and substance, they are human in structure and composition."[40] And significant change in the state of human knowledge may necessitate a change in that composition, a rearticulation of the traditional formulas -- a new interpretation necessary to preserve their religious significance in a changed intellectual atmosphere.[41] Thus Loisy could distinguish between the "material sense" of the dogmatic formula, its "external image", and its religious meaning and significance -- the latter capable of being reconciled "with new views of the constitution of the world and the nature of things in general."[42] This, then, is the door through which Loisy would bring a reinterpretation of Catholicism, one which would alter the meaning of doctrine, the significance of worship, the nature of authority, in the attempt to preserve the religious significance of the Church for a changed intellectual climate. The tree had developed from the seed; it was capable of further growth, in order that its life might be preserved in the future. And so Loisy affirmed, "How vain it is to proclaim the end of dogma because the doctrinal flower of this great life appears withered, and to imagine that the fruitfulness of Christian thought is definitely exhausted, and that the old tree can never again renew its adornment for a new epoch, a new springtime!"[43]

The response to L'Evangile et l'Eglise by Loisy's closest supporters was highly favorable, though in retrospect excessively optimistic.[44] Even among those less favorable in disposition, however, for some the book's refutation of Harnack tended to overshadow the grounds on which that criticism proceeded. And those grounds were rendered somewhat obscure by the book's manner of publication. Containing as it did the more historical portions of the livre inédit, and published in separation from the more theoretical parts, the "little red book" would be productive of much misunderstanding. For a time -- very brief -- that appeared to operate in Loisy's favor.[45] In the longer run it would be productive of more heat than light.

The year 1902 ended with the first of a series of articles from Abbé Hippolyte Gayraud, critiquing L'Evangile et l'Eglise. As a Dominican monk, Gayraud had taught scholastic theology at the Institut catholique at Toulouse. In 1893 he left the order to become a diocesan cleric and moved to Paris, where he became involved in the political and social questions of the day. Elected to the Chamber of Deputies as a firm supporter of the Republic[46], he constitutes an example of the odd juxtaposition of political liberalism and theological conservatism that contributes to the complexity of that era.[47] Gayraud possessed then, on the one hand, the knowledge of scholasticism and a commitment to its propagation[48], and on the other the polemical skills and disposition gained in the political arena. In 1893 he had written, "Assuredly, the best weapon against error is the exposition of the truth; from whence it follows that, even from the point of view of polemic, it is necessary to give to the defenders of the Church the true science of faith."[49] The science in question is that of scholastic theology, the "revealed theology" ably seconded by the scholastic philosophy, whose exemplar is St. Thomas, "the perfect type, the inimitable model of the scholastic doctor, the most authorized representative of this philosophy."[50] Admittedly, the synthesis of truths of the natural order and the revealed dogmas effected by the Angelic Doctor must be accomplished in a manner appropriate to the present day. Gayraud is thus a partisan of a renewed Thomism, one creatively adapted to the contemporary world. However,

> While waiting, the Thomist synthesis remains
> the greatest effort of human genius towards
> the unity of our knowledge; it forms the
> great foundation which bears the columns of
> the perfect synthesis whose glorious capstone
> the future, I hope, will see.[51]

Having established Gayraud's Thomistic credentials, his initial polemical encounter with Loisy may now be taken up.

As Loisy in L'Evangile et l'Eglise had occasionally accommodated his language to that of Harnack, Gayraud's treatment of Loisy manifests the same phenomenon. While metaphors are often similar between exegete and polemicist, still it is necessary to examine how Loisy's are interpreted, and the meaning which Gayraud places on those same metaphors.

Loisy's critic begins his series by admitting the legitimacy of a general thesis of evolution; contested are the exegete's applications of that thesis, which seem to run contrary to the theological tradition. Thus in the initial article Gayraud writes,

> That the progress of Christianity must be
> compared rather to the birth of a germ or of
> a plant than to a deductive or geometric
> construction, is something evident which no
> one, I believe would contest. Christianity
> is a real life, the highest degree of life
> for humanity. Thus it must grow and progress
> in the fashion of life. But what was there
> in the Christian germ from which Catholicism
> was the issue? That is precisely the
> question.[52]

The model of development proceeding by logical clarification and explication of the revealed deposit had the (scholastic) virtue of affirming the substantial identity of dogma throughout the developmental process. The conclusion of a syllogism draws forth a truth perhaps not entirely perceived, but, nonetheless, one which was implicitly present in the premises. Despite his disavowal of comparison with deductive construction, and his apparent agreement with Loisy's growth metaphors, Gayraud retains a commitment to the permanent and immutable nature of dogmatic truth which must be reflected in a substantial identity of the later tradition with the preaching and teaching of Jesus. Where Loisy seems to focus on the process of development present in his growth metaphors, and thus preserve continuity between primitive datum and present-day Catholicism, Gayraud seems to fasten on the contrast between embryonic source and the fully developed product. Struck with such contrast, he emphasizes their heterogeneity, the discontinuity present in the exegete's account.

> It can be held without doubt that this Christianity of history is of evangelical origin, that it has issued from the preaching of Jesus of Nazareth, and that the Catholicism of today is the legitimate product of the evolution of this doctrine of the kingdom. But who does not see how difficult it is to admit the identity of this primitive Christianity with our Catholicism? Their relations are no more those of a tree to its seed, or those of maturity to infancy, or of the man to the embryo. It seems rather that Catholicism is a strange engraftment placed on a trunk which was in no way destined by nature to bear an identical branch.[53]

For the official theology revelation consisted in truths revealed by God, attested by him and his infallible authority. This emphasis on the divine, coupled with the fundamentally ahistorical character of this paradigm, relegated the role of humanity to a rather peripheral status. Loisy's metaphors, comparing development to a natural process of growth, seemed to naturalize dogma. Despite the exegete's rhetoric affirming dogmas as divine in origin and in substance, his formulations appeared to lead to the conclusion that they are "uniquely the product of human conceptions". As Gayraud reads Loisy, dogmas represent the elaboration of the preaching of Jesus by a natural evolutionary process; as the product of human speculation, their "substantial foundation is only human thought."[54] Interestingly, in his final article Gayraud eschews the metaphorical language of growth and expresses himself in categories more congenial to his basic scholastic commitments. Quoting Loisy's assertion "that dogmas are divine in origin and substance, they are human in structure and composition", he goes on to observe:

> These words are capable of a very good meaning. If truly the substance of evangelical Christian thought is found

immutable under our dogmatic formulae, and if
the human part consists only in explicating,
elucidating, exposing the thought
methodically and scientifically, if such was
Loisy's doctrine, his language would be of
rigorous exactitude and conform to
traditional teaching. But it is not thus
that the learned critic understands the
elaboration of dogmas. What I see in his
discussion contra Harnack is precisely that
he does not find in the evangelical essence
of Christianity this permanent divine
substance of our dogmas, whose identity would
truly be the essential identity of the
Catholicism of our day and of the messianism
of Jesus.[55]

From Loisy's exposition Gayraud can only conclude that this does
not amount to a development of the self-same idea, but a
substitution of one idea for another. Consequently, Loisy's
reconstruction of the messianism of Jesus and contemporary
Catholicism are not the same religion.

The former Dominican had begun his series with the intention
of examining more closely Loisy's historical exposition of
Christian evolution, with a view toward determining "if under an
apparent agreement of words would not be hidden a profound
disagreement of ideas."[56] Though some apparent agreement of
words appears in Gayraud's treatment, there emerges rather
profound divergence of ideas.

In his Mémoires, Loisy observed regarding his critic:

Narrowly scholastic, he understood nothing of
historical criticism, and he applied himself
to fencing madly, in the name of dogmas and
theology, against my opinions as critic and
historian. . . . [T]he character and tone of
his lucubrations did not appear to me to
merit on my part an exception to the law of
silence which I had set myself vis-à-vis my
refuters.[57]

The second of Loisy's critics to be considered, Emile-Paul Le
Camus, surfaced his rejoinder in the form of a brochure, Vraie et
fausse exégèse.[58] At the time of its writing he was bishop of La
Rochelle, having been recently appointed in 1901. His background
was thoroughly scholastic: he had received a doctorate in
theology at Rome, and had attended the Vatican Council as
theologian to Mgr. Las Casas. As ordinary, his proposals for
reforming the curriculum of his diocesan seminary reflect the

less speculative and more positive theological orientation of the scholastic formation he received.[59] Nonetheless, while emphasizing the latter, he affirmed, "we have always reserved the rights of St. Thomas and of scholasticism to effect the rational synthesis of the dogmas whose apostolic origin we have previously demonstrated."[60] His approach to dogma follows the traditional line, and is expressed in the by now familiar categories:

> Development follows logically as a series of consequences included in the dogmatic principle bequeathed as deposit, and from which one must never depart. Who will pretend that successively drawing out the corollaries of a geometric theorem modifies the theorem itself? . . . so that, the Church having maintained its dogma substantially the same, without variations and with an ever growing clarity throughout the ages, we can really affirm that our faith is indeed the faith of the Holy Fathers, the faith of the Apostles, the authentic thought of Jesus Christ.[61]

Le Camus, during his theological formation, had also studied under Le Hir, the celebrated Hebraicist. Better acquainted with Scriptural exegesis than Gayraud, the bishop reflects this in his approach to L'Evangile et l'Eglise.[62]

In examining Vraie et fausse exégèse, one is struck by the predominance of spatial metaphors to refer to dogmatic development, and more generally to the role of historical exegesis vis-à-vis dogmatic theology. Samples: "the strength of Catholicism is partially in this divine flexibility which, combined with its dogmatic immutability, permits it to bend to the needs of all epochs, without leaving the indestructible rock on which it has been established . . . ."[63] Referring to "the precise sphere where exegesis can freely move", the author notes that, "This sphere is vast, for if Christian dogma marks its limits, true science must find there the necessary space to establish strong and victorious conclusions."[64] And,

> To the unreflective the banks which contain the river appear to constrain its movements; in reality they regulate its course and assure its salutary action. What are moreover the sciences which do not have arresting points beyond which they go so fatally to the drift? Have we not heard those who are among us, the most illustrious representatives complain of themselves being constrained in fixed paths which they could

not surmount? The limitation is traced for some by physical facts, for others by mathematical truths. For us, it is constituted by the rule of faith, and it is in not departing from this that our religious science has remained really science, establishing in the eyes of all that, going forth from the Gospel and the Tradition, Catholic dogma has developed, from age to age, according to the needs of the times, without having known variations. To address the questions of exegesis without having attentively recognized and without accepting the demarcation traced by the Church on the terrain where one is going to move, is to risk being caught suddenly outside the Catholic idea.[65]

In one of the cases where an organismic analogy is made, it is noteworthy that the comparison is structural, static, rather than dynamic: "The religion of Jesus Christ . . . is a doctrine, that is to say a collection of truths which are connected to one another to form a body so harmoniously constituted that, suppressing a part, or placing it in arbitrary dependence vis-à-vis another, is to compromise the entire body."[66] In the other case, where the comparison is made between the liberty of Catholic exegesis and a bird with clipped wings, the intent of the analogy is to show the salutary effect of a restricted field of movement.[67]

In Le Camus' writing there is also a noteworthy tendency to invoke military metaphors, reflecting the defensive posture of 19th century Catholicism, itself often referred to as a "fortress mentality". The language of defense and battle, weapons and tactics permeates the bishop's writings.[68] When one reflects that a goal of military campaigns is, after all, to capture territory, an affinity between this set of metaphors and those which are spatial emerges, converging, for example, in an expression such as "battlefield".[69]

These excerpts will suffice to indicate the mode of expression employed by the bishop. In light of Loisy's own assessment of Newman's work and his relation to it, the following is worthy of remark. In reference to the chapters on the development of dogma in L'Evangile et l'Eglise, Le Camus observed, "As he appears to understand it, this development is in reality a transformation. Nothing in common between this theory and that, very novel undoubtedly but otherwise balanced, of Cardinal Newman."[70] Obviously, scholastics and modernists had very different ways of reading Newman. Also obviously, scholastics had very similar ways of reading modernists: for both

Gayraud and Le Camus, Loisy's conception of development does not preserve continuity. Committed to a conception of substantial identity they read his theory as importing an illicit transformation.[71]

After reading the first of Gayraud's articles, Mgr. Mignot had written to Loisy, stressing the need for clarifying the conception of development set forth in L'Evangile et l'Eglise. Specifically, he advised some explicatory notes appended to a second edition of the book, stressing Loisy's distance from the sort of evolutionary naturalism imputed to Sabatier.[72] Loisy chose instead to write another book, written in the form of letters clarifying points of controversy raised by the "petit livre rouge". Mignot's observation to Loisy concerning Le Camus' effort has been noted earlier.[73] The exegete's own opinion found expression in a letter to von Hügel: "[Le Camus] does not have the air of suspecting why I have not availed myself of the fourth gospel, and he has learnedly refuted me with the texts of John. You may expect that indeed it is not difficult."[74] Accordingly, the third letter in Autour d'un petit livre was addressed "to a Bishop, on the criticism of the Gospels and especially on the Gospel of Saint John." A conversation of sorts is thus established between exegete and episcopal critic, one that Le Camus will continue in Fausse exégèse, mauvaise théologie (1904). Among the seven letters comprising Autour, the sixth is concerned with the origin and authority of dogmas, while the second included consideration of the development of religious ideas. Hence both of these will also be of interest here.

Although spatial and military metaphors occasionally crop up in Autour d'un petit livre, they apparently do so as conventional expressions rather than as expressive of a basic orientation.[75] Loisy's framework continues to receive formulation in the organic metaphors he found congenial in the Firmin articles and in L'Evangile et l'Eglise.

In this work of clarification, then, the theoretical portions of the exegete's apologetic resurface, this time for a much larger audience, and in terms more than faintly reminiscent of Firmin. The experiential character of revelation, the secondary status of doctrine and dogma, and the historical conditioning of truth are re-expressed in terms which develop but little those previously employed by Firmin.[76] In the letter directed to Le Camus, the exegete affirms, "Catholic doctrine is the intellectual expression of a living development, not the simple explication of an old text, nor the purely logical elaboration of an ancient creed."[77] Therefore, "To ask the historian to retrieve from the biblical texts the entire current doctrine of the Church is to ask him to see in an acorn the roots, the trunk and the branches of a century-old oak."[78] Or, in other words, to focus on the terminus a quo and the terminus ad quem is to misread both the metaphor and the reality to which it points. By contrast, Loisy places emphasis on the process of growth, the living evolution from germ to maturity: "the truth as a good belonging to humanity, is no more immutable than humanity itself. It evolves with it, in it, through it; and that does not prevent it from being the truth for it."[79]

With regard to the status of the sources, the gospels are not to be taken as historical biography but as assertion of faith. This is above all the case with the fourth gospel, for Loisy a "master work of mystical theology". As such it was discussed in L'Evangile et l'Eglise only in the chapter on Christian dogma, for it really belongs to the process of the development of Christology.[80] This turns on a distinction between fact and faith, on the claim for a legitimate autonomy for criticism in its sphere, for theology in its own.[81] For Loisy this was not the fruit of abstract consideration, but rose out of practical concern.

Autour d'un petit livre touched off a second barrage of criticism. If by reproducing the theoretical underpinnings of his apologetic Loisy succeeded in clarifying his position, he apparently succeeded also in strengthening the opposition. From the range of replies once again representatives of type will be offered: the polemicist, Gayraud; the episcopal representative, Le Camus; and this time a theologian, Bouvier.

Gayraud's series, again in L'Univers, increased by one over his previous set. Though six in number, his articles dwelt on five themes: history and theology, the historical value of the gospels, Christian development, the kingdom of heaven, and the Son of God. And once again his language manifests characteristics similar to the previous articles: metaphors which resemble those of his adversary, the tendency to read those in a way very different, and to resort to more scholastic terminology when pressed to state his position more precisely.

His preference for a more organic mode of expression is reaffirmed: "If I formulate a syllogism in order to condense the argument it is not, as their adversaries accuse the scholastics, that I reduce all progress of faith to the dry and cold form of geometrical deduction. I approve and like the classical comparison of life which grows through absorbtion and assimilation." But he soon adds, "But in the movement of Christian life I require the living germ and I accept it only from Jesus and his apostles"[82], implicitly introducing the requirement of substantial identity throughout development. The only acceptable sense in which progress of the faith is legitimate is that which supposes the permanence of the Christian idea, from Jesus to the present in eodem sensu et eadem sententia.[83] This last phrase runs like a refrain throughout the

60

series. Since this permanent identity of the primitive idea is found lacking in Loisy's system, Gayraud judges its conception of development deformative and in opposition to Catholic doctrine. The traditional conceptions of the latter remain the norm for assessing the adequacy of metaphorical renderings invoking growth:

> The identity of the person would not always be evident to the eyes of those, who having seen the infant, or even having raised him, recognize him at the age of maturity. The real question is this: are the Trinitarian and Christological formulae in use in the schools and consecrated by the councils, although imperfect and relative as all human language, the legitimate expression logically deduced from the teaching of Jesus?[84]

Where Loisy's position is concerned, Gayraud concludes in the negative, restating his conviction that to follow the exegete, growth by assimilation becomes growth by substitution. The criterion in eodem sensu et eadem sententia has nothing in common with a theory of succession of heterogeneous concepts. The proper word for the latter is not development, but replacement, indeed a replacement that proceeds entirely along human lines.[85]

The juxtaposition of organic metaphors and language of logical development in Gayraud's exposition stems from a conviction that the former is deficient of itself; it contains implications that are illegitimate when applied to dogmatic development. Hence the need to preserve an attachment to orthodox terminology as a control:

> But, by what disposition of mind has Loisy come to want to exclude from the historical development of the church its logical development? Why does he enclose himself so narrowly in the classical comparison of germ and life, that he can no longer see that it is defective for the Church, if one wants to make of it the absolute type of its evolution? In the germ, the plant is found only in power; in the Christianity instituted by Jesus, it is necessary that Catholicism already exist in substance, for there is no veritable progress in this matter unless it is accomplished in eodem sensu et eadem sententia. In that case, the Church is understood to be contained in the Gospels as in its premises, as the oak in the shrub, the animal in the embryo, as the man in the child . . . . Between the Galilean preacher of the

61

Janiculum and the Pontiff of the Vatican, the
chain of life, of thought, of faith, of
apostolic action appears uninterrupted in the
concentrated light of history and theology.[86]

Defective in its mode of expression, Loisy's thought remains
elusive in its style. In the concluding article of the series,
the critic had recourse to the contemporary art world to make his
point.

In truth, [Loisy's] thought most often slips
between the words, and, like an unseizable
fluid escapes from the grip of an argument.
The most subtle and indeed benevolent
dialectic sees itself forced to imitate those
painters who, powerless to render the
beauties of nature with their unskilled
paintbrushes, devote all their skill to
translating the impression that the objects
make on their eyes or on their nerves. This
is how the theologian proceeds with writing
sprinkled with errors or heresies.[87]

Before Gayraud's series had run its course, the Congregation
of the Holy Office intervened, placing the two controversial
"little books" in the Index, and adding three additional titles
of Loisy's. Authority had rendered judgment, but left to the
critics the task of specifying the offending points in Loisy's
presentation.

In 1904 Le Camus, invoking the biblical principle of "by
their fruits you shall know them", proceeded to examine the
fruits of Loisy's exegesis. The title of his brochure proclaimed
his verdict: Fausse exégèse, mauvaise théologie. The notable
preference for spatial and military metaphors characteristic of
his earlier effort is again apparent.[88] The bishop also employs
the traditional metaphor of "deposit" of dogma.[89] The latter
harmonizes more readily with an insistence on the immutable
character of dogmatic truth and with the now familiar commitment
to substantial identity throughout the tradition. As with
Gayraud, such terminology becomes a controlling principle in
reading organic metaphors. In this regard, an exemplary
illustration may be found in Le Camus' admission that, while
there may be cases where "it becomes difficult to see the oak in
germ in the acorn which produced it", nonetheless, "the tree was
not less in the seed from which it came." Quoting from the
tradition: "'There is certainly a considerable difference between
adolescence and the maturity of man. However, the mature man is
the same as the adolescent'", he concludes, "thus, with clarity,
the illustrious doctor renders precise the immutable character of
dogma as a deposit: 'It is, not something that you discover, but

something confided to you . . . .'"[90] Metaphors which for Loisy evoked the dynamic process of growth while preserving an element of continuity are here pressed into service of a conception whose movement is logical, whose concern is to preserve identity. In creating his own terms of comparison the bishop fastens on that of a jeweller cutting a diamond: "while leaving it always the same, [he] multiplies its facets, in order to increase the luminous irradiations."[91] Such is the work of the Church with respect to the development of dogma. (One receives the strong impression, however, that this is rather secondary to her task of "guarding" the deposit.[92])

For this conception which equates "development" with "clarification", Loisy's system appears "completely rationalist", one in which dogma "is formed and indeed transformed."[93] As for Gayraud, that system can only lead to a Christianity whose term is heterogeneous with its origin, and whose development is a completely human product.

Le Camus consecrates a significant portion of his rejoinder to a major point of contention between Loisy and himself, namely: the value of the gospels as historical witnesses for the life of Christ, and especially that of the fourth gospel. Their status is necessary to his arguments on several areas of disagreement: the foundation of the Church, the institution of the sacraments, the nature of the Eucharist. Some of this will be of concern to us later, and will be taken up in chapter 4.

Pierre Bouvier, S.J. (1848-1925) has received earlier mention in reference to his collaboration with Letourneau and Billot on the syllabus of errors extracted from Loisy's works. Prior to that Bouvier had shown himself an "intransigent spirit" in a controversy over the interpretation of another syllabus -- the Syllabus Errorum issued by Leo XIII's predecessor. The author of several historical and doctrinal works on Ignatian spirituality, the Jesuit turned to evaluating Loisy's work, publishing in March of 1903, L'exégèse de M. Loisy.[94] The latter catalyzed the collaborative effort to produce the small syllabus. Like the syllabus, Bouvier's brochure underwent expansion after the appearance of Autour d'un petit livre in October of that same year. What follows is based on that expanded version of 1904.

There is exhibited the familiar preference for spatial metaphors, occasionally juxtaposed with metaphors pertaining to light.[95] Thus the author admonishes, "It is not without impunity that the straight line of orthodoxy is abandoned, and that travel in the light of the Catholic Tradition is ceased."[96] Those who have been partisans of critical methods to excess "have ventured on . . . dangerous routes" and are poised on "the brink of the abyss" -- while Bouvier places himself "from the outset on Catholic terrain", making appeal to "all the documents preserved in the doctrinal deposit of the Church."[97] The resurrection of Christ is termed the "granite foundation of our faith."[98] Even on the single occasion where the author makes reference to the Church as a "living organism", the spatial and light metaphors qualify that:

> It is not that the Church is repugnant to progress, quite the contrary. Far from being petrified, the Church is a living organism, she is growing in knowledge . . . . Not that she adds truths to the deposit whose full plenitude she has originally received through the mediation of the apostles, or that she substitutes new truths for those whose protection and interpretation have been confided to her; but, in adapting herself to the needs and tendencies of the epochs that she traverses, sometimes makes resplendent some point of the divine revelation until then remaining in shadow, sometimes she disengages some conclusion heretofore unnoticed in the principles, sometimes she teaches with greater precision some article as yet proposed only under a general form and which was wavering in a half-light.[99]

Light metaphors evidence the controlling conception of clarification of revealed first principles via logical explanation. The progressive clarification of "the truth already taught" preserves the substantial identity of that truth: "the meaning of revelation once determined, either by the infallible magisterium, or by universal belief, remains from then on safe from all variations."[100]

The authoritative intervention by Rome in December 1903 occupied Loisy's attention into 1904, as he sought to determine his response to that.[101] Although the excommunication he expected did not materialize, it was clear to him that his projected renewal of Catholicism was unacceptable. From 1904 onward, then, Loisy's effective participation in the modernist movement all but ceases.[102]

From this survey of the exegete's turn-of-the-century work, and treatment of selected critical responses, there has emerged distinct preferences for kinds of metaphors and analogies on either side. A controlling metaphor in Loisy's work is that of life. Hence his language tends to be organismic and employed in a dynamic sense. Even where partisans of the dominant theology employ similar language, they do so in such fashion that organismic metaphors are read differently, or are interlaced with more static, often spatial terminology reflective of their own theological commitments. This is consistent with the tendency of the scholasticism of their period to be rather ahistorical, in which the truths of the faith were seen to be closely interconnected, such that a threat to one constituted a threat to all -- or really to the Church's authority which was held to undergird them. Thus while their metaphors may occasionally overlap those characterisitc of Loisy's work, their metaphors which actually are dominant -- those which are spatial and architectural -- are congruent with the general contours of the scholastic position. Constitutive of a fundamentally ahistorical position, such spatial metaphors reflect a distinguishable linguistic preference, and ensure that organismic metaphors are assimilated to a static perspective.

Following his treatment of Loisy's engagement of Harnack, Poulat was led to conclude, "At least this examination gives us two essential elements of our problem: the difficulty of the interlocutors in being understood and in explaining themselves; the reality of the disagreement which opposes them."[103] He states that these two elements will be found again between Loisy and the Roman theologians. In the foregoing survey real and divisive issues centering on and surrounding the development of dogma have emerged. Conscious articulations of difficulties in mutual understanding have also surfaced. Possessing some sense of the language characteristic of exegete and adversaries, it is time to approach the latter more analytically, inquiring into the dynamics of that.

ii

> The basic unity in [a theological] constellation could be clarified by reference to a root metaphor that was shared by all members of the group. Theologians of different orientation often disagreed because they were working on the basis of different metaphors which they took for granted and did not subject to serious questioning.[104]

A point of departure for this analytical section can be found in Kuhn's statement that scientific revolutions have "transformed the scientific imagination in ways that we shall ultimately need to describe as a transformation of the world within which scientific work was done."[105] In accepting a new paradigm, then, the practitioner must undergo fundamental change in his orientation toward the world, often acquiring new conceptualizations which reconstitute the world in a new way, new methods which open new problem areas for access and vitiate solutions of previously "solved" problems. Given the large element of discontinuity within science (and theology) seen as a revolutionary enterprise, it is less than surprising that proponents of competing paradigms would fail to make complete contact with each other's viewpoints. Kuhn termed this phenomenon "incommensurability" and saw it engaging three major aspects of paradigms: data, methods, problems; language; and world view.

The issues which are encountered as problematic, and the language employed to explicate/ debate said problems are not independent of one's basic way of looking at the world. The modernists viewed the profound changes that had followed in the wake of empirical science as having created a different world, a different intellectual culture. In doing so they came into direct conflict with the world conception of neo-Thomism. This confrontation of theologies has been interpreted as a reflection of a cultural collision.[106] And something of that interpretation is reflected in Wernz's comment that, "The misunderstanding and criticisms that arise can in part be laid at Loisy's door. But I am more inclined to explain the confusion on the basis of the distance from which the orthodox view Loisy. He shares neither their vocabulary nor their thought-world."[107]

In speaking of world views we are at one step remove, as it were, from theology: the focus is not on developed theologies of God or of salvation (or of development), but rather on the contour of a "world", such that certain ideas of God, salvation, or development, and not others, seem peculiarly appropriate.[108] So in the face of his critics, Loisy kept repeating that he was only stating "the facts", and the facts witnessed to a process of development. "The facts are there. They cannot honestly be denied, when they are known . . . ."[109] In response to the exegete's conclusions his critics largely reiterated the conciliar decrees and continued to quote Scripture in a rather literalistic way, without regard for the literary genres contained therein. Le Camus, for example, could write: "We must take our Gospels such as they are, as the exact, faithful, unimpeachable expression of what the apostles saw, heard and told of Jesus."[110] At issue here is not simply the authenticity of a given evangelical text, or even a methodological difference in evaluating the gospels as four biographies of equal value versus developmental products of faith and reflection; the divergence engages a set of background assumptions against which methodologies are accepted as legitimate (or not), texts assume a variable historical veracity (or not). Differing world views constitute differing networks of assumptions within which certain arguments "make sense", while others appear naive or beside the point.

It would appear that not only certain ideas, but means of expressing those ideas, particularly linguistic expressions, would be compatible with a given world view. This engages the second aspect of paradigm incommensurability: language. As Kuhn remarks, "Two men who perceive the same situation differently but nevertheless employ the same vocabulary in its discussion must be using words differently. They speak, that is, from what I have called incommensurable viewpoints."[111] This phenomenon has emerged at a number of points along the way. Loisy's habit of using the traditional language, but of not organically relating that to his argument is both symptomatic of underlying divergence in Weltanschauungen and a complicating factor in its own right. Hence, Le Camus could remark Loisy's use of the traditional language, while adding that he was not always sure what the exegete meant by it: "Amidst language where conventional but very unclear formulas of 'Easter Message' and 'Easter Faith' are mixed in profusion, language assuming German cloudiness and of which many readers will understand nothing, one asks oneself if M. Loisy admits the resurrection of Jesus Christ, yes or no."[112]

The fact of linguistic incommensurability presumably has been well established. At the close of chapter 1, however, the task was set of inquiry into its dynamics. As a first step in that, the notion of "polysemy" will be examined -- for that, as the "basic condition for symbolic discourse", constitutes "the most primitive layer in a theory of metaphor, symbol, parable, etc."[113] Polysemy refers to "that remarkable feature of words in natural languages which is their ability to mean more than one thing."[114] Which meaning a word will assume at any given point is specified by context -- really a variety of contexts. Paul Ricoeur lists these as: the linguistic environment of the actual words, the speaker's and hearer's behavior, the situation common to both, and the horizon of reality surrounding the speech situation.[115] Since written texts are under analysis here, the first and fourth of these assume primary importance. And since something of the horizon of reality has been suggested with regard to the respective world views (or "cultures") underlying modernist and scholastic positions, the linguistic environment will receive immediate attention. Later we should be in a position to connect the two.

An author's metaphors -- the most basic as well as the most prevalent -- constitute an important portion of the linguistic environment within which terms assume their meanings. Indeed, according to Ricoeur metaphors themselves can be understood as a creative use of polysemy.[116] Just as polysemy is a semantic phenomenon -- the polysemic word assumes meaning within the context of the sentence through a dialectical process in which context narrows the range of possible meanings that a word may take -- so must metaphor be understood as a semantic phenomenon. Metaphor does not occur only at the level of the word[117] -- as an evocative, ornamental way of communicating what could otherwise be said in more mundane terms -- but at the level of the sentence. As the product of a context, it emerges in the interaction between words and sentences (and, indeed, between series of sentences that constitute a text).

In a now classic article[118] Max Black expresses the interaction via the terms "focus" and "frame". A word (the focus) by being placed in a given context (the frame) produces a change of meaning by virtue of that interaction. The new context imposes extension of meaning upon the focal word. In order to understand Black's view of how this process occurs it is probably best to proceed with a specific example. In Autour d'un petit livre Loisy wrote, " . . . the Gospel and the Church are in an identical relation to the kingdom; they immediately prepare it; they are its terrestrial root, whose trunk mounts toward eternity."[119] In Black's terminology, "root" constitutes the "focus" ("trunk" would constitute another, but in the interests of simplification it will be ignored here); the rest of the sentence, the "frame". The interaction occurs first by the frame acting upon the focus. To call Gospel or Church "root" is to evoke in the focus "root" a series of opinions and preconceptions which are the common possession of a linguistic community. Called by Black a "system of associated commonplaces", for roots these would include notions like trunk or stem (that which is rooted), growth, decay perhaps, the soil in which something is rooted, more generally -- stability. The frame, then, evokes this system but in that very process emphasizes some of those notions and "filters" out others. In the process those evangelical and ecclesiastical traits most susceptible to being talked about in "root-language" will be rendered prominent, while any that cannot will be pushed into the background. Interaction also occurs in the focus acting upon the frame. The metaphor "root" organizes a view of Gospel and church by applying a subsidiary subject (root) to the principal subject(s). The application of the metaphor "selects, emphasizes, suppresses, and organizes features of the principal subject by implying statements about it that normally apply to the subsidiary subject."[120] Gospel and Church are not literally like roots. But by bringing these two realms together, similarity is metaphorically created between Gospel and Church on the one hand, and roots on the other.

While recognizing several strengths in Black's analysis, Ricoeur points to a fundamental problem. As Black himself admits, his rendering of metaphor is itself metaphorical: a metaphor is a filter. For Ricoeur this begs the question of the emergence of metaphorical meaning.[121] This is a significant lacuna, although one apparently not easily rectified: much of the literature on how metaphors work that has emerged since Black's groundbreaking article has been concerned with explaining just how metaphor creates new meaning and generates insight.[122]

Black's system of associated commonplaces limits, in

68

Ricoeur's mind, the work of metaphorical interaction to connotations already established. As such metaphor can produce extension of meaning, but cannot be said to be truly innovative, in the sense of creative of novel meaning. Black does make allowance for "specially constructed systems of implications, as well as . . . accepted commonplaces"[123]; for Ricoeur this provides an avenue to a more adequate understanding of metaphor.

The foregoing exposition of Black's theory highlighted a tension between two subjects -- one primary, the other subsidiary. This can amount virtually to locating the tension between two terms: e.g., Church and roots. Ricoeur will want to place this tension rather between two interpretations of the sentence itself. The metaphor would involve the purposive creation of a semantic discrepancy in the sentence (i.e., a literal contradiction which is a logical absurdity). The Church is not a root, if root is something which holds a tree in the ground and through which it draws nourishment from the soil. A sentence which predicates a root of the subject Church may be a syntactically correct sentence, but will be literally absurd, that is "semantically impertinent" (incorrect) with respect to meaning. The predicate in this instance is not pertinent to the subject; it does not fall within the range of permissible meanings. Where a literal interpretation fails, the metaphor forces a new interpretation, the establishment of a new semantic pertinence out of the impertinence at the literal level.[124] "The function of metaphor is to make sense with nonsense, to transform a self-contradictory statement into a significant self-contradiction."[125]

In discussing polysemy, it was seen that the function of context -- sentence, discourse, text -- was to reduce polysemy: to fix a meaning appropriate to the sentence from the possible range of meanings that the word could assume. Contrary, however, to the normal interchange of word and sentence, the metaphor is not a potential meaning, but establishes meaning. In establishing a new pertinence at the level of the sentence, the metaphorical word changes meaning. "The metaphorical interpretation presupposes a literal interpretation which self-destructs in a significant contradiction. It is this process of self-destruction or transformation which imposes a sort of twist on the words, an extension of meaning thanks to which we can make sense where a literal interpretation would be literally nonsensical."[126] The metaphor exists in the tension, the conflict of two interpretations. As long as the tension is maintained, the metaphor is living. When that tension ceases, the metaphorical word assumes a standard linguistic identity and passes into the language as an enrichment of the polysemy of words. Such "dead metaphors" have been alluded to previously, although they were termed "conventional". Le Camus' use of military metaphors is based on the conventional metaphor:

argument is war.[127] As but one instance, "Theology will still be able to cope with the attacks of rationalism, even without recourse to a peace signed with it on the evolutionist terrain. There are auxiliaries who, without suspecting it, do the work of enemies."[128] Light also can assume a conventional status, as in an expression as the "light of faith".

From Ricoeur's analysis living metaphor emerges as the vehicle for the creation of new meaning that the prior polysemy could not contain by itself. This is why the meaning of metaphor cannot be reduced exhaustively by translating it into a series of literal statements. Meaning is created out of the tension of self-contradiction; metaphor as a creative enterprise breaks through previous categorization to "establish new logical boundaries on the ruins of preceding ones."[129] In doing so it creates a new gestalt, as it were, a new viewpoint.[130] In an intuitive experience-act the similar is seen in the dissimilar. It is not a case of bringing together two systems of associated commonplaces and linking their already established meanings; it is a matter of establishing resemblance on the metaphorical level while the contradictory usage of a literal meaning remains intact.[131] While retaining the clash between the "same" and the "different" -- through its retention of the tension of interpretations -- metaphor creates a meaningful similarity between two ideas previously thought incompatible. Powerful metaphors empower the user to experience reality in a new way:

> The strategy of discourse implied in metaphorical language is . . . to shatter and to increase our sense of reality by shattering and increasing our language. The strategy of metaphor is heuristic fiction for the sake of redescribing reality. With metaphor we experience the metamorphosis of both language and reality.[132]

In other words, through a "heuristic fiction" -- an imaginative schema or proposal which, though literally false, is a useful tool for the uncovering of a previously undiscovered dimension of reality -- the metaphor creates a tension which can be overcome only by a change in perspective. It does so by weakening the first-order reference of ordinary language through a literal contradiction, in order to open up a figurative, second-order reference which gives rise to a new interpretation of reality.

Such metaphoric redescription may occur in practice through networks of metaphors. Black, for instance, remarks that a metaphor may involve a number of subordinate metaphors among its implications. Such subordinate metaphors play a role in constructing the system of implications that illuminate/

70

configure the primary object. Normally they belong to the same field of discourse as the primary metaphor. When a primary metaphor is powerful enough to organize metaphoric networks consisting of the partial metaphors borrowed from the diverse fields of experience and thereby assure them a partial equilibrium, it constitutes a "root metaphor". Stephen Pepper has explained the notion in this way:

> The method in principle seems to be this: a man desiring to understand the world looks about for a clue to its comprehension. He pitches upon some area of common-sense fact and tries if he cannot understand other areas in terms of this one. This original area becomes then his basic analogy or root metaphor. He describes as best he can the characteristics of this area, or, if you will, discriminates its structure. A list of its structural characteristics becomes his basic concepts of explanation and description. We call them a set of categories. . . . He undertakes to interpret all facts in terms of these categories. . . . Since the basic analogy or root metaphor normally (and probably at least in part necessarily) arises out of common sense, a great deal of development and refinement of a set of categories is required if they are to prove adequate for a hypothesis of unlimited scope.[133]

Thus root metaphors possess the capability of organizing metaphoric networks in service of greater understanding, i.e., they assemble. But on the other hand, their analogical nature gives them the ability to engender a conceptual diversity: a number of potential interpretations at a conceptual level.

The root metaphor employed by Loisy in the works considered could be rendered as "living organism". References to the church as a "living being", as "ecclesiastical organism"; to Christianity as a "living reality", to revealed religion as "a life, an active organism" dot these writings.[134] The attendant vocabulary develops the foundational metaphor via networks drawn from various fields of experience: "acorn", "roots", "trunk", "century-old oak", "flower" (doctrine); "germ in a seed" (dogma); "root", "stem" (Christianity); "budding", "animal life from birth until adult life", "embryo" and "maturity" (development); "man at fifty . . . day of his birth" (Church/ Gospel).[135] From these metaphorical networks are drawn structural characteristics that provide descriptive and explanatory concepts: organisms obviously exhibit "growth"; they may proceed through "assimilation", which

71

results in a "transformation" of the living thing.[136] But living things are also "subject to imperfection", and they can "decline and perish".[137] While metaphorical networks are drawn from a number of contexts throughout Loisy's "modernist" writings, in L'Evangile et l'Eglise "vegetative" language and its accompanying implications seem especially prominent. Very likely the latter stems from Harnack's choice of "kernel"/ "husk" metaphors to describe dogma/ development. In any event, vegetative metaphors are more developed.

The gospels provided Loisy with seed and plant imagery, and the acorn/ oak image was classical within the tradition: Vincent of Lérins used it. The exegete developed his metaphorical networks out of his underlying concern to emphasize the element of transformation in dogma, while at the same time preserving some sense of continuity. For Loisy, the unitary construction effected by the dominant theology suppressed diversity in the historical record.

> The work of traditional exegesis, from whence dogma may be said to proceed by a slow and continuous elaboration, seems in permanent contradiction with the principles of a purely rational and historical interpretation. It is always taken for granted that the old Biblical texts and the witness of tradition must contain the truth of the present time, and the truth is found there because it is put there.[138]

The conception of revelation present in scholasticism and the status accorded to dogma in consequence have rendered this theology myopic with regard to the variability and relativity that history attests and is manifest to a scientific criticism. To want to place the full doctrinal flower of present-day Catholicism in the primitive germ is to ignore the historical record -- and the record of history will not be so accomodating. "If you place all that in the Gospel, you suppress history, and history does not let itself be suppressed; you do violence to the texts, and the texts testify against those who torture them."[139] The exegete's choice of language also attests his intention to argue that the process of transformation was a necessary one, if the Church were to survive. That process is intrinsic to living things; as living the gospel had to change in order to adapt, had to be transformed in order to go on living. Thus a contradiction on the literal level (living, growing plants/ living, growing ideas, rituals, institutions) serves to insinuate a shift in viewpoint. At issue, really, is a redescription of the reality of dogma (and its attendant constellation of theological notions). In line with Ricoeur's treatment, metaphor not only shatters the previous structures of language, but shatters also

72

the previous structures of what we call reality: "with metaphor we experience the metamorphosis of both language and reality."[140]

This can be better appreciated after examining the metaphors characteristic of the neo-Thomists who have received treatment. The root metaphor could be captured in a word such as "deposit" -- something put in place, given over: revealed truths, forms of worship, institutional offices. That which was deposited with the primitive Church has been handed on to subsequent generations, intact. Something of definable quantity and definite character to be preserved from any addition, to be transmitted without omission. Part of this deposit receives specification via metaphors centering on logic: "geometric theorem" (revealed truth) and "corollaries" (the dogmas of the tradition).[141] The preciousness -- and indeed, the strength, indestructability -- of that which has been given (divine truth) is implicit in "diamond".[142] The spatial nature of deposit is reflected in its cognitive component: without due caution one may be "caught suddenly outside the Catholic idea".[143] The structural features that provide descriptive and explanatory concepts follow: corollaries are "logically deduced" from theorems; a jeweller painstakingly cuts the diamond to multiply its facets and increase its radiance (development).[144] As something to be preserved intact, the deposit must be carefully "guarded", "defended".[145]

These metaphorical networks permit change of a sort, but not of such fashion as to touch the substantial identity of the object of that activity. The diamond remains substantially the same diamond before and after the application of the jeweller's skill. The theorem remains itself unchanged by the activity of logical deduction: what was contained implicitly is rendered explicit in its corollary. Hence, even where a metaphorical network of a different sort is employed -- as in the seed/ plant imagery supplied by the tradition -- these networks exert a controlling force on how those organic metaphors are evaluated. The same tradition which supplies the language of childhood and adulthood also supplies its interpretation: the emphasis on identity over difference.[146] That same force is felt in the evaluation of Loisy's metaphors: the natural process of growth is all too natural; or, in reality it is not development, but "engraftment".[147]

To summarize: These metaphorical networks and their structural entailments are the producers of an approach that is static, constituting an attitude which was oriented toward keeping truth from being infiltrated by error. And since truth was unchanging (else how could it be true?), the stress fell on identity. So:

dogma is guarded in Scripture and in the

tradition by the Church which interprets,
defends, imposes it. That is what we have
always understood and taught in theology.
The theories of truth evolving in humanity,
with it, through it, and for it are
irrelevant here; and we see nothing to change
in the traditional conception of dogma which,
fixed in its essence and perfectible in its
development, is marvelously adapted to the
double law of stability and movement called
to govern the harmoniously constituted body
of the Catholic Church.[148]

Parenthetically, it may be noted that, given this background
of world view and metaphor, the divergent interpretations of
Newman advanced by neo-scholastics and modernists become more
intelligible. It has already been stated that Newman's own
formulations were composed of many elements -- not always
mutually reconcilable if drawn to their logical conclusions.
Given this characteristic of the Cardinal's approach to
development, it is unsurprising that his psychological theories
were somewhat puzzling to partisans of both camps. They asked if
he were speaking of logical or biological development, and,
failing to obtain a precise answer, emphasized that aspect which
was most congenial to their own conceptions. Conceiving
revelation as a deposit of propositional truths, and armed with a
deductive theological method, neo-scholastics naturally
empathized with the logical aspects of Newman's thought. Largely
leaving aside the examination of the intellectual life of society
in its psychological, historical, and sociological aspects, they
were content to study only the logical consistency of theological
systems in their completed state. Modernism, on the other hand,
having come to birth in an atmosphere of evolutionary awareness,
reflected that bias in its psychology. This vitalist orientation
influenced innovators' reading of the Essay on Development, while
informing their own attempts at theoretical solution. In
general, then, the modernists tended to criticize Newman for
having allowed logic too much play, all the while stressing the
biological; their neo-scholastic opponents did exactly the
reverse.[149]

But Newman's work was not the only such to produce a variety
of interpretations. Returning to Loisy, it will be recalled that
several factors have been invoked to account for the difficulties
encountered by his interpreters. First, Loisy tended not to
relate his positions to those of the orthodox theology in any
explicit fashion. When he used the terminology of the scholastic
tradition it did have some effect on toning down the
revolutionary implications of his writing, but he did so without
really integrating it into his overall position. More
characteristically he employs the vocabulary of the critical

historian -- in orthodox eyes, that of the rationalists. To this must be added his rather functional use of concepts to mediate elements of his position.[150] Note, for instance, the role of "truths" pointed to earlier. "Tradition" and "the Christian consciousness" assume something of the same status -- which is to say the same vagueness. If a metaphor sets up a gestalt, an intuitive perception of similarities that is influenced by context(s), then the overall context of Loisy's style has hardly contributed to orthodox acceptance. Reading those metaphors from very different contexts -- from a linguistic environment dominated by static, often spatial metaphors, themselves reflective of an underlying world view committed to an emphasis on the immutable, neo-Thomists would hardly be sympathetic to Loisy's presentation and, unsurprisingly, read his vocabulary as fluid and ambiguous -- at best; and, at worst, heretical.

The third level of incommensurability advanced by Kuhn engages the level of problematic. Summarily put, Loisy took seriously the discontinuities in the tradition which he perceived in the historical data; the problem was to take those into account in an apologetic that would affirm the continuity of the contemporary Catholicism with primitive Christianity. Thus in the exegete's treatment of development the discontinuities are prominent against a background of continuity. Elements of discontinuity are handled by the accordance of a secondary status to doctrine and dogma. If religion is primarily a life, its conceptual expression becomes auxiliary rather than fundamental. And thus a change in the form of dogmas is not crucial. Tied to this is Loisy's stress on the ineffability of the religious objects; human concepts can never adequately express the reality they seek to communicate. "Faith addresses itself to the unchangeable truth, through a formula, necessarily inadequate, capable of improvement, consequently of change."[151] Another source of discontinuity stems from "the needs of the times". As the state of knowledge advances, dogma must likewise progress: "The external forms of religious truth will be modified thus in contact with science, or indeed the faith will be in danger."[152] These elements of discontinuity do not place dogma in continual flux, however. There are several principles of continuity present in his thought on development, although the organic metaphor renders their specification more difficult. Among these principles are the unchanging identity of the religious object ("Truth alone is unchangeable, but not its image in our minds."[153]), the historical facts themselves -- once established accurately -- they will not be modified, and tradition.

His neo-Thomist critics felt their problem to be that of demonstrating the substantial identity of the present-day Church with the teaching of Jesus, in face of clear differences between the two. Committed to a conception of truth as unchanging, to a conception of revelation as a repertoire of propositional truths, to a notion of theology as providing an integrated synthesis of these supernatural revealed truths with the aid of human reason, and to a method predominantly deductive, their approach to dogmatic development reflected these commitments. The fundamental issue of continuity was really conceived as identity. Since the fulness of revelation had been given in the so-called deposit of faith, the subsequent history of dogma became one of deductively drawing out truths present in the initial premises. Given this orientation, the only acceptable solution was development as clarification; any solution seeking to go beyond this implied a transformation. Thus the contemporary dogmas provided the starting point of theological work; the tradition was read in light of that approach, with appropriate ramifications for methodology and data.

Thus language enters into the very formulation of problems and in part poses the terms of their solutions. More pervasively, language is expressive of world view, but is also in part constitutive of it.[154] The choice of root metaphor(s) is certainly influenced by underlying premises concerning the nature of reality, but metaphor in turn tensively constructs reality, shapes the contours of a Weltanschauung through the areas it throws into relief as well as those it suppresses. Loisy's efforts to express his commitments to a reality that admitted of historicity, of progressive development, and therefore of a measure of relativity via a metaphor of organic life highlighted elements of discontinuity more than it reassured on the level of continuity. His critics, committed to a set of presuppositions that were quite other, expressed in metaphors appropriate to that vision, could only exhibit a degree of incommensurability with regard to the exegete's formulations. Given the divergences on deeper levels, Loisy's failure to communicate effectively with his critics on the one hand, and to adequately express historicity and continuity on the other, achieves a measure of inevitability.

The analysis of metaphor has yielded further explication of Kuhn's incommensurability of language. The specification of characteristic metaphorical networks and the identification of controlling root metaphors in partics to the controversy has targeted an aspect of theological discourse significant for understanding the phenomenon of polarization. The "tensive" theory of metaphor, with its appreciation of language as constitutive of reality has engaged the deeper level of world view. It has also entered into problem perception and definition, and underlies the plausibility (or nonplausibility) of methodologies and the problem-solutions they produce. In the following chapter deeper divergences will be explored at greater length, by moving from a semantic analysis of metaphor to a treatment of narrative. Through application of Hayden White's work on historical discourse, applied to L'Evangile et l'Eglise as a species of historical apologetic, the role of language in figuring historical reality will be examined. White's conceptualization provides some insight into how language may be taken as constitutive of world view, and in that way advance the linguistic preoccupations that have guided this analysis. In the final chapter a number of more specific issues will be taken up -- eucharist, sacrament, and Church, in order to shed some light on "the reality of the disagreement which separates"[155] Loisy and his neo-Thomist critics -- while retaining a focus on the language characteristic of each party to the controversy.

[1]Loisy, Autour d'un petit livre, (Paris: Alphonse Picard et fils, 1903), p. 218. François Thureau-Dangin, a former student of Loisy's, was the comparison's source.

[2]Quoted in Owen Chadwick, From Bossuet to Newman, (Cambridge: Cambridge University Press, 1957), pp. 186-187.

[3]Loisy to von Hügel, 26 Dec. 1896. Loisy, Mémoires I, p. 426.

[4]W.J. Williams, Newman, Pascal, Loisy and the Catholic Church, (London: Francis Griffiths, 1906), p. 302.

[5]Nicholas Lash, Change in Focus, (London: Sheed and Ward, 1973), p. 35.

[6]Loisy, Mémoires I, p. 449.

[7]Ibid.

[8]"B. Holland justly says that Newman's writings 'fell in with, and accelerated, the line of thought that Loisy was already pursuing.'" Alec Vidler, The Modernist Movement in the Roman Church, (Cambridge: Cambridge University Press, 1934), p. 93n. Cf. Williams, pp. 302-303.

[9]Nicholas Lash, Newman on Development, (Shepherdstown, West Virginia: Patmos Press, 1975), p. 143.

[10]Ibid. Loisy's "vitalistic" emphasis will emerge below. For its prominence in the work of others associated with theological renewal, see Williams. Also Vidler, Variety, particularly chapt. 4.

[11]Alfred Firmin Loisy [A. Firmin], "Le développement chrétien d'apres le Cardinal Newman", RCF XVII (1898), p. 14.

[12]Cf. Lash, Newman on Development, pp. 56-57; J.-H. Walgrave, O.P., Newman the Theologian. Translated by A.V. Littledale. (New York: Sheed and Ward, 1960), pp. 283ff.

[13]Loisy [A. Firmin], "Le développement chrétien", pp. 18-19. Cf. p. 6.

[14]"L'idée de la révélation", RCF XXI (1900): 250-271. "Les preuves et l'économie de la révélation", RCF XXII (1900): 126-153.

[15]Loisy [A. Firmin], "La théorie individualiste de la religion", RCF XVII (1899): 202-215; [A. Firmin], "La définition de la religion", RCF XVIII (1899): 193-209.

[16]". . . a religious institution cannot be immobile since it is living, . . . all movement supposes a change, and . . . all change which will be a progress in the development of the institution will not necessarily have to be considered as a forfeiture of its principle . . . ." "La théorie individualiste", pp. 204-205.

[17]Ibid., p. 213.

[18]See note 14 supra.

[19]"If one admits that in the depths of the religious soul, upon contact with the divine, a living light bursts forth for the intelligence, communicable to other souls, one admits that revelation is the production, divinely effected, of a truth substantially divine, although always humanly perceived and formulated." Loisy [A. Firmin], "L'idée de la révelation", p. 258.

[20]Ibid., p. 251.

[21]Ibid., p. 254.

[22]Ibid, pp. 267-268.

[23]Ibid., p. 268.

[24]Cf. Loisy [A. Firmin], "Les preuves et l'économie de la révelation", p. 152. "If this identity is taken in an entirely material and rough sense, as would be the identity of a statue which would have subsisted for hundreds of years without deteriorating, certainly the thought of the Church is not met with, and an error more gross than many others is committed. . . . [W]hen [the Church] affirms the identity of the Gospel of the present day with that of yesterday, of the Catholic Church of the 19th century with the apostolic Church, she in no way intends to speak of a completely material and exterior identity, but of a substantial identity, one could say a personal identity, which is perfectly compatible in the Church as in every living being with a real development of the organism and a growing manifestation of force and activity. The conservation of dogmas in eodem sensu et eadem sententia excludes from doctrinal development contradiction, substitution of one meaning for another under the same formula, but not the interpretation of a traditional truth by means of notions connatural, if it is permissable to express oneself thus, to the first expression of these truths." Loisy, "Le développement chrétien", p. 19.

[25]Loisy, "L'idée de la révélation", p. 270.

[26]Loisy, "Le développement chrétien", p. 5.

[27]RCF XXIV (1900): 337-363.

[28]See Introduction, note 13.

[29]Cf. A. Sabatier, The Vitality of Christian Dogmas. Translated by Mrs. E. Christen. London: Adam and Charles Black, 1898:

"The question is only whether divine revelation consisted in doctrines and in dogmatic formulas. We say no. . . . But God, in entering into contact with the soul, has made it go through a certain religious experience, out of which, by means of reflection, dogmas have issued. Thus, what constitutes revelation, what should be the norm of our life, is the creative and fruitful religious experience as it originally existed in the soul of the prophets, of Christ, and of the apostles." pp. 36-37.

". . . languages are organisms and . . . words have a life of their own, quite analogous to that of animals or plants. It is through this vital power which belongs to them that their continuance and their transformations are explained. . . . It is the same with the dogmas of a Church, which form likewise a living organism, and which are, if rightly considered, only a kind of theological language by which the consciousness of the Church or the piety of its members reveals itself outwardly, and grows stronger by this self-revelation." pp. 20-21.

"In the case of religion and dogma, the intellectual element is only the symbolical expression of religious experience." p. 31.

These will suffice; they could easily be multiplied. For an exposition of Sabatier's work, see Thomas Silkstone, Religion, Symbolism and Meaning. Oxford: Cassirer, 1968.

[30]Loisy, "L'idée de la révélation", pp. 253-254.

[31]Wernz, pp. 87-88.

[32]GC, p. 16. An extensive analysis of Harnack's and Loisy's positions and their interrelation can be found in Bernard Scott, "Adolf von Harnack and Alfred Loisy: A Debate on the Historical Methodology of Christian Origins", Ph.D. dissertation, Vanderbilt University, 1971.

[33]GC, p. 16. Scott points out that Loisy's use of the term "essence" differs from Harnack's, and in fact represents an accomodation to the latter's terminology. "There is no essence, in the accepted sense of the term, of Christianity for Loisy, but rather all of Christianity is the expression of its essence." Scott, Harnack and Loisy, p. 167.

[34]GC, p. 17.

[35]Ibid., p. 19.

[36]Ibid., p. 215.

[37]Ibid., p. 214.

[38]"Setting aside all theological subtleties, the Catholic Church, as a society founded on the gospel, is identical with the first circle of the disciples of Jesus if she feels herself to be, and is, in the same relations with Jesus as the disciples were, if there is a general correspondence between her actual state and the primitive state, if the actual organism is only the primitive organism developed and decided, and if the elements of the Church to-day are the primitive elements, grown and fortified, adapted to the ever-increasing functions they have to fulfil." Ibid., p. 171.

[39]Ibid., p. 210.

[40]Ibid., p. 211.

[41]Ibid., pp. 216, 217.

[42]Ibid., p. 216.

[43]Ibid., pp. 221-222.

[44]See Loisy, Mémoires II, pp. 156-157 for those of Mignot and von Hügel.

[45]Ibid., pp. 172ff. Cf. Duel, p. 229.

[46]For a resumé of the circumstances surrounding his election see Edouard Lecanuet, L'Eglise de France sous la troisième république 4 vols. Les signes avant-coureurs de la séparation, (Paris: Félix Alcan, 1907-1930), t. 4: 98ff.

[47]See Robert F. Byrnes, Antisemitism in Modern France, (New York: Howard Fertig, 1969), pp. 208-209.

[48]Hippolyte Gayraud, "A propos des études ecclésiastiques en France" (1893); "L'avenir de la philosophie scholastique" (1895); "La réforme des études ecclésiastiques dans les séminaries" (1897). These were gathered, together with articles more directly political in nature, in Questions du jour.

[49]"A propos des études ecclésiastiques en France", pp. 270-271.

[50]"L'avenir de la philosophie scholastique", p. 333. Cf. p. 357.

[51]Ibid., pp. 356-357.

[52]Abbé Hippolyte Gayraud, "L'Evangile et l'Eglise", L'Univers, 31 Dec. 1902.

[53]Gayraud, L'Univers, 2 Jan. 1903. In the fourth article of the series Gayraud wrote in a similar vein. Commenting on Loisy's rendering of the development of the dogma of the divine consubstantiality of Jesus, he queries, "Is that a progressive development of the evangelical Christian idea? Would it rather not be a heterogeneous product, in which there no longer remains anything of the early thought, the latter having been only the occasion of this dogmatic work, instead of being the permanent and immutable substance of doctrine and of tradition?" L'Univers, 9 Jan. 1903.

[54]Gayraud, L'Univers, 9 Jan. 1903.

[55]Gayraud, L'Univers, 10 Jan. 1903.

[56]Gayraud, L'Univers, 31 Dec. 1902.

[57]Loisy, Mémoires II, p. 178.

[58]Emile-Paul Le Camus, Vraie et fausse exégèse. Paris: Librairie H. Oudin, 1903.

[59]E. Le Camus, Lettre de Monseigneur l'Evêque de la Rochelle et Saintes réglant la réorganisation des études ecclésiastiques dans son grand séminaire de la Rochelle. La Rochelle: Imprimerie Rochelaise, 1901. E. Le Camus, Lettre sur la formation ecclésiastique de ses séminaristes. Paris: H. Oudin, éditeur, 1902. See L'Episcopat français: depuis le Concordat jusqu'à la Séparation (1802-1905), (Paris: Librairie des Saints-Pères, 1907), pp. 698-700.

[60]Le Camus, Lettre 1902, p. 7.

[61]Le Camus, Lettre 1901, pp. 17-18.

62Poulat offers a comparison of Le Camus and Gayraud. Beginning with the former's critique, he observes, "it surprises by the breadth of the concessions it makes, certainly not to the exegete whom it wishes to refute on his ground, but to the name of <u>true</u> exegesis put at the service of traditional faith. Two mentalities coexist here, of different age and unequal authority, whose <u>modus</u> <u>vivendi</u> it is curious to observe. The theological spirit affirms its primacy uncontested, but it has lost its absolute power; the critical spirit has only a consultative voice, but it intervenes as a listened-to expert and in no way suspect; the one refuses 'innovation', and the second does not fear to furnish 'newness'. And it is precisely this which distinguishes Mgr. Le Camus from a man like Abbé Gayraud, for example, who also refers to criticism but doesn't know the first elements of the craft. The second remains, in his way of thinking, a pure scholastic, even though he shows himself informed or does not give way before a concession; a new equilibrium is observed, on the contrary, in the course of the first, but with something provisional which gives it a hybrid transitional aspect." Poulat, <u>La crise moderniste</u>, pp. 234-235.

63Le Camus, <u>Vraie et fausse exégèse</u>, p. 11.

64Ibid., p. 12.

65Ibid., pp. 10-11.

66Ibid., p. 18.

67"The comparison borrowed from Renan, of the bird whose wings are clipped a little, is not cause to be alarmed, when I bear in mind that in the end, if the possibility is removed from a dear and imprudent bird of going to throw himself in the talons of a vulture, he is left the right to take rather useful frolics and to sing with a liberty which, for being limited, remains not less a liberty itself of the best, real and sufficient." Ibid., pp. 9-10.

68See especially <u>Lettre</u> 1902.

69The role of biblical exegesis is rendered by Le Camus via a network of military metaphors in the following: Protected by the authority of the Church, "biblical exegesis will be only more surely a noble and good science opening vast and luminous horizons to those who apply themselves to it." Its task: that "of preparing, in order to resist the attacks of free thought, a line of firm defense that a new tactic will render victorious. In fact, there is something more decisive to the war than the ardent light horsemen going off terribly recklessly as scouts: it is the army organized in a disciplined fashion and marching to combat with a regular, practiced and sure step. The former can inform against the enemy, harass him, even draw him to the battlefield where he will meet defeat; from this point of view one owes them some gratitude, even when their foolhardy and compromising incursions are criticized. It is the latter's duty to do battle with method, and to execute useful strategic exercises, in the desired order, according to the needs of the struggle." Le Camus, Vraie et fausse exégèse, p. 39. Cf. Poulat's less metaphoric rendering of Le Camus' position, note 62 supra.

[70]Vraie et fausse exégèse, p. 38.

[71]Having examined a representative polemicist and a member of the episcopacy, there remains to be heard the voice of the professional theologian. Pierre Bouvier did produce an antiloisyste brochure (1903) following the appearance of L'Evangile et l'Eglise. Since he published an expanded version after Loisy's publication of Autour d'un petit livre, consideration of the Jesuit's contribution will be deferred until the second round of criticism is examined.

[72]Mignot to Loisy, 1 Jan. 1903. Mémoires II, p. 178.

[73]See page 4 of the Introduction.

[74]Loisy to von Hügel, 5 Feb. 1903. Mémoires II, p. 213.

[75]Examples of Loisy's use of spatial metaphors may be found in APL, pp. 52, 63, 141, 192, 256; military metaphors appear on pp. xix, 182-183.

[76]"The truths of revelation are living in the assertions of faith before being analyzed in the speculations of doctrine. Their native form is a supernatural intuition and a religious experience, not an abstract consideration or a systematic definition of their object." APL, p. 200.

"Revelation is not immutable in the sense that its symbols, once given, escape all transformation, but because it remains always, for faith, substantially identical with itself, and because the changes which are produced in its exterior determination and in its formulae are something secondary in relation to the unity of its spirit and the continuity of its development." Ibid., pp. 198-199.

"The conditions of religious knowledge, even in the order of revelation, which does not change the quality of the human mind nor the forms of its activity, do not permit that the representation of the most essential truths be otherwise than relative and imperfect, enclosed as it is in symbols which figure these truths only by analogy, without expressing them adequately." Ibid., p. 143.

[77]Ibid., p. 65.

[78]Ibid., p. 66.

[79]Ibid., p. 192. This is from the sixth letter.

[80]Ibid., pp. 106-107, 94.

[81]Ibid., pp. 49-50.

[82]Gayraud, L'Univers, 16 Nov. 1903.

[83]in the same meaning and in the same underlying significance.

[84]Gayraud, L'Univers, 16 Nov. 1903.

[85]"I dare say that, according to this manner of viewing it, Catholicism is attached to Jesus only by a link completely human and purely historical, a little like present-day Europe is a continuation of that of the Middle Ages." Ibid.

[86]Gayraud, L'Univers, 1 Dec. 1903.

[87]Gayraud, L'Univers, 28 Dec. 1903. Impressionism had constituted something of a "heresy" in the eyes of the art establishment -- an interesting context for this particular analogue. See F.W.J. Hennings, The Life and Times of Emile Zola. New York: Charles Scribner's Sons, 1977 for the impact of this movement.

[88]Emile-Paul Le Camus, Fausse exégèse, mauvaise théologie. Paris: Librairie H. Oudin, 1904.

[89]E.g., "rock", pp. 64, 94, 121; "weapons", "battle", "soldiers": pp. 7, 9, 60, 62, 65, 126.

[90]Ibid., pp. 15, 16, 79, 118, 122.

[91]Ibid., p. 16.

[92]Ibid. The analogy emphasizes the structure of a thing identical with itself. Even where the analogy is expressed in organic terms, the structural emphasis takes precedence over the developmental: e.g., "all that constitutes dogma properly so called has its origin in principle in Jesus Christ, and its point of departure from the Gospel, as the tree in full bloom, with its branches, its flowers and its fruit, originates completely from the trunk which carries it. . . . It is from him indeed, and him

alone, developed by human work, but not changed." p. 121.

[93]Ibid., pp. 15, 99.

[94]Ibid., pp. 67, 17.

[95]Aubert, "Deux documents antimodernistes inédits", p. 564n.

[96]These latter have something of a conventional status. Parties on both sides of the controversy employ light metaphors, although my impression is that they occur with greater frequency among Loisy's critics than in the exegete's own work.

[97]Pierre Bouvier, L'exégèse de M. Loisy 2nd ed., (Paris: Victor Retaux, 1904), p. 16.

[98]Ibid., p. 17. Cf. pp. 61, 67. Again, one finds that a "deposit" must be "guarded".

[99]Ibid., p. 67.

[100]Ibid., p. 68. Cf. p. 32.

[101]See Duel, pp. 247ff. for a recital of the events.

[102]Commentators agree on 1904 being a watershed in Loisy's career. Cf. Normand Provencher, O.M.I., "The Origin and Development of Loisy's Modernism", Science et Esprit XXXII (1980), p. 325: "from 1904 his attitude changed, and he progressively separated himself from the Church and orthodoxy." From its side the Church rendered that separation official with Loisy's excommunication in 1908.

[103]Poulat, La crise moderniste, p. 112.

[104]Avery Dulles, S.J., Models of Revelation, (New York: Doubleday and Company, Inc., 1983), p. viii.

[105]Kuhn, SSR, p. 6.

[106]As with Bernard Scott's utilization of Lonergan's "classicist" and "historical" cultures.

[107]Wernz, pp. 94-95.

[108]John C. Gager, Kingdom and Community: The Social World of Early Christianity, (Englewood Cliffs, New Jersey: Prentice-Hall, Inc., 1975), pp. 10-11.

[109]Loisy, Simples réflexions, p. 91.

110Le Camus, _Vraie et fausse exégèse_ , p. 17.

111Kuhn, Postscript, p. 262.

112Le Camus, _Vraie et fausse exégèse_, p. 33. Cf. p. 37-38. Cf. Bouvier, p. 65.

113Paul Ricoeur, "From Existentialism to a Phenomenology of Language", _Philosophy Today_ 17 (1973), p. 95.

114Paul Ricoeur, "Creativity in Language", _Philosophy Today_ 17 (1973), p. 97.

115Ibid., p. 100.

116Ibid., p. 105.

117This way of regarding metaphor is the product of classical rhetoric. It is summarized in Paul Ricoeur, _Interpretation Theory_, (Fort Worth: Texas Christian University Press, 1976), p. 49.

118Max Black, "Metaphor" in _Proceedings of the Aristotelian Society_ 55 (1954): 273-294. All references here will be to its reprinting in Max Black, _Models and Metaphors_, (Ithaca, New York: Cornell University Press, 1962), ch. 3.

119APL, p. 159.

120Black, pp. 44-45.

121Paul Ricoeur, _The Rule of Metaphor_. Translated by Robert Czerny et al. (Toronto: University of Toronto Press, 1979), pp. 84-90. Cf. Paul Ricoeur, "The Metaphorical Process" in Mark Johnson, ed., _Philosophical Perspectives on Metaphor_, (Minneapolis: University of Minnesota Press, 1981), pp. 232-233. J. Martin and R. Harré, "Metaphor in Science" in David S. Miall, ed., _Metaphor: Problems and Perspectives_, (New Jersey: Humanities Press, 1982), pp. 90-95.

122For a survey of this literature see "Introduction" in Johnson. Andrew Ortony, ed., _Metaphor and Thought_ Cambridge: Cambridge University Press, 1979 contains many of the articles/ authors referenced in Johnson.

123Black, p. 43.

124Ricoeur, _Rule_, pp. 130-131.

125Ricoeur, "Creativity in Language", p. 111.

[126]Ricoeur, Interpretation Theory, p. 50.

[127]For a treatment of conventional metaphors, see George Lakoff and Mark Johnson, Metaphors We Live By. Chicago: University of Chicago Press, 1980. Cf. Barry Schwartz, Vertical Classification. Chicago: University of Chicago Press, 1981.

[128]Le Camus, Fausse exégèse, mauvaise théologie, p. 65.

[129]Ricoeur, "Creativity in Language", p. 111.

[130]"When we look at something after the metaphoric process has taken place, our observation is different from what it was before. Kuhn might say that we have been subjected to a paradigm-shift." Mary Gerhart and Allen Russell, Metaphoric Process, (Fort Worth: Texas Christian University Press, 1984), p. 126. In view of Masterman's use of metaphor to explicate paradigm-shift, it is interesting to see that reversed.

[131]Metaphorical meaning is not "drawn" from a system of associated commonplaces -- or from anywhere else. It is a semantic innovation, a creation of language which has no status in established language, either as designation or connotation.

[132]Ricoeur, "Creativity in Language", p. 111.

[133]Stephen C. Pepper, World Hypotheses, (Berkeley: University of California Press, 1970), p. 91. Cf. Max Black, "Models and Archetypes" in Models and Metaphors, pp. 239-241.

[134]Loisy, "Le développement chrétien", p. 19 and APL, p. 161. Cf. GC, p. 171; "La théorie individualiste", p. 210; "L'idée de la révelation", p. 270 respectively.

[135]APL, p. 66. Cf. p. 159. GC, pp. 221-222 (doctrine); GC, p. 214 (dogma); GC, p. 19 (Christianity); GC, p. 214. "Le développement chrétien", pp. 18-19. APL, p. 17 (development); GC, pp. 170-171 (Gospel/ Church).

[136]APL, pp. 117, 180, 254; GC, pp. 194, 195; GC, pp. 213, 214. Cf. APL: "The universal idea of salvation and of the Savior . . . exists really under this particular form, as a living germ, which is entirely ready to burst its envelope and which already pierces it." p. 132.

[137]GC, p. 177; GC, pp. 149-150.

[138]Ibid., p. 219.

[139]APL, p. 225.

[140]Ricoeur, "Creativity in Language", p. 111.

[141]Le Camus, page 57 supra.

[142]Le Camus, page 63 supra. Cf. Vraie et fausse exégèse, p. 13.

[143]Le Camus, page 58 supra. Cf. Gayraud, L'Univers, 2 Jan. 1903.

[144]Gayraud, page 61 supra. L'Univers, 1 Dec. 1903. Le Camus, page 63 supra. Cf. Le Camus, Vraie et fausse exégèse, pp. 6-7; Fausse exégèse, mauvaise théologie, pp. 18, 98-99.

[145]Bouvier, p. 61. Le Camus, Fausse exégèse, mauvaise théologie, pp. 15-16.

[146]Le Camus, pages 62-63 supra. Cf. Gayraud's correctives applied to Loisy's language, noted in several of the texts quoted earlier in this chapter. The "structural" use of organic metaphors by Loisy's critics has been pointed out already. Cf. note 92 supra.

[147]Gayraud, page 55 supra.

[148]Le Camus, Fausse exégèse, mauvaise théologie, p. 15.

[149]Walgrave, pp. 283-299.

[150]This way of describing Loisy's work is derived from Wernz, who judges that, at worst, the exegete achieves a mere assertion of harmony between the cognitive and affective/ experiential, faith and fact, Catholic orthodoxy and his idea of religion. At best, Loisy constructs only a "functional" relationship, i.e., "the building of theological constructs without either filling in their frameworks or tying them together." Wernz, p. 360.

[151]GC, pp. 217-218.

[152]Loisy, "L'idée de la révélation", p. 254.

[153]GC, p. 217.

[154]This dialectical relationship is explored in Peter L. Berger, The Sacred Canopy, (Garden City, New York: Anchor Books, 1969), ch. 1 and 2. Cf. Peter L. Berger and Thomas Luckmann, The Social Construction of Reality. Garden City: Anchor Books, 1967.

[155]See note 103 supra.

Chapter 3

The Language of Structure
and the Structure of Language:
The Tropics of Alfred Loisy's
Modernist Apologetic

i

Conceptualization

In history . . . the historical field is
constituted as a possible domain of analysis
in a linguistic act which is tropological in
nature. The dominant trope in which this
constitutive act is carried out will
determine both the kinds of objects which are
permitted to appear in that field as data and
the possible relationships that are conceived
to obtain among them. The theories that are
subsequently elaborated to account for
changes that occur in the field can claim
authority as explanations of 'what happened'
only insofar as they are consonant with the
linguistic mode in which the field was
prefigured as a possible object of mental
perception. Thus, any theory which is framed
in a given mode is foredoomed to failure in
any public which is committed to a different
mode of prefiguration.[1]

In summary and highly compressed fashion, the preceding quote
sets out Hayden White's tropological approach to the analysis of
historical discourse. Even in this succinct formulation,
however, a careful reading will detect resonances with Kuhn's
notion of incommensurability, and the treatment of metaphor
(especially the notion of root metaphor) in the chapter just
previous. The intent of the present chapter is to pursue the
linguistic analysis of Loisy and representative neo-Thomist
critics, moving from the primarily semantic analysis of metaphor
engaged by Ricoeur and others to the hermeneutical level of
historical narrative practiced by White. In this fashion the
incommensurability of metaphorical networks may be grounded in a
study of linguistically shaped world views.

White's thought has been characterized as "close to a genetic
structuralism"[2]; before outlining the structure of his
conceptualization, some clarification of its roots in structural

91

linguistics will likely prove helpful. After suggesting some aspects of structuralism by way of orientation, then, a summary exposition of White's position and its general application to the two theological orientations under study will be presented. With that, a route will be open to proceed to the object of central concern in the present chapter: an examination of Loisy's historical apologetic, focusing on his most noteworthy work, L'Evangile et l'Eglise, and the critical readings of that. Having analyzed Loisy's book tropologically, I shall conclude by indicating how White's conceptualization lends further specificity to Kuhn's notion of incommensurability. That should yield some enhanced understanding of the polarization between modernists and neo-Thomists that is such an outstanding characteristic of the theological crisis at century's turn.

Structuralism traces its more or less proximate roots to the work of Ferdinand de Saussure in linguistics, dating from the early part of this century.[3] Essentially, his work may be organized around four theoretical dichotomies: the synchronic and diachronic; language (langue) and speech (parole); signified (signifié) and signifier (signifiant); and lastly, syntagmatic and paradigmatic dimensions.

Departing from the type of linguistics prevalent in the comparative philology of the 19th century, which emphasized the evolution of a language, Saussure viewed language synchronically, i.e., as a living whole which exists at a particular point of time. Viewed as such language may be distinguished as language-in-use (parole): the individual utterances of speakers of the language in everyday situations; and language-system (langue): the totality of a language deducible only from an examination of the experiences and memories of all language uses. Parole, then, is only the tip of the whole langue iceberg; moreover, the speech available to an author is a function of the language-system of relations -- a network which informs individual utterances and sets limits on how things can be expressed.[4]

In the language system conceived synchronically as relational network, two dimensions of these relationships were singled out by Saussure as being particularly important: syntagmatic (or "horizontal") relations and paradigmatic or "associative" ("vertical") relations. The former refers to the linear sequence of signs (which are made up of signifier and signified, standing in arbitrary relationship), to the meaning that words will have as a function of their relation to words that precede or follow. Thus, on the level of the sentence, individual words derive their meaning in their functioning as subject, verb, object, or appropriate modifiers, and in their relation to other words that so function. Paradigmatic relationships, on the other hand, occur between words that are expressed and those that have something in common and are associated in memory -- words that may be synonyms, antonyms, of the same grammatical function, which help by <u>not</u> being chosen, to define the meaning of the words which have. While the example here is given in terms of words-sentences, these relationships hold on a number of structural levels: to include texts or even the total linguistic system.

The thrust of Saussure's analytical framework is to focus attention <u>from</u> "reference", the world toward which the meaning of the text <u>points</u> (i.e., <u>what</u> the text means), to "sense", to linguistic structures themselves as "closed", self-sufficient systems (i.e., <u>how</u> the text means). Moreover, the emphasis regarding linguistic structures is relational: <u>langue</u> as relational network, relation between <u>langue</u> and <u>parole</u>, syntagmatic and paradigmatic relationships. This stress on the relational constitutes a defining characteristic of structuralism: "In every instance it is the structure, the relationships among . . . elements of discourse, and not the elements by themselves that produces meaning."[5]

The result of the Saussurean revolution in linguistics was to place emphasis on language as <u>form</u>, not as <u>content</u>. As self-regarding, self-regulating form, as the characteristic means of encountering the world, language could be regarded as constituting the characteristic human structure. The further step -- that language also constitutes the characteristic structure of human reality -- was taken by American structural linguistics. Independently of Saussure's work Edward Sapir noted that language structured its speakers' abilities to differentiate among some sounds while remaining "anaesthesized" to others (what gives foreign speakers their "foreign" accents). From language's influence on the structuring of sounds Sapir, and later Benjamin Lee Whorf, proceeded to language's influence on the structuring of culture. Language, in short, was held to structure not only our hearing, but our very perception of reality. "The assumption is not that reality itself is relative, but that it is differently punctuated and characterized by participants of different cultures, or that different aspects of it are noticed by, or presented to, them."[6]

In the hands of more recent structuralists, such as Roland Barthes, this takes the form of the assertion that we "encode" our experience of the world in order that we <u>may</u> experience it. In proceeding from the semiotic focus on the sign to the semantic concern with discourse, sense is once again related to reference. Writing style, therefore, does not simply reflect reality, but also shapes it, acting as an institutionalized carrier/ encoder of values.[7]

All of this may now be drawn together, that it might serve as a basis for understanding the nature of White's project. Structuralism distinguishes between surface structure (cf. Saussure's _parole_) and deep structure (cf. _langue_). A text exhibits a "vocabulary", a surface gestalt that is the manifest union of form and content, which covers an underlying "grammar" which lies implicitly and unconsciously beneath, around, or alongside of the text. This may be clarified by Daniel Patte's distinction between structures of the enunciation and deep structures. In the case of a text or discourse, constraints are imposed on the author by his/ her conscious intentions regarding what is to be communicated and the audience to whom it is to be communicated. Such stylistic structures (structures of the enunciation) are a "manifestation" or actualization of the potentialities of deeper structures. These latter proceed from the structure of human consciousness itself, and are reflected in the system of concepts and their interrelations which prefigure reality, prior to any conscious articulation of it.[8] The point here may be taken as two-fold: first, the attempt to articulate an area of reality, to give verbal expression to some "finite province of meaning" proceeds via a linguistic encoding -- a creative and, on one level, a conscious process; second, that this conscious articulation will be subject to the deeper constraints of language itself, which through its conceptual apparatus and relational network will provide a code that is implicit, unconscious, yet will also creatively shape what is perceived/ said/ written regarding the meaning of reality. In summary, "The structures of a text are the semantic potentialities of this text. All these structural meanings were passively assimilated by the author. He assumed them while he, as a creator of significations, was concerned to communicate a specific meaning."[9] Or, to put it yet another way, structuralism focuses primarily upon the significations imposed upon the author, rather than on the author as semantic agent.

In introducing his approach White distinguishes between the "surface" of the historical text, which for him includes "data", theoretical concepts explicitly used by the historian for "explaining" these data, and the narrative structure for presentation; and a "deep structural content which is generally poetic, and specifically linguistic, in nature, and which serves as the precritically accepted paradigm of what a distinctively 'historical' explanation should be."[10] This two-fold distinction can be unpacked to encompass several levels of conceptualization in the historical work, together with various modes of prefiguring the historical field itself.[11]

Conceptualization: 1. chronicle: This refers to the arrangement of the events to be dealt with in the temporal order of their occurrence. (Even at this stage the interpretive element is operative, insofar as every chronicle exhibits some selection from the unprocessed historical record.[12])

2. story: The chronicle is transformed by the characterization of some events in terms of inaugural/ transitional/ terminating motifs. "Periods" are identified, cutting points are introduced.

3. mode of emplotment (explanation): The story is fashioned into a story of a particular kind by stressing/ subordinating/ excluding events. A plot structure endows the story with a comprehensible process of development, resembling the articulation of a novel. Hence White adapts the typology developed by Northrop Frye in his theory of fictions to the historian's enterprise. In White's usage, a "romantic" emplotment stresses conflict between hero and enemy, of good and evil, in which good triumphs and the hero transcends a fallen world. "Romance" is employed to make sense out of the historical process conceived as struggle, as conflict between essential virtue and a hostile, though ultimately transitory, vice. Alternatively, the story may take the form of comedy, tragedy, or satire.[13] The interpretive element, present in the periodization of events, is even more apparently operative here. Emplotment is linked to a further level, namely,

4. mode of argument (representation): This is the level of metahistorical presuppositions about the nature of the historical field. These presuppositions constitute different notions about the nature of historical reality, and therefore generate different conceptions of the kinds of explanations (level 3) that can be employed validly in historiographical analysis. White adapts his paradigms of the form that an historical account may be conceived to take from the world hypotheses advanced by Stephen Pepper. Historical reality may be conceived under a "formist" mode of representation which directs attention to "the qualities and relations of particular events". In consequence, "The historian describes events as they have occurred. If he finds that they are causally related, he describes the causal relations as part of the existential events. But his interest is primarily in the character of the events that occurred, not in the laws which they may exemplify."[14] In formism, stress falls on the uniqueness of the elements which constitute the events to be explained: agents, acts -- while the "scene" in which they appear is recessive. In work subsequent to his formulation of this framework in Metahistory White has substituted the term "idiography" for Pepper's formism, as better reflective of historical concerns. Consonant with the four-fold typology of modes of emplotment, modes of argument also are quadriform. Alternatives to the idiographic mode are organicist, mechanistic, and contextualistic approaches.[15]

5. mode of ideological implication: The existence of alternative modes of representing the historical field entails for the historian a choice. White sees that decision informed by precritically held opinions about the nature of humanity and of society, opinions which are ideological in

nature. Thus he holds that every historical account of any scope presupposes a specific set of ideological commitments which inform its very notion of "science", "objectivity", "explanation". Essentially, ideologies are held to constitute a set of prescriptions for action in the world. White adapts the work of Karl Mannheim to preserve symmetry with previous typologies, identifying anarchism, conservatism, radicalism, and liberalism.[16]

While there is an element of interpretation present at all five levels of conceptualization, the interpretive dimension is especially prominent in the latter three. According to White, then, "a historiographical style represents a particular combination of modes of emplotment, argument, and ideological implication."[17] Further, such combinations are not arbitrary; "elective affinities" are held to exist among elements of the various levels, e.g., romantic emplotment, idiographic argument, and anarchist ideology -- although departures from these links are not uncommon, and indeed constitute something of the genius of certain historians who can combine them in ways that make creative use of the tension among disparate elements.[18]

Prefiguration: Emplotment, argument, and ideology are linked not only among themselves, but are also a product of a deeper interpretive ground in which the historical field itself is prefigured. That is to say, before bringing the conceptual apparatus to bear upon the data of the historical field the historian must constitute the field itself as an act of mental perception. This prefigurative act is precognitive and precritical within consciousness, and is constitutive of a domain which the historian can treat as a possible object of mental perception, of the concepts that he/ she will use to identify the objects of that domain, and of the possible modes of relationships that these concepts can sustain with one another. "In the poetic act which precedes the formal analysis of the field, the historian both creates his object of analysis and predetermines the modality of the conceptual strategies he will use to explain it."[19] Since historical accounts assume the form of verbal models, or "icons" of particular segments of the historical process, the prefiguration assumes the form of a preconceptual linguistic protocol, which White argues can be classified according to the four-fold distinction among tropes: metaphor, metonymy, synecdoche, and irony. "In short, the theory of tropes provides us with a basis for classifying the deep structural forms of the historical imagination in a given period of its evolution."[20]

Historical narratives, therefore, do not simply reproduce the events reported in them, but describe those events in such fashion as to inform the reader what to take as an "icon" of the events in order to render them meaningful. Put another way, historical narrative does not so much provide a map of the historical terrain as give directions for map-making. It serves less as an image of what it indicates, but rather it evokes images of the things it indicates, in a fashion White finds analogous to that of metaphor:

> The metaphor does not image the thing it seeks to characterize, it gives directions for finding the set of images that are intended to be associated with that thing. . . . [I]t does not give us either a description or even an icon of the thing it represents, but tells us what images to look for in our culturally encoded experience in order to determine how we should feel about the thing represented.[21]

Past events assume meanings in historical narratives over and above appeal to causal laws, via the metaphorical similarities they evoke between sets of real events and the conventional structures of types of fictions.

The various strands of the structuralist outlook presented earlier form a backdrop against which White's project can be projected, and hopefully clarified. Put in Saussure's terms, White's levels of conceptualization as those are employed by a particular historian in a given work constitute a parole, while the deeper structures of preconscious prefiguration constitute a langue. The concern will be to explicate how the latter is determinative of the former, as the linguistic mode in which the taxonomy of the field is cast will implicitly rule out certain modes of representation and modes of explanation regarding the field's structure while tacitly sanctioning others.[22]

In somewhat different terms, one could, I think, equate modes of emplotment with the syntagmatic, or "horizontal" dimension. The paradigmatic dimension would then reach "vertically" "down" to include (conceptually) the modes of argumentation and ideological implication. And it would reach beyond to encompass (preconceptually) the linguistic protocol in the form of the dominant trope, which is constitutive of the historical domain and that which inhabits it.

Rather apparent in White's conceptualization is a stress on the creative function of language. Historical facts and their interrelationships do not simply "emerge" from the unprocessed historical record, waiting only for the historian's attention to be directed toward them as a catalyst. On the contrary, in the encodation of events as elements of different story types (emplotment), a larger framework (argumentation, ideology) having deeper roots in consciousness (tropological prefiguration) functions to constitute the very data themselves and set limits regarding favored/ excluded relationships among them.[23]

Compressed as this summary is, it is now possible to return to the quotation with which this section began and view it with enhanced understanding. Essentially, he argues that theories which account (or seek to account) for the sequence of changes that occur within the historical process are not simply "read off" the historical data. Historical accounts are not so much verbal pictures as verbal icons -- they evoke, rather than provide a mirror reflection. This is so because the kinds of objects that appear in them as data, and the relationships that obtain among the data are constituted in the process of historical reflection -- at some levels consciously and conceptually; at a deeper level preconsciously, prefiguratively, preconceptually. This prefigurative act is tropological in nature, and one corollary that White draws is that people who are working from different master tropes in prefiguring the ground out of which their developed theories emerge will not likely find one another mutually convincing. Or to put it another way, the linguistic roots of incommensurability are deep structural and tropological in nature. This issue will be taken up at the end of the chapter.

Prior to any enhanced understanding of incommensurability that may emerge from White's conceptual scheme, that conceptualization must be applied to the treatment of history characteristic of the two theological orientations in question. Since the neo-Thomist texts which have been considered represent critical responses to Loisy's work, application of White's scheme will proceed more by way of indication. The nature of L'Evangile et l'Eglise better lends itself to more extensive treatment; that will be reflected in the analysis which follows.

ii

Conceptual Application
The Tropics of Neo-Thomism

Do not the testimonies of those who have seen the superhuman acts, and heard the discourses which they were called to confirm, suffice to constitute an historic fact? It is on this fact that our reasoning is established: Jesus has declared himself God in his discourses, he has proven this affirmation by miracles.[24]

The character of neo-Thomism as a supernatural science of faith, as a science of revealed truths has been set forth. The consequences for history -- particularly ecclesiastical history -- have been suggested, and its conception of development specified. The task here is to indicate how those consequences translate into White's conceptual terms.

The historical drama is the drama of salvation. The contours of God's salvific plan have been revealed; history is the field on which that is worked out, on which successive generations work out their salvation by the grace of God and the quality of their lives. The mode of emplotment, therefore, may be characterized as "romantic" (in White's sense): "It is a drama of the triumph of good over evil, of virtue over vice, of light over darkness, and of the ultimate transcendence of man over the world in which he was imprisoned by the Fall."[25] Frye, in his discussion of the romantic type specifies conflict as its hallmark, and themes of conflict with evil and redemption as characterisitic of this mode as it permeates religious literature. To an ecclesiastical mentality which saw itself surrounded by the hostile forces of a society increasingly characterized by unbelief, conflict was an operative -- indeed dominant -- reality. Le Camus' use of military metaphors is not, then, an individual preference, an "idiolect" peculiar to himself, but is symptomatic of a more pervasive ecclesiastical stance. To such a standpoint a "romantic" vision of history not only grasped the redemptive role of Christ's messianic mission within the scriptural sources, but obtained strong plausibility in light of that continuing conflict as experienced in the contemporary ecclesiastical milieu. Romantic emplotment is held to have an "elective affinity" for an idiographic mode of argumentation, and that is apparently the case here.

Stephen Pepper explicitly identifies neo-scholasticism with the formist world hypothesis, indicative of its Aristotelian roots and correspondence theory of truth.[26] On the plane of historical explanation, formism stresses "the uniqueness of the different agents, agencies, and acts which make up the 'events' to be explained is central to one's inquiries, not the 'ground' or 'scene' against which these entities arise."[27] To a theology which placed the high Christology of the fourth gospel on a plane equal in historical veracity to the Synoptics ("We possess four biographies in order to establish the history of the Master . . . ."[28]); which in emphasizing the divinity of Christ stressed his uniqueness, his difference from his environment; which regarded his teaching as a supernaturally revealed deposit -- an idiographic mode of representation would be congenial indeed.

By contrast, Loisy's concern to give due weight to the Jewish environment of Jesus, to indicate its influence on his ideas and practices could only be construed as reductive. In Gayraud's judgment,

Jesus of Nazareth, such as the loisyste criticism conceives and envisages him, must

have had only the ideas of his epoch and
environment, as he had its manner of living,
its habits and its language. Thence his error
on the nature and on the proximity of the
great messianic coming. He was human, he
appeared only human; his human self still was
not conscious of himself as God and Messiah.
. . . This loisyste prejudice is truly the
key to the system expounded in the two little
books.[29]

A romantic mode of emplotment and an idiographic mode of
asrgumentation are said to have an elective affinity with the
mode of ideological implication White labels "anarchist".
Whatever the structural affinities among these three modes, here
it must be said that on the level of conscious intention and
overt action neo-Thomists were conservatives, "inclined to
imagine historical evolution as a progressive elaboration of the
institutional structure that currently prevails, which structure
they regard as a 'utopia' -- that is, the best form of society
that men can 'realistically' hope for, or legitimately aspire to,
for the time being."[30] That ideological position is concretized
in a theology that stressed the divine nature of the Church over
the human, conceived it in largely juridical terms as a "perfect
society", and informed its role in history accordingly.[31] Again
reflecting the nature of the neo-Thomist texts as critical
responses, the connection between argument and ideology may be
observed in negative commentary on Loisy's apologetic:

But if in the essence and the germ of
Christianity ones places, as M. Loisy does,
only the preparation of the kingdom of heaven
taken in the eschatological meaning, if Jesus
were mistaken regarding the extent and
grandeur of his mission, if he did not teach
that he is Son of God in the sense in the
consubstantial sense of the word, if the
Catholic doctrine of the Redemption is not of
evangelical origin, but only Pauline, cannot
it likewise be concluded that 'historic
Christianity, especially Catholicism, is an
adventitious institution, foreign and
contrary' to the pure essence of the Gospel?
. . . It seems to me that, in M. Loisy's
opinion . . . the hierarchical, dogmatic and
liturgical development of the Church is only
a human contribution of elements foreign to
the work and the doctrine of Jesus and not
the progressive elaboration of a thought
always identical to itself in its basis, or
the normal growth of a living substance. This

would be a grave error in theology.[32]

The uniqueness of Jesus must be adequately preserved if the "utopian" character of the Church is to be maintained.

On a deep structural level, the dominant trope undergirding this theology and its approach to history is that of metaphor. To prefigure the historical field in the mode of metaphor is to sanction an interest in events in their particularity and uniqueness.[33] As such it is linked with idiography, whose root metaphor is that of similarity: its root metaphor, in other words, is metaphorical. This emerges rather clearly in its correspondence theory of truth -- characteristic of formism and fundamental to neo-Thomism. The way in which this perception of similarity gets worked out is well characterized by White:

> The Christian apprehends the world as one term of a Metaphor, the other and dominant term of which, that by which the world is given its meaning and identity, is conceived to exist in another world. And, far from recognizing the claims of a Metonymical or Ironic comprehension of the world, the Christian strives for the transcendence of all the tensions between the ideal and the reality which these very modes of comprehension imply.[34]

This surfaces in the scholastic distinction between supernatural and natural truths, and their mode of interrelation. As a way of rounding off this summary treatment of neo-Thomism it might be useful to encapsulate that interrelation in a specific example on the terrain of biblical history.

The privileged status granted Scripture as revealed truth had early on generated a literalist reading of the creation narrative in Genesis and with it a chronology of world history. By computation relying on the geneological information provided in the Old Teatament the date of the origin of the world and hence of human history itself had been arrived at and set at 4004 B.C. Despite advances in the geological sciences during the 19th century which increasingly called that chronology into question[35], neo-Thomism, by the very logic of its position regarding revealed truth and literalist approach to Scripture, was compelled to defend the traditional chronology. Thus, when Cardinal Mazzella, defending in his De Deo Creante the view that the days of creation were indeed days of twenty-four hours, dealt with the fossils, which geology proves to have been in the earth for long periods of time, he applied a theological solution to the dilemma: God must have created them in statu perfecto, just

101

as they are found today by the geologist![36] In the case of
perceived conflict, the tendency is to accommodate scientific
data (the mundane term of the metaphor) to the revealed norm of
faith as that was conceived (the extra-mundane term). It was no
less the case with historical data, and it was here that
neo-Thomism came into sharp conflict with the results of
historical criticism.

Loisy's Historical Apologetic:
Tropological Analysis

> Thus the best apology for all that lives lies
> in the life itself. All the scaffolding of
> theological and apologetical argument is only
> an element, and a necessary one, to figure
> the relation of the past to the present as
> well as the continuity of religion and
> religious progress from the beginning.
>   Alfred Loisy[37]

In focusing on L'Evangile et l'Eglise we are not focusing on
a work of history, strictly speaking. Ostensibly a reply to
Harnack's Das Wesen des Christentums on the terrain of history[38],
it contained in reality resources for liberalizing Catholicism,
for reconciling it with the contemporary culture. While we are
dealing, then, with a more reflective work than that of
historical narrative, we are not dealing with a highly reflective
work on the philosophy of history. While the book consisted not
only of history, but of philosophy as well -- a fact recognized
by a number of Loisy's assessors as well as the exegete himself[39]
-- it remains primarily on the historical rather than a highly
reflective philosophical plane. Accordingly, it is here
characterized as historical apologetic to distinguish it from
straightforward historical narrative on the one hand, and
speculative philosophy of history on the other. White's
conceptualization encompasses both of the latter, distinguishing
them by the relative prominence accorded to the story line in
relation to the conceptual context which interprets it. In
Loisy's work the developmental framework is more prominent than
would be the case for historical narrative -- his historical data
serve more for illustration. But that framework is subjected to
less philosophical rigor than would be the case for speculative
philosophy of history. His work falls within the range of
White's framework, without conforming precisely to either polar
category.

According to his perception of the historian's task, Harnack
set out to determine what was of permanent value in the gospel.
His dominant metaphor is that of kernel/ husk.[40] It is this that
Loisy objects to -- to the quest to find amidst the diversity of

102

history an unchanging essence. Continuity, then, for Harnack would imply an unchanging essence (kernel) preserved in new circumstances (husk). The problem becomes that the husk may be mistaken for kernel. In his criticism of Harnack's metaphor Loisy's own metaphorizing of the process of historical development of Christianity emerges: "Herr Harnack does not conceive Christianity as a seed, at first a plant in potentiality, then a real plant, identical from the beginning of its evolution to the final limit and from the root to the summit of the stem, but as a fruit, ripe, or rather overripe, that must be peeled, to reach the incorruptible kernel . . . ."[41]

Thus for Loisy it is not essence which constitutes continuity; that is provided by the process of living growth itself, as the plant grows from the seed to assume a different form, while yet preserving its identity throughout its phases of growth with the principle that gave it life.

> The historian cannot but refuse to regard the essence of living Christianity a germ that multiplies without growing. Rather he should return to the parable of the mustard seed, comparing the new-born Christianity to a little grain. . . . The grain, nevertheless, enclosed the germ of the tree that we now see
> . . . .
>   The particular and varied forms of the development, in so far as they are varied, are not of the essence of Christianity, but they follow one another, as it were, in a framework whose general proportions, though not absolutely constant, never cease to be balanced, so that if the figure change, its type does not vary, nor the law that governs its evolution. The essence of Christianity is constituted by the general features of this figure, the elements of this life and their characteristic properties; and this essence is unchangeable, like that of a living being, which remains the same while it lives, and to the extent to which it lives.[42]

While for Harnack, change threatens the essence, adding layer upon layer of husk which may well camouflage the kernel and, indeed, be taken for it, for Loisy the essence is preserved in the very process of change; when there is no change the tree is dead.

Turning to White's conceptualization, we are led naturally to the level of mode of argumentation, for Loisy's organic metaphors are indicative of an organicist mode of representing the historical field. In part, the latter is a function of the historicism which informed his use of critical method. As expressed by Maurice Mandelbaum, historicism refers to the "belief that an adequate understanding of the nature of any phenomenon and an adequate assessment of its value are to be gained through considering it in terms of place which it occupied and the role which it played within a process of development."[43] Contrary to a view for which historical events have an individual character which can be grasped apart from their situatedness in a process of development, historicism regards the latter context as essential for their understanding. Such events assume meaning only when seen as part of a stream of history.[44] Further, an adequate understanding of the process of development involves more than a mere tracing of a succession of changes -- "on the contrary, the historian is concerned with a developmental process in which some subject manifests itself in successive forms, each of these forms expressing a tendency which is characteristic of the whole."[45]

On the level of historical argumentation White characterizes the organicist mode as attempting to depict the particulars discerned in the historical field as components of a synthetic process. The historian utilizing this mode of argumentation "will tend to be governed by the desire to see individual entities as components of processes which aggregate into wholes that are greater than, or qualitatively different from, the sum of their parts."[46] And as Pepper notes, the interest will fall less on depicting the individual elements than in indicating the integrative process itself. The organicist metaphors employed by Loisy -- seed/ plant, acorn/ oak, child/ adult -- stress both the aspect of qualitative difference among forms, and the process of growth as a whole.[47] It is worth noting that the theory of development functions as a framework for Loisy's apologetic, in reaction to the fixist scheme that was a feature of the deposit model. He does not himself undertake the demonstration of the homogeneity of dogma as explication of an initial given.[48]

Loisy's organismic metaphors have the effect of strongly embedding historical personages, ideas, and events in their environment. "The gospel was not an absolute, abstract doctrine, directly applicable at all times to all men by its essential virtue. It was a living faith, linked everywhere to the time and the circumstances that witnessed its birth."[49] This has the effect of subjecting them very seriously to changes in that environment:

But a better and entirely different knowledge
of the universe and of the terrestrial globe,
of human history, of humanity itself, has
changed the face of science, so that, without

exaggeration, one could say that the believer, possessing traditional dogma, finds himself, with regard to the contemporary world, in the same situation as the first apostles when they brought the faith of the Messiah to the Greco-Roman world.[50]

An organicist mode of argumentation thus entails a conception of truth that differs significantly from the correspondence theory which Pepper sees as informing formism. He identifies it as a coherence theory and notes as one of its consequences that truth admits of varying degrees. Each developmental level exhibits more truth through the higher integration of the facts.[51] So with Loisy the progressive development of the Christian tradition places Jesus "higher", gives "a more comprehensive idea of his mission" -- "as a larger view of the world and of humanity is disclosed to intelligent faith."[52] While the exegete did not develop a systematically worked out epistemology[53], he did evidence a commitment to truth as "something necessarily conditioned, relative, always perfectible, and also subject to diminution" for humanity, and contrasted that with the received ideas of the dominant theology.[54]

On the level of emplotment, organicism is seen to hold an elective affinity for comedy -- which views change and transformation as resulting in occasional reconciliations of the forces at play in the social and natural worlds.[55] Significantly, historicism also has an affinity for comic emplotment, stressing reconciliation on the collective level of social forms.[56] Loisy's answer to Harnack's individualism in religion was to emphasize the intrinsically social nature of Christianity, his apologetic for that nature taking the form of stressing its evolutionary adaptation and achievement of provisional equilibrium in face of environing pressures. The following text is illustrative:

The Church became, at important moments, what it had to become in order not to decline and perish, dragging the gospel down with it. . . . An organ which up to one moment seemed rudimentary, and of little vigour, took on the proportions and structure that an imminent necessity demanded: then it existed in this acquired form, except for accessory modifications produced on the the occasion of other developments to preserve the equilibrium of the whole. This equilibrium was seldom established without internal movement, having all the characters of a serious crisis. Such, as a matter of fact, is the law of all development, and the natural growth of living things knows similar experiences.[57]

Interestingly, organicism has a structural affinity for a conservative ideological implication. "Equilibrium" can have distinctly conservative overtones, implying a dynamism among the parts that contributes toward stabilizing the whole. Loisy's orientation, on the other hand, has been intimated to have been rather radical in its implications, perhaps as much a commentary on the state of the dominant theology as on the inherent tendencies of his position. The exegete himself appears to have been aware of the overtones of the organicist strategy, and their utility for making the proportions of his reforming project less threatening. In Choses passées he states his conscious intention in L'Evangile et l'Eglise: "I did not confine myself to a criticism of Professor Harnack, but paved the way, discreetly but definitely, for an essential reform in Biblical exegesis, in the whole of theology, and even in Catholicism generally." Regarding the book itself, he notes in the same paragraph: "One half of my book could be accepted by all Catholics; the other half, notwithstanding my caution as to the language employed and the fact that it masqueraded, so to speak, under the cloak of the more apologetic portion, was calculated to awaken opposition."[58]

This more than suggests the existence of two levels in the work, a factor to be taken into account in moving to the tropological level of analysis. On one level, the dominant trope underlying Loisy's organicist presentation would be that of synecdoche, as that stresses part-whole relationships in an integrative way. ("By the trope of synecdoche . . . it is possible to construe the two parts in the manner of an integration within a whole that is qualitatively different from the sum of the parts . . . ."[59]) As the quote which introduces this subsection suggests, and as other texts we have noted render explicit, for Loisy the essence of Christianity is not reductive but integrative; it is the life process as a whole, rather than any particular phase that is emphasized. To but reinforce what has gone before, note the synecdochic resonance of the following:

Why not find the essence of Christianity in the fulness and totality of its life, which shows movement and variety just because it is life . . . . Why should the essence of a tree be held to be but a particle of the seed from which it has sprung, and why should it not be recognized as truly and fully in the complete tree as in the germ?"[60]

The link between synecdoche and organicism[61] is once again reinforced by the connections of both to historicism. Of synecdoche White asserts, "The 'methodological projection' of this trope is that Organicism which modern historians of historical thought have identified as 'Historicism.'"[62]

On another level, there are several indications that an ironic perspective may be at work in L'Evangile et l'Eglise. White has observed that "irony sanctions the ambiguous, and possibly even the ambivalent, statement." Though itself a kind of metaphor, it "surreptitiously signals a denial of the assertion of similitude or difference contained in the literal sense of the proposition, or at least sets a crucial qualification on it."[63] Certainly ambiguity/ ambivalence have been persistent themes in critical reactions to Loisy's book. The private reflections subsequently published in Choses passées show that such criticisms were not entirely lacking in substance. And the chosen mode of presentation within L'Evangile et l'Eglise, itself provides further indication of a studied ambiguity. While both Harnack and Sabatier were prominent in the Firmin articles, it was the former who was targeted in the "petit livre rouge". Gabriel Daly interprets this as reflecting more than the impact of Harnack's book, arguing that Loisy's "debt to Sabatier was too great, and the similarity of his position to Sabatier's too marked, for him to achieve a convincing discrimination between them."[64] This judgment is reinforced by Loisy's admission to Houtin that, "Out of the fact of controversy, I often had the air of being farther from Harnack than I was in reality; I criticized him on nuances while I was in agreement on basics."[65] The apparent differences between German Protestant and French Catholic were highlighted, allowing their exegetical similarities to remain recessive. This constitutes yet another admission on Loisy's part that the little red book was not simply what it appeared to be: a critique of Harnack's position allowed the insinuation of an apologetic for Catholicism based on critical historical method.

Loisy, then, was conscious of affirming tacitly something other than was presented manifestly. His critics also exhibit awareness that things are not simply what they seem. Given this conscious awareness, White's framework raises the question of what is operative on a preconscious, tropological level in the exegete's discourse?

There is a further indicator of irony raised by White which may be discerned more explicitly in the more theoretical portions of Loisy's apologetic which preceded and followed L'Evangile et l'Eglise. Irony is essentially dialectical, in the sense that it represents a consciousness of the inadequacy of metaphor -- a recognition of the problematical nature of language itself to adequately characterize reality. It is dialectical "in its apprehension of the capacity of language to obscure more than it clarifies in any act of verbal figuration."[66] If the ahistorical character of neo-Thomism enabled/ reinforced a tendency toward reification of language, a temptation to "forget" the "un-truth of metaphor"[67], Loisy's historicism pointed to the relativity of human formulations as such -- doubly problematic when religious language engaging the divine was at stake. In the Firmin articles, for example, in speaking of revelation the exegete noted, "One could amass the most varied metaphors on this subject without rendering it more clear. For our most consistent ideas in the religious order are always only metaphors and symbols, a sort of algebraic notation representing ineffable quantities."[68] Irony, then, is congenial to an awareness of the historically conditioned and imperfect nature of human conceptions, to a mode of thought self-critical not only with respect to a given representation of the world of experience but to the very effort to capture its truth in language. This would implicate a radical tendency in Loisy's position.

Another observation made by White suggests further possibilities. When there is an awareness of the possibility that events may be emplotted in either a comic or a tragic mode, and when thereby a comic resolution of the drama is called into doubt, organicist explanations of history may give way to a desire for mechanistic or contextualistic explanatory techniques. While in October of 1902 Loisy affirmed his belief in the Church as "still the chief moral resource of civilization", he noted the alternative viewpoint of the Church as "the great enemy of human progress" if "wholly unsusceptible of amendment."[69] As Loisy's belief in the possibility of a renewed Catholicism shattered under the repeated blows of ecclesiastical censure, one might expect his organicist representation of Christian origins to undergo change in the direction of other modes of argumentation and emplotment. That possibility will not be pursued here, however, as it lies beyond the scope of Loisy's "modernist" writings.

These several indicators point to the need for a closer examination of Loisy's text for evidence of the trope of irony.

Irony implies the insinuation of a reversal of perspective. It affirms, but frames its affirmation in such a way as to inspire second thoughts about the nature of what is said, or the adequacy of that statement. It affirms, but does so in such a way as to render doubtful, suspect -- perhaps going so far as to present its object as faintly absurd. Having "loosened" the hold of its object, it may then signal a more "enlightened" understanding: one more self-critical with respect to that object or even to the linguistic representation of it.

Given Loisy's chosen stance toward Harnack in L'Evangile et l'Eglise, one would expect to find on the surface of his discourse strategies for insinuating the questionableness of rendering the Christian tradition into an originally "pure"

108

essence and successive accretions which obscured/ deformed it. Instances of Loisy's use of an ironic tone rather than direct argument contra Harnack can be found, for example, in chapter I of the section, "The Christian Dogma". To cite but a portion of that:

> Great admirer of Luther that he is, Herr Harnack holds the Protestant Reformation to have been incomplete. In matters of dogma, there are a crowd of problems that Luther did not know, much less was able to solve; 'he was, in consequence, unable to separate the kernel from the husk. . . . generally speaking, [he] did not know how to draw a clear distinction between dogma and the gospel. . . . The inevitable consequence was, that intellectualism was not destroyed, but formed a new scholastic dogma, considered essential to salvation, so that there remained two classes of Christians, those who understood the doctrine, and those who accepted it from those who understood and thus continued spiritually minors.' In this respect, Protestantism threatens to become an inferior type of Catholicism. Let the Evangelical Churches beware of becoming Catholicized! If they would remain truly evangelical, they must have no orthodoxy.[70]

For Harnack, trying to recapture the authentic spirit of the Reformation, to distinguish the accretions that constitute the "husk" from the "kernel" or essence of the gospel, Protestantism certainly in no way represented an "inferior type of Catholicism". And while he sought to purify Christianity of a "husk" which has become identified with orthodox belief, his project was to repristinate orthodoxy, not dispense with it altogether. A few pages later, by representing developments within Christianity as "indispensible", "necessary", by portraying a philosophically articulate Christianity as "the bridge between the new religion and the science of antiquity", as a "vital manifestation . . . which enabled the Church to link her own tradition to the science of the age", Loisy insinuated his own, more enlightened perspective. By contrast to Harnack's position on development of dogma, portraying the latter as weighing "so heavily on all Christian orthodoxies, binding them to an effete doctrine and to the science of Plato and Aristotle, long since passed by modern knowledge", development was necessary for Christianity to transcend its Jewish environment, to strike root into Greek soil and to live.[71] This values that development as necessary to its time, but also implies a certain relativity to that time. Since irony is "relativizing" in its intention, it becomes a mode of figuration congenial to insinuating that aspect of Loisy's historical apologetic. With this in mind, we may proceed to look for indications of its operation with respect to the received theology.

One does not have to search far. Early in the following chapter of that same section on dogma, Loisy first alludes to Harnack's position, then proceeds to engage that of the dominant theology:

> Doctrinal Christian development was inevitable, therefore, and in principle, legitimate; on the whole, it has served the cause of the gospel, which could not exist as a pure essence, but being constantly transformed into living doctrines has itself lived in these doctrines, whose development is therefore justified in fact.
> It is easy to say that the Catholic Church does not even recognize the existence of this development, and condemns the very idea of it. Perhaps it would be nearer the truth to say that she has never had consciousness of it, and that she has no official theory concerning the philosophy of her own history. That which is taught by Vincent of Lérins, modern theologians (except Cardinal Newman) and the Council of the Vatican, touching the development of dogma, applies in reality to the definitely intellectual and theological phase of its development, not to the first budding and formation of beliefs, or at least includes in an abstract definition, much work for which this definition is no adequate expression. It is just the idea of development which is now needed, not to be created all at once, but established from a better knowledge of the past. The acquisition of this new dogma will have no different effect to that of the old ones. These latter were not contained in primitive tradition, like a conclusion in the premises of a syllogism, but as a germ in a seed, a real and living element, which must be transformed as it grows, and be determined by discussion before its crystallization into a solemn formula. They existed as more or less conscious facts or beliefs, before they were the subject of learned speculations or of official judgments.[72]

The position that the Church proscribes the very idea of development is "easy to say"; second thoughts are raised by the expression "nearer the truth", by giving an alternative reading: not proscription exactly -- but more a lack of prescription. Development was there (note the appeal to "facts" -- twice), but conscious awareness of it was lacking, and hence no "official theory" could materialize. Note that the contrasts are established rhetorically, rather than argued. Current Church teaching on development "in reality" is circumscribed within intellectual limits -- by implication not addressing other phases of dogmatic development. Or if extended to include such, such teaching in its very "abstract" character is not "adequate". Loisy's use of language cumulates to cast suspicion on the adequacy of the reigning position -- on its ability to do justice to the full reality of development, to its very consciousness of the true nature of that phenomenon. A more enlightened perspective is signaled in the juxtaposition of "facts" with "speculations", in the ability of "a better knowledge of the past" (exactly what the historical critical method can provide: "the assured results of criticism") to enable an adequate idea of development. This idea of development even provides its own legitimation: present "in fact", its presence "grows" in consciousness (as a seed grows and is transformed). Hence, the difference between Loisy's (and Newman's -- by assimilation) idea of development and that of Vatican I is explained by the exegete's controlling metaphor of "life". The life of the Church is a transformative process, dynamic; as only a portion of that process its intellectual aspect "crystallizes" into formulae -- solidify as it were, convey a static substantial nature to dogma. Once again, Loisy's discourse conveys a broader understanding of its object: dogma and the process of development, one more critical with respect to "the facts", and more capable with regard to their representation. The "second thoughts" inspired by an ironic perspective are to loosen the hold of the received theology, to allow the force of his use of organic metaphors to be felt by the reader -- in short, to impart a plausibility to his assertion that "Doctrinal Christian development was inevitable . . . and in principle, legitimate . . ." The text -- and one could find others which work in similar fashion -- serves to impart a sense that things are not what they seem, and to reveal the way they they really are.

Summing up this segment, White has distinguished aesthetic, epistemological, and ethical levels conceptually with his four-fold typologies of emplotment, argumentation, and ideological implication respectively; and a deep structural level that is tropological in nature. In such terms, neo-Thomism may be rendered as utilizing a romantic mode of emplotment, formist argumentation, and conservative ideology -- prefigured via metaphor. Loisy's historical apologetic, on the other hand, employed a comic emplotment, organicist mode of representation, in some respects radical in ideological tendency -- and prefigured via synecdoche. There are also indications of the trope of irony in the latter's perspective as well. Attention will now be directed toward the interaction of these two configurations.

Incommensurability: Again

Novelty is often error for those who are
unprepared for it, from the refraction with
which it enters into their conceptions.
John Henry Newman[73]

From the foregoing analysis it would appear that White's conceptualization is not only taxonomic, but genuinely illuminative of Loisy's work, and suggestive of further avenues of investigation.[74] As a final analytical payoff, I would like to pick up on the last sentence of the quote with which this chapter began -- to the effect that mode of prefiguration is influential for the kind of reception accorded a position. I noted there that White's framework might be linked to paradigm incommensurability; the issue of Loisy's "irony" raises some possibilities for pursuing that further.

Neo-Thomism, as dominant theological paradigm, reacted violently to modernism, and had the authority structure to translate rhetoric into action. In this case Pepper's observation that "Formism and organicism are especially hostile to each other" emerges as something of an understatement.[75] More is at stake here than explicit mode of argumentation, however. White's metahistorical analysis makes it clear that language reaches deeper than consciously explicit levels, to the deep structural level of prefiguring the field of discourse tropologically.

In dealing with the assertions Loisy makes concerning his publications and with assessments made by critics, one remains on the "surfaces" of discourse: on the level of conscious intention rather than preconscious figuration. Closer examination of two texts from L'Evangile et l'Eglise has identified the presence of irony tropologically, on a preconscious plane. In taking up incommensurability once again, it will be useful to examine how the shift in perspective insinuated by irony impacted critics[76], and how it shaped their understandings. In addition to their readings of L'Evangile et l'Eglise, their reactions to the clarifications introduced by Autour d'un petit livre will also be of interest. Wayne Booth has provided a schema for the reconstruction of irony on the reader's part, which will serve to

112

organize the critics' commentary.[77]

In the first step, or element, supplied by Booth, the reader is required to reject the literal meaning. This will proceed from recognition of some incongruity among the words in the text, or between the words and something else which the reader knows. Gayraud's comment in his initial article engaging L'Evangile et l'Eglise is illustrative: "But it is necessary to examine a little closer this doctrine of Christian evolution, such as M. Loisy sets it forth to us in the light of history, to see whether under an apparent agreement of words would not be hidden a profound disagreement of ideas. I have every reason to fear it."[78]

In a second stage, alternative interpretations or explanations are tried out -- all in some degree incongruous with what the literal statement seems to say: e.g., the author was careless in his expression, did not see the implications that his statement entails, the reader missed something earlier. In Le Camus' estimation, "pious souls will be frightened by a language which is nearly always that of a rationalism which seems to be ignorant of itself."[79] Bouvier lamented, "Ten times perhaps I read and re-read these pages, searching for an explanation to dispel meaning which presented itself too naturally as his own."[80] Gayraud manifested his own hesitation: "But I prefer to believe that I do not grasp entirely M. Loisy's point of view, method, and that his thought eludes me in this thoroughly scientific discussion against M. Harnack."[81]

This leads, thirdly, to a decision about the author's knowledge or beliefs. While one can, in a certain sense, speak of the work's intentions (as White's analysis would legitimate), Booth holds that ironic interpretation depends in part on some conception of the author, and of what he could have intended. Admittedly, an author's intentions may not be easily inferred. Regarding Loisy's, one may note some hesitation on the part of critics, though not unmixed with suspicions. Bouvier's citation of the opinion of the Bishop of Autun is indicative:

> Nearly every page one wonders whether if the author intended to say such a thing or the contrary; if he intends to reply to the objections of the Protestant professor whose conferences on 'The Essence of Christianity' he is analyzing or if indeed he approaches them, all the while trying either to attenuate them or accomodate them somehow or other to the traditional teachings of Catholic theology.[82]

Bouvier himself would be less circumspect. With regard to the exegete's exposition on the Eucharist, he observed, "One finds in the book a page where all seems calculated to let the initiated understand what is not dared to be said openly."[83] Autour d'un petit livre, which was to have served to clarify Loisy's position, succeeded in strengthening an apprehension of his work as subversive of the Catholic tradition and destructive in its ramifications.

Fourthly, there results a reconstructed meaning which will be in harmony with the unspoken beliefs the reader has decided to attribute to the author. This is encapsulated in Cardinal Perraud's reaction to Autour d'un petit livre, recounted to Loisy and told in Choses passées:

> The Cardinal had read as far as the seventh letter without encountering the heresy that simply must be there. The light dawned on his intelligence almost at the last page, when he read this obvious statement concerning the sacrament of ordination: 'In proportion as the Eucharist took on the character of a liturgical act, those who regularly presided over it acquired the standing of priests.' 'So they did not, then, have it from the beginning!' he cried. And this monstrous assertion, contrary to the definitions of Trent, enabled him retrospectively to find plenty of other errors in the volume.[84]

Prior to the appearance of that work of clarification, however, critics such as Le Camus had judged Loisy's exposition "no longer speaking the language of the great Church."[85] Despite the appearance engendered by the exegete's language, Gayraud estimated that he did not fundamentally safeguard the substantial identity of Catholicism and the Christianity of Jesus Christ.[86]

Booth admirably sums this up to make the essential point:

> it is also clear by now why irony causes so much trouble. An aggressively intellectual exercise that fuses fact and value, requiring us to construct alternative hierarchies and choose among them; . . . floods us with emotion-charged value judgments which claim to be backed by the mind; accuses other men not only of wrong beliefs but of being wrong at their very foundations and blind to what those foundations imply -- all of this coupled with a kind of subtlety that cannot be deciphered or 'proved' simply by looking

closely at the words: no wonder that 'failure
to communicate' and resulting quarrels are
often found where irony dwells.[87]

In his work on irony, Kierkegaard voiced the expectation that
irony must dwell to a certain extent at every world historical
turning point.[88] For him irony was not so much a matter of
words, of characters, but of a total perspective which does not
wish to be directly and universally understood. At a shift in
"cultures" of the proportions exhibited in the modernist crisis,
it is therefore not surprising to detect the operation of an
ironic perspective and to view its consequences in a "failure to
communicate".

White has argued that because of a preconceptual,
preconscious apprehension of the field, historians

> actually see different objects in that field,
> provisionally group them into different
> classes and species of historical existence,
> conceive the relationships among them in
> different terms, and explicate the
> transformations of those relationships in
> different ways, in order to figure different
> meanings for them by the structure of the
> narratives they write about them.[89]

In Kuhnian terms, commitments at the level of world view
inform problems, methods, and data. That level has figured in
the analysis of languages of development. Greater specification
of problem incommensurability may be rendered by proceeding from
a focus on the process of development to consider what actually
develops. While all three levels are inevitably engaged at any
point in this analysis, White's framework has directed primary
attention to underlying world view as tropologically prefigured,
and the metaphoric examination of chapter 2 to incommensurability
of language itself. The final chapter will center on Loisy's
presentation of the Eucharist as a way of examining more closely
incommensurability of data/ methods/ problems. To contextualize
that, some accompanying discussion of Church, and sacrament in
general will be necessary.

[1]Hayden White, _Metahistory_, (Baltimore: The Johns Hopkins University Press, 1973), p. 430.

[2]Dominick La Capra, _Rethinking Intellectual History: Texts, Context, Language_, (Ithaca: Cornell University Press, 1983), p. 77.

[3]This section is indebted to the following: Terence Hawkes, _Structuralism and Semiotics_, (Berkeley: University of California Press, 1977), chapt. 2; Edgar McKnight, _Meaning in Texts_, (Philadelphia: Fortress Press, 1978), chapt. 4; Daniel Patte, _What is Structural Exegesis?_, (Philadelphia: Fortress Press, 1976), chapts. I and II; Robert Detweiler, _Story, Sign, and Self_, (Philadelphia: Fortress Press, 1978), chapt. 1. For a critical perspective see Rosalind Coward and John Ellis, _Language and Materialism_, London: Routledge and Kegan Paul, 1977.

[4]"Ultimately, it seems that the very concepts a language expresses are also defined and determined by its structure." Hawkes, p. 27.

[5]Detweiler, p. 18.

[6]Dorothy Lee, quoted in Hawkes, p. 32.

[7]Just as metaphor can no longer be taken as "ornamental" in the theories of Black, Ricoeur, and others, so with style here: "The focus on surface qualities [of a text] does not relegate style to mere 'decoration' as many classical rhetorical theories would have it. Style is more substantive than 'figures of speech' that simply embellish the presentation of an argument to make it more pleasing and, hence, convincing. Style is a matter of technique, but it is not only technique." Wesley Morris, _Friday's Footprint_, (Columbus: Ohio State University Press, 1979), p. 147.

[8]Patte, pp. 22-25.

[9]Ibid., p. 15.

[10]White, _Metahistory_, p. ix.

[11]Ibid., Introduction.

[12]See Hayden White, "Interpretation in History" in _Tropics of Discourse_, (Baltimore: The Johns Hopkins University Press, 1978), p. 51.

13Both comedy and tragedy are stories of reconciliation, although of different forms. Comedy holds out the possibility of at least partial and provisional release from a fallen world -- in the long run the conflicting elements in world and society are seen to be harmonizable with one another. The convention of comedy makes some kind of happy ending inevitable. The reconciliation achieved in tragedy is more somber: at narrative's end the protagonists have become conscious of the inalterable conditions under which they must live in the world -- and resigned to those conditions which limit human aspirations and achievements. Satire, on the other hand, represents a parody of the romantic drama of redemption, positing humanity as ultimately a captive of the world rather than its master. As noted, White draws these from Northrop Frye's work, taking care to disclaim that the typology is exhaustive, but rather usefully imported from the study of literature as particularly apt for application to historical works. Northrop Frye, Anatomy of Criticism, (Princeton: Princeton University Press, 1973), Third Essay. For White's summary adaptations, see Metahistory, pp. 8-11. Cf. "Interpretation in History" in Tropics, pp. 61-62.

14Pepper, p. 182.

15Briefly, where in formism the stress is placed on the unique event, in mechanism the concern is with generic typifications of events and ultimately with the laws which govern history. The organicist attempts to display the integrative nature of the historical process as a whole: individual entities are seen as components of processes which aggregate into wholes, whose importance is greater than their constituent parts described in the course of the narrative. As its name implies, contextualism explains events by recourse to the "context" of their occurrence. As such it is less dispersive than formism, though the relationships among events which it discerns are not granted the status of mechanist historical laws. A primary axis for distinguishing broadly among the four, then, is their tendencies toward dispersion or integration. Idiography and contextualism tend toward the former, while organicism and mechanism evidence the latter. In the exposition of Loisy's position and that of neo-Thomism, the modes of argumentation that engage those approaches will be discussed at greater length. White's discussion of the four may be found in Metahistory, pp. 13-21.

16All four ideological positions are oriented towards change, hence their interest in history. Regarding change, both conservatives and liberals view it as being most effective when particular parts of the totality are changed, rather than structural relationships. For radicals and anarchists change is necessarily structural for society to be transformed. While all four are change-oriented, the latter two positions are characteristically more critical toward the status quo, desiring

117

its transformation or dissolution, while conservatism and liberalism tend to be more generally accepting of the current state of affairs. Further differentiation of positions is made by taking into account other factors. See White, _Metahistory_, pp. 22-29. He observes, "I cannot claim that one of the conceptions of historical knowledge favored by a given ideology is more 'realistic' than the others, for it is precisely over the matter of what constitutes an adequate criterion of 'realism' that they disagree." p. 26. Using Kuhn's terminology, this could be expressed as epistemological incommensurability. It suggests the lines along which White's conceptualization will ultimately link up with the larger conceptual framework operative in the thesis.

[17]Ibid., p. 29.

[18]White has expressed these affinities in tabular form:

Mode of Emplotment	Mode of Argument	Mode of Ideological Implication
Romantic	Formist	Anarchist
Tragic	Mechanistic	Radical
Comic	Organicist	Conservative
Satirical	Contextualist	Liberal

[19]Ibid., p. 31.

[20]Ibid. "Irony, Metonymy, and Synecdoche are kinds of Metaphor, but they differ from one another in the kinds of _reductions_ or _integrations_ they effect on the literal level of their meanings and by the kinds of illuminations they aim at on the figurative level. Metaphor is essentially _representational_, Metonymy is _reductionist_, Synecdoche is _integrative_, and Irony is _negational_." p. 34. For description of each trope, see pp. 31-38. In the introduction to _Tropics of Discourse_, White notes that troping is "both a movement _from_ one notion of the way things are related _to_ another notion, and a connection between things so that they can be expressed in a language that takes account of the possibility of their being expressed otherwise." p. 2. Consistent with the structuralist roots of his framework, White's analysis emphasizes relationships over entities. "Histories, then, are not only about events but also about the possible sets of relationships that those events can be demonstrated to figure. These sets of relationships are not, however, immanent in the events themselves; they exist only in the mind of the historian reflecting on them. Here they are present as the modes of relationships conceptualized in the myth, fable, and folklore, scientific knowledge, religion, and literary art of the historian's own culture. But more importantly, they are, I suggest, immanent in the very language which the historian must use to _describe_ events prior to a scientific analysis of

118

them or a fictional emplotment of them." "Historical Text as Literary Artifact" in *Tropics*, p. 94.

[21]Ibid., p. 91.

[22]White, "The Fictions of Factual Representation" in *Tropics*, pp. 127ff.

[23]"Many historians continue to treat their 'facts' as though they were 'given' and refuse to recognize, unlike most scientists, that they are not so much found as constructed by the kinds of questions which the investigator asks of the phenomena before him." White, "The Burden of History" in *Tropics*, p. 43. The reference to scientists evokes a connection with Kuhn's analysis: as noted in chapter 1, data ("facts") are themselves paradigm-dependent. That is to say, the significance attributed to data, and how data are to be utilized in explanation are part of the regulative dimension of paradigms. In chapter 4 Loisy's use of the fourth gospel in relation to the status accorded it by his critics will illustrate this.

[24]Le Camus, *Fausse exégèse, mauvaise théologie*, p. 80.

[25]White, *Metahistory*, p. 9.

[26]Pepper, p. 141. One may note in passing that scholasticism is not as dispersive as Pepper's characterization of it as purely formist would entail. This is particularly true of neo-Thomism, in its self-conception of a master-synthesis of the great scholastic thinkers.

[27]White, *Metahistory*, p. 14.

[28]Le Camus, *Fausse exégèse, mauvaise théologie*, p. 62.

[29]Gayraud, *L'Univers*, 28 Dec. 1903. Cf. Bouvier: "Is he God, this Christ whose reason is subject to failure and whose logic is found at fault?" p. 27.

[30]White, *Metahistory*, p. 25.

[31]See Sanks, pp. 108ff.

[32]Gayraud, *L'Univers*, 9 Jan. 1903. Cf. Bouvier, p. 52.

[33]White, *Metahistory*, p. 167.

[34]Ibid., p. 125. One might argue that a perennial danger of this formist-metaphorical linkage is a tendency to "forget" its metaphorical character and reify its categories. Paul de Man has observed, "The degradation of metaphor into literal meaning is

not condemned [by Neitzsche] because it is the forgetting of a truth but much rather because it forgets the un-truth, the lie that the metaphor was in the first place. It is a naive belief in the proper meaning of the metaphor without awareness of the problematic nature of the factual, referential foundation." Paul de Man, Allegories of Reading, (New Haven: Yale University Press, 1979), p. 111. In the integralist theology that came increasingly to dominate the Roman Catholic theological scene, for which neo-Thomist categories mirrored the truth and any theological difference was treated as theological deviance, this tendency was realized.

35See Stephen Toulmin and June Goodfield, The Discovery of Time, (Chicago: The University of Chicago Press, 1982), pp. 59ff. and chapt. 7.

36Joseph Perrier, The Revival of Scholastic Theology in the Nineteenth Century, (New York: The Columbia University Press, 1909), pp. 39-40.

37GC, pp. 220-221.

38"Since the learned professor announces the work as historical, it shall be discussed solely according to the data of history." GC, p. 3.

39E.g., von Hügel, Genocchi, and by Loisy himself. See Francesco Turvasi, The Condemnation of Alfred Loisy and the Historical Method, (Roma: Edizioni di Storia e Litteratura, 1979), pp. 75-76, 104. Cf. Le Camus, Fausse exégèse, mauvaise théologie, p. 5. Gayraud, L'Univers, 16 Nov. 1903.

40Adolf von Harnack, What is Christianity? Translated by Thomas B. Saunders. (New York: Harper and Row, Publishers, 1957), p. 15.

41GC, p. 19.

42Ibid., pp. 17-18. Loisy later makes the same point utilizing the metaphor of human growth: "To be identical with the religion of Jesus, [the Catholic Church] has no more need to reproduce exactly the forms of the Galilean gospel, than a man has need to preserve at fifty the proportions, features, and manner of life of the day of his birth, in order to be the same individual. . . . The Church, to-day, resembles the community of the first disciples neither more nor less than a grown man resembles the child he was at first. The identity of the Church or of the man is not determined by permanent immobility of the external forms, but by continuity of existence and consciousness of life through the perpetual transformations which are life's condition and manifestation." GC, pp. 170-171.

[43]Maurice Mandelbaum, History, Man, and Reason, (Baltimore: The Johns Hopkins University Press, 1971), p. 42 (italics omitted).

[44]"The world of man is in a state of incessant flux, although within it there are centers of stability (personalities, institutions, nations, epochs), each possessing an inner structure, a character, and each in constant metamorphosis in accord with its own internal principles of development. . . . There is no constant human nature; rather the character of each man reveals itself only in his development." Georg G. Iggers, The German Conception of History, (Middletown, Conn.: Wesleyan University Press, 1983), p. 5. Cf. Loisy's critique of Harnack's attempt to delimit an essence of Christianity; for the former, "essence" lies in the totality of the process of Christianity's development.

[45]Mandelbaum, p. 47.

[46]White, Metahistory, p. 15.

[47]Francesco Turvasi's work suggests that Loisy's use of organicist metaphors is not entirely consistent with other aspects of his position. The following is suggestive: "Loisy had appealed to the image of 'germ', but maintained that the development of Christological dogma took place through external dialectics, by dint of philosophy, as cause and effect. On the basis of this philosophy, faith defined its essence, transforming itself substantively along the various phases of its evolution." From this he concludes, "The image of germ which Loisy uses to qualify his conception of dogmatic development is improper. A germ has immanent in itself a determined plant which it is destined to realize. The seed of a pear can never produce a banana. The environment can favor or hinder its development, but not determine it in its nature. For Loisy, if Jesus . . . becomes Son of God and himself transcendent God, this occurs solely on account of Greek philosophy of transcendence." Turvasi, p. 107 and 107n.

In terms of both dominant metaphors and mode of argumentation, Loisy's position is apparently organicist. Wernz's observation regarding the "functional" nature of several of the exegete's central concepts raises the possibility that an organicist reading may not be exhaustive, however. Wernz pointed out the tendency to assert connections between the cognitive, conceptual aspects of revelation and dogma and the experiential, intuitive dimension; between the realm of fact and that of faith. Often the nature of such connections remains underdeveloped in Loisy's thought, leaving them open to specifications being supplied by his critics -- specifications which were at variance with his assertions. For example, though he noted a divine role in the process of revelation, his critics read this position as reductive: dogmas become merely human products. By extension, it could be said that Loisy asserts organicist connections, reflected in his language of "principles" or "ideas" that inform the developmental process as a whole. But his failure to work that out at greater length, coupled with other references to "laws" that govern evolution point to the possibility of another, recessive mode of representation. White notes that organicist integration can coexist with a mechanist search for impersonal causal agencies that relate elements of the historical field in terms of part-part relationships. "For the mechanist, then, the historical field is considered to have been 'explained' when he has satisfactorily distinguished between causal agencies and the effects of these agencies' operations, and then provided the necessary and sufficient conditions for their specific configurations at specific times and places within the whole process." Tropics, p. 66. With his language of "principles" Loisy wishes to assert a dynamic internal to Christianity that allows it to dominate what it assimilates. His invocation of external factors, as impersonal causal elements could be construed to be at variance with this -- as Turvasi points out, and as critics reflect.

[48]Poulat, La crise moderniste, p. 96.

[49]GC, p. 177.

[50]APL, p. 129.

[51]Pepper, p. 310.

[52]APL, p. 120.

[53]See Wernz, pp. 260ff.

[54]APL, pp. 191; 190.

[55]White, Metahistory, p. 9.

[56]Hayden White, "Romanticism, Historicism, and Realism: Toward a Period Concept for Early 19th Century Intellectual History" in Hayden White, ed., The Uses of History, (Detroit: Wayne State University Press, 1968), pp. 54-56.

[57]GC, pp. 149-150.

[58]CP, p. 247; Duel, p. 228.

[59]White, Metahistory, p. 35.

[60]GC, p. 16.

[61]"Synecdoche is integrative in the way that Organicism is." Metahistory, p. 36.

[62]Ibid., p. 177.

[63]White, Tropics, p. 73. Or, to put it another way: "The aim of an ironic statement is to affirm tacitly the negative of what is on the literal level affirmed positively, or the reverse." White, Metahistory, p. 37.

[64]Daly, p. 66. Cf. Mémoires I, pp. 452ff.

[65]Loisy to Houtin, 17 March 1906. Mémoires II, p. 270. This was also recognized from Harnack's side. Cf. Poulat, La crise moderniste, p. 93n.

[66]White, Metahistory, p. 37.

[67]See note 33 supra.

[68]Loisy, "L'idée de la révelation", p. 267.

[69]CP, pp. 242-243; Duel, p. 225.

[70]GC, pp. 186-187.

[71]Ibid., pp. 190-191.

[72]Ibid., pp. 213-214.

[73]Quoted in Maisie Ward, Insurrection verses Resurrection, p. 21.

[74]White's approach has been criticized for being too taxonomic -- to the point of harboring a "Procrustean tendency to see texts as embodiments of patterned variables or model sets of tropes, emplotments, arguments, and ideologies." La Capra, p. 81. As long as the cautions raised with regard to Kuhn's paradigm analysis are borne in mind, however, the objection does not appear overwhelming. See chapter 1, note 40.

[75]Pepper, p. 147.

[76]Loisy's representation of his position vis-a-vis Harnack's occasionally engendered suspicion, as with Gayraud in his initial article on the book: "I will say only that one would wish that the exposition of M. Harnack's opinions were more clear, more distinct, that M. Loisy's arguments stood out more clearly from this exposition and that the ad hominem reasons were separated from those which constituted the thesis itself." Gayraud, L'Univers, 31 Dec. 1902. Gayraud's not having read Harnack would absolve Loisy from some of the responsibility for the confusion,

but only to a point. Perhaps more telling are the responses of others, manifesting not only confusion, but suspicion. The antimodernist Canon Henri Delassus may be taken as a representative: "A very high dignitary of the Church has said of [Loisy's] attitude: 'It is a feint.' And in fact it seems indeed that the pretended refutation of Harnack was only an enterprise to shelter from all condemnation, and to enable the errors which M. Loisy had already professed on several occasions and which were scarcely other than those of Harnack himself, to penetrate more easily. Thence, the fleeting forms employed in his style to attack the fundamental dogmas under pretext of defending them." Quoted in Houtin, Q bib. XX, p. 79n.

[77]Booth cautions that his schema may not always represent sequential steps but elements of an experience that could be described as having a gestalt-like character. In the critical readings of Loisy, however, the temporal factor does seem operative, with earlier interpretations being more tentative than those which followed, particularly after Autour d'un petit livre. Wayne C. Booth, A Rhetoric of Irony, (Chicago: University of Chicago Press, 1974), chapts. 1 and 2.

[78]Gayraud, L'Univers, 31 Dec. 1902.

[79]Le Camus, Vraie et fausse exégèse, pp. 37-38.

[80]Bouvier, p. 22.

[81]Gayraud, L'Univers, 4 Jan. 1903.

[82]Bouvier, pp. 17-18.

[83]Ibid., p. 48.

[84]Duel, p. 244.

[85]Le Camus, Vraie et fausse exégèse, p. 30.

[86]Gayraud, L'Univers, 10 Jan. 1903.

[87]Booth, p. 44.

[88]Soren Kierkegaard, The Concept of Irony. Translated by Lee M. Capel. (Bloomington: Indiana University Press, 1968), p. 278.

[89]White, Metahistory, p. 274.

Chapter 4

The Exegete and the Eucharist

[Modernism] left nothing standing of the work of dogmatic unification realized by the councils of Trent and the Vatican. After having disorganized and ruined at the base the classical demonstrations of the existence of God, of his personality, of the distinction of the soul and of the body, the innovators declared that the concepts of creation, of the supernatural, of miracle, of dogma, of nature, of person, of transubstantiation, of objective and subjective certitude, of morality founded on the will of God had become not something false, but, what is more serious, unthinkable.[1]

. . . orthodoxy is only unchangeable in the imagination of those who believe it such . . .
Alfred Loisy[2]

Ernest Renan, the French rationalist critic, was once characterized as "le rat nourri de pain béni".[3] Loisy, who had attended Renan's lectures in order to learn the tools to meet the critic on his own ground, ironically enough became known as a second Renan, worse than the first.[4] This second Renan's thoughts on the "pain béni" will provide a focus for the present chapter. Certainly the difficulties experienced by Loisy and his critics in being understood and in explaining themselves, and the reality of the disagreement which opposed them to one another (to retrieve Poulat's factors) emerged in the discussion of development in chapter 2. By examining respective positions on the eucharist, it is felt that greater specification can be lent to the terms of that opposition. Whereas chapter 2 centered more on the rhetoric of development to explicate incommensurability of language, while retaining that concern this one will examine incommensurability of data/ problems/ methods via a particular object of development. Inevitably, incommensurability of world view cannot be ignored, nor can that of language.

In undertaking an exposition of Loisy's thought on the eucharist, it will be necessary to move materially beyond the two little red books which have figured so prominently in previous discussions to include matter in his biblical commentaries. It will be useful to move beyond the temporal limits observed thus far (1904) to examine briefly Loisy's replies to official

censures which descended in 1907, in the dual form of the
syllabus Lamentabili and the encyclical Pascendi insofar as they
bear on this subject. The texts of Loisy's three critics
utilized earlier will not be supplemented, as they will suffice.
Since the excerpts from their work cited in chapter 2 established
the basic unanimity of position among them (or shared paradigm),
here -- as in the previous chapter -- on a given occasion one may
be allowed to represent all three. Also, it will be expedient to
provide a larger context for eucharist by engaging positions on
Church, and sacrament in general.

i

One can very well say that the facts are on
one side and the formulas on the other: in
such a case one is Loisyste.
                    Joannès Wherlé[5]

Chapter 2 took up Loisy's reformulation of the so-termed
"theological postulate": the essential invariability of the
fundamental religious ideas. That revision, to be accomplished
within a framework of organic development, would enable
reformulation of a third, "ecclesiastical postulate", i.e., "The
Church, with the essential stages of its hierarchy, its
fundamental dogmas, and the sacraments of its worship, has been
directly instituted by Christ."[6] The middle term of this
postulate, dogma, has been discussed at some length. The first,
and especially the third, will be objects of investigation here.

It is within that developmental framework -- established in
the Firmin articles -- that the argument in L'Evangile et
l'Eglise moves. The central work of Jesus was represented in the
preaching of the kingdom, a future event very near at hand. As
preacher of the kingdom, Jesus is the predestined Messiah --
assuming that status fully only with the end of the present age
and the arrival of this "great hope". Under the influence of
this eschatological perspective, Loisy held that Jesus could not
have consciously and intentionally founded an enduring Church
with an explicit sacramental structure. Both developed after the
death of Jesus in response to the various environments in which
the followers of Jesus found themselves. "Jesus foretold the
kingdom, and it was the Church that came; she came, enlarging the
form of the gospel . . . ."[7]

The sacraments are thus part of this process of enlargement,
and in the course of this process their meaning changed. Within
the earthly ministry of Jesus the last supper is intimately tied
to the central theme of his preaching: the coming kingdom.

The supper of the eucharist, then, stands out
as the symbol of the kingdom, that the

126

sacrifice of Jesus is to bring; and more
distinctly still, this communion, on the day
of its first celebration, signifies the
abrogation of the ancient worship and the
approaching advent of the kingdom, rather
than the institution of a new ritual, as the
thought of Jesus was bent, as always, on the
idea of realizing the kingdom of Heaven
rather than the direct idea of founding a new
religion and a Church.[8]

After the death of Jesus a natural process of development
occurred by which the preacher became the preached; the center of
the message was no longer the kingdom but Jesus as Messiah. The
eucharist could not but be affected by this shift. During this
early period,

Everything is living, the faith and the rite,
the baptism and the breaking of bread; the
baptism is the Holy Ghost the Eucharist is
the Christ. There is no speculation about
the token, no hint of physical efficacy of
the sacrament in baptism, nor of
transubstantiation in the Eucharist; but what
is said and believed goes almost beyond these
theological assertions. The worship of that
primitive age might be defined as a kind of
spiritual realism, knowing no pure symbols,
and essentially sacramental by virtue of the
place that rites hold in it as the vehicle of
the Spirit, and the means of Divine life.[9]

Under these conditions the eucharistic supper no longer
symbolizes the kingdom, but rather memorializes the passion of
Jesus and anticipates the festival of the Messiah -- all in the
presence of Jesus with whom real communion is possible by
partaking of the consecrated bread. The rite became increasingly
detached from its Jewish origins and the manner of its
understanding came to be influenced by the Gentile environment.[10]

Loisy's developmental framework thus informs his exposition
of the evolution of sacramental understanding and practice. The
alteration of the theological postulate to admit of doctrinal
change and development renders possible the conclusions
concerning the ecclesiastical postulate: the seven sacraments
were not directly instituted by Christ (the early Church knew
only baptism and eucharist), and even in the case of the
eucharist which is directly traceable to Jesus' action, its
meaning within the Church is not identical with its original
meaning for Jesus. That development is held to be legitimate,
however; for to live is to grow, to change. And the logical

extension is that future developments, also legitimate, can and must occur as the Church continues to live.

> The period at which the Church fixed the number of the sacraments, is only a special point in the development, and marks neither the beginning nor the end. The starting-point of the system is . . . the baptism of Jesus and the Last Supper. The end is still to come, as sacramental development, continuing to follow the same general lines, can only end with the Church herself.[11]

To a mentality for which authentic teaching is that which has been taught "always, everywhere, and by all" such assertions could only provoke an attack of theological vertigo.[12] Trent had taught there were seven sacraments, not more, not less, because Jesus had directly instituted seven sacraments, not more, not less. Any attempt to sunder the connection between the acts of Jesus and the sacraments of the Church could only be perceived as an attack on the foundations of the existing theological edifice -- which, indeed it was, as the paradigm analysis has intimated and the reactions of critics have evidenced.

But how did Loisy justify his assertions? In _Autour d'un petit livre_ he explicated some of his underlying premises. Basic to these is a distinction between the historical and theological points of view, between the realm of historical fact and the realm of faith. In line with this distinction the exegete asserts that conciliar definitions have as their object dogmas, not history. Thus with respect to the sacraments, "The decrees of Trent determine the meaning which the Church attaches to the sacramental institution, not the historical form of this institution."[13] As expressed in the decrees of that council, then, the general idea of sacramental institution would not be an historical representation of either what Jesus did or what the apostolic Church thought. Rather it is "an authentic interpretation . . . authorized by faith, of the traditional fact." As such this interpretation does not concern the historian qua historian, "since it does not concern, since it could not concern history directly."[14] It does not have to be defended on the terrain of primitive history since it does not address that level of reality. Moreover, as the exposition in _L'Evangile et l'Eglise_ has made clear, it could not be defended on that level: the texts will not support such a position. The claim for a legitimate autonomy for history vis-à-vis theology, which surfaced in the paradigm analysis, reappears here in the fact/ faith differentiation.

The Tridentine position numbering the sacraments at seven, holding them to be directly instituted by Christ himself, deeming them necessary to salvation, and instruments of divine grace given by the fact of their conferral is "perhaps a view of faith, true, in its manner, for faith; but if you take it as the letter of history it will be an absurd and untenable position."[15] To attempt to place the conciliar position in the gospel would constitute an attempt to suppress history -- and as Loisy avowed to Le Camus, history will not let itself be suppressed.[16]

Essentially, then, if an individual is to find a truth-value in the traditional asserta, he must do so by assent through faith, not on the basis of historical demonstration:

> The historian can only verify that the Church is the vital and logical continuation of the Gospel. He can also affirm that Christ has always lived and that he still lives in the Church, but he realizes this verification only by experience of faith, not through the critical examination of the texts and of the facts.[17]

The Tridentine definitions, like all dogmatic definitions, are a product of their times. And just as the times have changed, patterns of language and ways of thinking have altered, so must those decrees undergo reformulation. They do not stand outside of history, and so cannot impose themselves on all subsequent ages without adaptation.[18]

If Loisy's approach to the traditional teaching was critical, his assessment of its value bore radical implications. The uneasy tension between truths of history and truths of faith, which he had registered during his student days at the Institut catholique[19], became resolved by attributing primacy to historical fact. As for truths of faith, stress was placed on their experiential character, with their cognitive component described as "symbolic". In the Firmin articles the relation of these two dimensions tended to be mediated by functional concepts which left their relationship imprecise. Autour d'un petit livre does not resolve that ambiguity; if anything, in reacting to the intellectualist emphasis present in the scholastic theology, it reinforces the experiential by underscoring the practical, moral aspect. By the mid-1880s Loisy could assert, "But what are beliefs, even, if not symbols which derive their value from their moral efficacy? Was not this moral efficacy the one thing needful?"[20]

This line of interpretation is present in the treatment accorded the eucharist within Autour d'un petit livre. What is said there, however, is brought out more fully in two other works, Etudes évangéliques (1902), which contained sections of Loisy's complete commentary on the fourth gospel which appeared only in 1903: Le Quatrième évangile.[21] These two works will now be drawn upon to provide a brief portrait of the exegete's conception of the eucharist, as that possessed a truth-value for faith.

In John 6 the multiplication of the loaves furnishes the occasion for the evangelist to say all he wants on the eucharist. In the language of the discourse on the bread of life is an echo of the eucharistic institution. That is not to say that the discourse itself is historical; it is rather a theological exposition reflecting the understanding of the eucharist in the contemporary environment. No more than the synoptic accounts of the last supper itself can this chapter be taken as a legitimation for a connection of the eucharist as expressed in the traditional theology with the direct intentions of Jesus.[22]

The discourse of the fourth gospel reflects, then, the tendency -- as set forth in L'Evangile et l'Eglise -- on the part of the apostolic Church to make Jesus the center of the message, to make the preacher the preached. The theology of John's gospel is consistent with the Pauline association between Christ's passion and the eucharist. The breaking of the bread is the commemorative sign of the death of Jesus. And the partaking of the consecrated bread is communion with Christ in the symbol of his death; "the presence of Jesus in the eucharist is, in a sense, more strongly impressed, more deeply felt in the teaching of the fourth gospel than in the decrees of the Council of Trent."[23] The other major theme of the Johannine theology of the eucharist is that of agapaic love. It is present in the account of the multiplication of the loaves and the accompanying discourse, but appears more prominently in the washing of the feet (Jn. 13, 1-20), substituted by the evangelist for the symbolic distribution of the bread and wine. The passion and death of Christ, the servant Christ washing the feet of his disciples, and the eucharist as symbolizing both are interconnected. For in his death Jesus is made, by love, the servant of humanity. Symbolizing Christ's death, the eucharist also expresses the love of one who has given his life for his friends; it unites them with the source of this love unto death, and commissions them to express this love to one another.

> Jesus having represented in the washing of the feet the totality of the service of salvation which he rendered to humanity, principally in his death, it is this service, as Jesus effected it on the cross, as he represented it in the eucharist, which is recommended to the Christian; it is in the spirit of Jesus dying that the Christian must participate in the eucharistic agape and

130

exercise charity, in order to remain united to Jesus by the one and by the other, by the one in the other. Christ is going to proclaim happy those who will follow his example . . . .[24]

Such is the "moral efficacy" of the eucharistic symbol. Although the substance of the traditional interpretation cannot remain untouched by changes in people's intellectual surroundings, the ritual has an enduring value in communicating the moral message. The participation of members of a religious society in acts which bring about their union and sensibly represent it, is an ongoing necessity. Thus the eucharist continues to reunite the faithful "in this extreme love which becomes their law."[25]

Loisy, then, distinguishes between fact and faith, between the historical Jesus who is preacher of the kingdom, and the glorified Christ who founds the Church. Just as the resurrection is not properly a fact of the historical order, is not demonstrable by the sole witness of history, but instead is a fact of the purely supernatural order -- so with the Church. Its divine institution is an object of faith, not a historically demonstrable fact -- "founded on Jesus more than by him."[26] What is open to historical inspection is the existence and progress of faith, not the object of faith which is supra-historical. In examining the history of faith, the historian discovers the progress won by the Church in response to circumstances. Under the influence of relative necessities the Church assumed the organizational form of contemporary Catholicism. The evolution of an ecclesiastical hierarchy and the forms and powers it assumed were necessary to the life of the Church, to her adaptation to changing environments, to her continued survival. But that also entails the necessity of continued adaptation: "the ecclesiastical power, as a service to the Gospel, is necessary to the conservation and propagation of the Gospel itself. I also said that the applications of this power and the forms of its use could be modified."[27] To cling to the received forms in face of the changed demands of modern society would represent an illegitimate attempt to arrest the process of development, in effect to deny the living character of the gospel. The framework is organic; the Church's continuing life legitimates Loisy's attempt to reconcile Catholicism with the modern world.

Consistent with the understanding of Christ's role in founding the Church is his role in the institution of the sacraments. The latter, like the institution of the Church, are the work of the glorified Christ; as such, they are objects of faith, not of history. As in the case of the Church, the historian can consult the historical record, the process and the circumstances of their development reflecting the influence of

131

historical context. As with the Church, he discerns in them a "vital and logical continuation of the Gospel."[28] And he can conclude that, like the organizational structure of the Church, their ritual expression and theological conceptualization are capable of further modification.

> It matters little that sacraments are held to be composed of form and substance; there would be nothing unsuitable in abandoning these notions of ancient philosophy, artifically applied to the sacraments, and considering them in themselves, taking them for what they are, namely, religious acts, endowed with supernatural efficacy.[29]

So with the eucharist, the contemporary expression of faith is conditioned by a mode of philosophical expression that cannot be read back historically into primitive Christianity. To the historian there is available only the externals, the surfaces of the movement; that underneath, "there is really the immortal Christ and the action of his Spirit" is discerned by "the Christian consciousness".[30] In keeping with the experiential emphasis Loisy sought to communicate via such terms as the latter, the meaning of the eucharist for faith is couched in terms of moral efficacy.

In face of Loisy's assertions regarding the gradual acquisition of the sacraments by the Church, the nonessential character of their traditional philosophical rendering in terms of matter and form, and the possibility of their undergoing future development, Pierre Bouvier reiterated the Tridentine decrees. To the exegete's conclusions, the fruits of his criticism, there is opposed -- characteristically -- the authoritative pronouncements of the tradition. This is consistent with the principle of theological control characteristic of this theological paradigm. Or as Bouvier put it, "There is criticism and there is criticism. But one sees . . . that if it is useful to have doctrinal tradition as conducting-wire in the intricacies of documentary criticism . . . ."[31] Lacking the sound navigational principles furnished by the teaching authority of the Church, one risks straying from safe waters -- with potentially dire consequences. On the other hand, guided by "the principle of authority . . . if there be peril of shipwreck, one can return prudently toward the shore."[32] Clearly, Bouvier thought Loisy to be navigating in dangerous waters indeed. Concerning the eucharist in particular the critic was led to query,

> . . . one anxiously asks oneself with anxiety what the institution of this sacrament and of the sacrifice, by a Christ who is Son of God

in hope only and who does not actually
foresee the church, can indeed become in the
new system. . . . [C]an one truly recognize
still the integral doctrine of the Church on
transubstantiation and the real presence? I
pose the question without daring to take on
myself a response to it.[33]

One suspects that the illocutionary force of Bouvier's
question is more rhetorical than real. Gayraud, for one, in his
series on L'Evangile et l'Eglise had already provided an answer.
In the final article he remarked that perhaps "the most dangerous
blow" struck by Loisy at the gospel texts was aimed at the
institution of the eucharist.[34] Juxtaposing a rather
literalistic reading of the gospel accounts of the eucharistic
institution to the exegete's developmental perspective, he
arrives at a conclusion consistent with his reading of Loisy's
organic process of evolution with regard to dogma in general: "It
is always the substitution of human thought for that of Jesus
Christ."[35] In the second series of articles which followed
publication of Autour d'un petit livre, that line of criticism is
reinforced. In Loisy's system the dogmas of Catholicism become
volatilized into symbols whose meaning and value become relative
to the epoch in which they have been conceived and formulated.
The eucharist is reduced in this system to "a realization by the
faith of Christ conceived as always living and present in his
Church."[36] Again, the exegete's position is not so much engaged
as dismissed; the terms of that dismissal betray an
incommensurable mode of regarding the evangelical data, and
method of utilizing it theologically. "Dialectic condemns more
and more the poor reasoning of the loisyste criticism. No, truly
M. Loisy does not have a single valid reason for denying the
authenticity and perfect historicity of the Gospel texts on the
institution of the Eucharist."[37]

Underlying the felt lack of cogency in Loisy's position,
then, is a much different evaluation of the nature of the sources
themselves and the role of authority in their regard. This is
reinforced by the divergent conceptions of development
characteristic of the dominant theology and the exegete
respectively. If the effect of an organismic metaphorical
network was to situate Jesus squarely within his Jewish
environment, a consequence was to heighten the rupture with that
environment occasioned by the Church's expansion into a Gentile
world. The discontinuities Loisy perceived in the historical
record could not be met with a theology of development by logical
clarification. Acorn and oak are just too manifestly different,
and their continuity can only be legitimated by the process of
growth that furnishes the principle of identity. It will be
recalled that Loisy's reliance on organic metaphors was
criticized as a narrow over-reliance, and reduced the process of

development to a merely human product -- a complaint that re-emerges specifically in relation to the eucharist.

The different readings of development are grounded in different modes of argumentation, or, to put it another way, in divergent epistemological commitments. Loisy's organicism is expressed in a certain historicism, which his critics tend to read as deformative. The exegete is charged with advocating a reductionistic apologetic: in focusing on the data of history his approach remains confined to the phenomenal, and the realities of Christian history are reduced to human proportions. Further, he is criticized for a deterministic strain in his thought, an evolution shaped by fixed externals. This is not in fact what Loisy holds. As the texts have evidenced, he is careful not to assert that historical investigation exhausts any reality, especially that of religious facts. And he affirms that Christianity contains its own principles which allow it to dominate that which it assimilates. A significant portion of his problem appears to be that these positions are asserted rather than systematically argued. Certainly the divine aspect of revelation is repeatedly emphasized in Loisy's presentation, its presence coordinated with the human.[38] But assertion only indicates a coordination without explaining it. A role for the supernatural is stated, but its operation is never explicated. Instead, emphasis falls on the human side of the relationship and attention is given to the role of history with its aspect of relativity.

Despite Loisy's assertions, then, his failure to state what revelation's divinity implied appeared to critics in effect to eliminate the supernatural. While this reading is not exactly on target, neither is it entirely off the mark, however. In distancing theological expressions -- historically contingent and necessarily inadequate -- in which the inexpressible religious facts come to symbolic expression, from the mystery to which the symbol points, the relationship between object of revelation and its expression becomes problematic. In what sense can it be affirmed that the religious symbol is true or false as a statement about the transcendental reality to which it points? Loisy's reaction against a scholastic intellectualistic emphasis directed him toward intuitive, affective, and ultimately moral dimensions of dogma. While a reading of the tradition which highlights its practical implications for the life of the believer was a needed corrective to the dominant theology's emphasis, it begged important aspects of the question. This reappears to haunt his conception of development: does the standard by which continuity in dogma might be judged become in effect unspecifiable, if the relation between dogmatic assertion and religious reality is left vague? An organic framework conveys the necessity of development; it is less helpful in specifying criteria for legitimate development. Loisy's assertions to the effect that "the Catholic Church . . . is identical with the first circle of the disciples of Jesus if she feels herself to be, . . . if the elements of the Church to-day are the primitive elements, grown and fortified, adapted to the ever-increasing functions they have to fulfil"[39] were hardly satisfying to a neo-Thomist criterion of substantial identity. But if, from the side of the official theology there is an incommensurable grasp of the problem in relation to Loisy's view of it, does not their uneasiness nonetheless expose a vulnerable point in the exegete's exposition?

In a fashion analogous to revelation, despite his allusions to the principles of Christianity, Loisy's stress on the historical environment directed critics' attention to the external. References to "the law of all development", to development as a necessary process were read as entailing a determinism. Loisy's developmental metaphors were read in a way consistent with this interpretation.

The eschatological perspective which informs (and in the minds of his critics deforms) the exegete's treatment of the eucharist, threatens the direct institution of the seven sacraments by Jesus himself, and calls into question the very divine institution of the Church. The teaching of Trent is reiterated, and the gospel testimonies are marshalled in support of the seven sacraments, for "the institution of the sacraments serves indirectly to prove the divine institution of the Church. They have, indeed, justification only if Jesus Christ has constituted a society charged with administering them." To establish the historical basis on which the institution of the sacraments rests, then, is to "establish subsidiarily that the institution of the Church is an historically demonstrable fact."[40]

Le Camus put it succinctly: "If Jesus has not founded the Church, then what did he do in his Messianic ministry?"[41] Loisy's answer, of course, was that he preached the kingdom, and ministered in expectation of this "great hope". For the scholastics, to admit a Jesus who, influenced by ideas prevalent in his environment, held (erroneously) a belief in an imminent kingdom, impugned his divinity and undercut the orthodox Christology. To admit such a Jesus called into question his conceiving the necessity for a Church with organized ritual and hierarchical structure and undermined the received ecclesiology. To do so was to admit a break between Jesus and the apostolic Christianity which succeeded him. It was to place the Church after that ministry had ended, allowing that hierarchy, cult, doctrine had evolved under the action of circumstances, of events, somewhat as the French Republic succeeded historically, naturally, legitimately, from the monarchy of Clovis -- to borrow Gayraud's comparison.[42] That points to a reduction of the Church to a merely human product, its elements foreign to the work and doctrine of Jesus, the artifacts of Paulinism, Johaninism, Hellenism, Romanism, and the like. In this there is historical succession, and indeed historical transformation, "not progression or explication of an identical religious thought."[43] The nature of that identity is supplied by Bouvier: "Jesus Christ, before leaving earth, founds and organizes this supernatural society, and he leaves it, with its doctrine and sacraments, a hierarchy destined to govern it throughout the centuries."[44]

Loisy had seen that Newman's developmental hypothesis had to be expanded to encompass the Scriptures themselves. That organic conception was countered by the logical theory of his critics, and their evaluation of the evangelical sources as eyewitness accounts. This entailed the further rejection of the fact/ faith distinction invoked by the exegete in support of his position. One could not put the historical facts on one side and the formulas of faith on the other -- for the latter were demonstrable by the former. All of these factors: logical development, the nature of the scriptural sources, and the historical demonstrability of the institution of the Church by Christ come together in the following text from Le Camus' Fausse exégèse, mauvaise théologie:

> The institution of the Church by Jesus Christ is thus established by a series of facts rising absolutely from history. From that time it is historically demonstrable, and not only an object of faith, in M. Loisy's sense. Christ's will, on this point, remains verifiable for the historian. Without very much effort it could even be recognized that the Church has been constituted under the monarchical form, a form especially propitious for maintaining order, while assuring life and progress by the sovereign authority in questions of jurisdiction or teaching. Undoubtedly Peter did not see all the deductions that later would be drawn from the words by which he has established the essential foundation of the new society . . . but he certainly understood that he was instituted chief of the Apostles, and he exercised his primacy from the outset. . . . Yes, by the simple criticism of texts we can, whatever M. Loisy says, demonstrate the divine institution of the Roman pontificate and determine the legitimate conditions of its exercise.[45]

It would seem that the polarization of position between Loisy and the official theology could hardly have been more complete. And yet, in a way it could: in the authoritative intervention of the ecclesiastical hierarchy which added official censure to theological critique. The discussion of Kuhn's framework in relation to theology raised the issue of authority. This is held to function in theological communities in a way discernibly different from its role in scientific communities. Accordingly, critical discourse in theology may become authoritative critical discourse. When the latter is also incommensurable as a rival theological discourse, it can be expected that words will be translated into social control measures. Language inescapably contains a sociological dimension: the status of neo-Thomism as dominant theological paradigm engages that here.

Loisy's critics found official support with the issuance of the syllabus <u>Lamentabili Sane Exitu</u>, which appeared in July of 1907.[46] The 54th proposition reaffirmed the "ecclesiastical postulate", condemning the opinion that, "Dogmas, sacraments and hierarchy, both their notion and reality, are only interpretations and evolutions of the Christian intelligence which have increased and perfected by an external series of additions the little germ in the gospel."[47] This struck directly at Loisy's developmental interpretation of the sacraments, seeing in them the influence of the Church as it adapted to the circumstances and events of the various times and places in which it found itself. The eucharist was expressly dealt with by proposition 45, which condemned the position that, "Not everything which Paul narrates concerning the institution of the Eucharist (I Cor. 11: 23-25) is to be taken historically." As Loisy admitted in his <u>Simples réflexions sur le décret du saint-office "Lamentabili sane exitu" et sur l'encyclique "Pascendi dominici gregis"</u> (1908), this proposition viewed a position taken in <u>Autour d'un petit livre</u>. Just as the treatment of the eucharist in the fourth gospel links it to Jesus' passion and death, so is this process of theological interpretation present in Paul. On the basis of the results of his critical exegesis since the latter book, Loisy felt able to conclude that the words of institution over the bread and wine were not original to the primitive tradition of the last supper. Those elements were only presented to the disciples by Jesus, with the avowal that he would eat and drink with them henceforth only in the banquet of the kingdom of heaven. As "theologian of the redemptive death" Paul visibly interpreted, according to his theory of universal expiation, the supper commemorative of Jesus' death.[48]

Contrary to Loisy's developmental reformulation of the ecclesiastical postulate, the Tridentine decrees are reaffirmed as still valid and binding. Condemned is the notion that "The opinions concerning the origin of the sacraments which the Fathers of Trent held and which certainly influenced their dogmatic canons are very different from those which now rightly exist among historians who examine Christianity." (proposition #39).[49] There are several propositions which deal with the institution of the Church, its constitution, and the Petrine primacy. In each case the evolutionary position evident in Loisy is rejected.

The syllabus not only declared itself contrary to the exegete's position on sacraments and Church, but also rejected the distinction between history and faith by which he sought to justify it. In #23: "Opposition may, and actually does, exist between the facts narrated in sacred scripture and the Church's dogmas which rest on them. Thus the critic may reject as false facts the Church takes as most certain." This position is stated and proscribed.

The syllabus Lamentabili was followed in September by the encyclical Pascendi. Again the position that the sacraments have not been instituted by Christ is censured, being attributed to the agnosticism of the modernists, their espousal of the laws of immanence and evolution, and their use of history (as all these are interpreted by the encyclical). The symbolic interpretation of the sacraments is noted as one of the "gravest errors" which the modernist system leads to ("for the Modernists the sacraments are symbols or signs, though not devoid of a certain efficacy . . . inasmuch as they have become the vehicle for the diffusion of certain great ideas which strike the public mind"), and their dual function of "giving some sensible manifestation to religion" and "propagating it" through "sensible form and consecrating acts" is also cited as an erroneous position.[50] The modernist appreciation of Church is presented in terms consistent with the encyclical's description of sacrament. In that document's view the Church is reduced to a society in which faith can be shared and propagated, and the common good promoted. To a theology which emphasized the divine character of the Church, stressed the "vertical" dimension, the modernist position appeared to stress reductively the "horizontal".

In the encyclical's description of how sacraments and Church are linked with Christ its cognizance of Loisy is readily discernible:

> Still it is to be held that both Church and
> sacraments have been founded mediately by
> Christ. But how? In this way: all Christian
> consciences were, they affirm, in a manner
> virtually included in the conscience of
> Christ as the plant is included in the seed.
> But as the shoots live the life of the seed,
> so, too, all Christians are to be said to
> live the life of Christ. But the life of

138

Christ is according to faith, and so, too, is
the life of Christians. And since this life
produced, in the course of ages, both the
Church and the Sacraments, it is quite right
to say that their origin is from Christ and
is divine.[51]

Once again, when the controlling notion is "substantial
identity", an organismic rather than logical framework is read as
succession, "engraftment" -- transformation.

Both syllabus and encyclical speak to other issues which have
surfaced in these pages, e.g., the nature of theology and its
relation to auxiliary and profane sciences, the nature of truth.
The foregoing should suffice, however, to suggest the extent of
the polarization that existed between modernists and
neo-Thomists, a polarization not confined to Loisy and a number
of critics but engaging what might usefully be termed conflicting
paradigms. For official Catholicism, modernism indeed
represented "the synthesis of all heresies" and Loisy was
identified as its chief architect.

Having set forth, at some length, representative texts, it is
now possible to proceed to a more analytical treatment of the
issues they raise.

ii

Truth alone is unchangeable, but not its
image in our minds.
                    Alfred Loisy[52]

Truth is no more immutable than man himself,
since it evolved with him, in him, and
through him.
          Condemned by Lamentabili (#58)

The paradigm analysis in chapter 1 attempted to define Kuhn's
notion in a way useful to theology, and apply it to the
modernists at the level of a shared conception of science which
influenced their perception of theology -- particularly as the
latter relates to its various subdisciplines and auxiliary
disciplines. Loisy's position regarding the autonomy of critical
historical investigation in relation to theological
pronouncements flowed from his commitment to a scientific
criticism. How that conception got worked out more concretely
with regard to Church, sacraments, and the eucharist in
particular, has emerged from the textual exposition of the
previous section.

Undergirding Loisy's appreciation of science, his evaluation of theology, and the specification of their mutual interrelation are epistemological and metaphysical presuppositions. Given his pragmatic tendencies, Loisy largely manifested impatience with philosophical speculation; hence, while there are clear epistemological and metaphysical tendencies in the exegete's thought, many of his concepts have a rather unspecified character. Lack of clearly formulated concepts is attributable only in part, then, to the refractory character of the levels of reality being addressed.

Scientific knowledge, knowledge of empirical fact, is knowledge of phenomena. Historical facts fall within this category, e.g., Jesus proclaimed himself Messiah. Religious knowledge, knowledge of religious facts, is acquired immanently. The latter, in adding a dimension to the historical, are visible only to faith, e.g., the "depth" of Jesus' relation to the Father. Between these two orders Loisy attempted a sort of coordination: history will not let itself be suppressed by faith, nor yet can history contradict faith; rather faith can grow out of history -- though this last relationship is left unspecified -- and perhaps cannot be.

> For harmony to subsist between these two witnesses, which are but one, taken hold of at different moments, one need only take them for what they are, the first [historical] as the root of the second [dogmatic], and the latter as the development of the former.[53]

In addition to historical facts and to the believer's experience of their faith dimension, there are also attempts to express that depth dimension symbolically -- personally, Scripturally, ecclesially. Although these attempts may be the best possible expressions at the time of their formulation, they are bound to the thought-patterns and conceptualizations of their times and thus inescapably possess an historical relativity. Furthermore, given the insufficiency of any expression to exhaust that depth dimension of truth, they possess an intrinsically relative character. No formula, dogmatic or theological, could be unchangeable or sufficient.

Regarding the realm of historical fact, then, Loisy's position expresses an axiomatic historicism. For him the gospel had an existence independent of those who studied it, and could be understood in itself before it was interpreted in the light of the exegete's own preferences and needs.

Regarding the realm of faith, the dogmatic and theological assertions which give expression to this are assigned a distinctly secondary role in the life of religion. In line with Loisy's emphasis on the empirical, factual dimension is his

140

emphasis on the experiential over the cognitive, although the importance of the latter is affirmed repeatedly.

In the exegete's writings the two realms of faith and fact are related through purely functional concepts as bridging notions, or metaphorical expressions. The positive content of these mediating notions is difficult to specify: neither they nor Loisy's assertions that the two orders were not entirely independent and that he was not propounding a sort of "double truth" theory were sufficient to quell orthodox criticism.

> . . . Loisy's assertions of an organic connection between history and faith are not visibly grounded. When Jesus' divinity, his founding of the Church and his institution of the sacraments were removed from the plane of the historically ascertainable, Catholic traditionalists would not be assuaged by bare assertions. . . . [T]he application of insubstantial notions and suspect associations to the bases of Rome's self-understanding could not escape stricture.[54]

If conceptions of science and theology are themselves undergirded by philosophical infrastructures, these conceptions are in turn regulative of data, methods, and problems.

The data against which Loisy assessed the traditional teaching, including that on Church and sacraments, was Scripture. In his critical handling of the sources, the Scriptures are subject to the same rules of composition and therefore to the same rules of criticism as other ancient documents. Questions of authorship, period and place of composition are to be decided on grounds of internal evidence, not on the attributions made subsequently by the tradition. As post-resurrectional documents, the New Testament books reflect the faith and the situation of the early Church as well as the teaching of Jesus. As such, one must be wary of attributing to him what really belongs to a later stage of development in the life of Christianity. By contrast, the writings of the critics represented in this study present the literalistic, proof-texting approach to Scripture described in the paradigm analysis. Even Le Camus, who is critically informed to a degree, upheld the gospels as "the exact, faithful, unimpeachable expression of what the apostles saw, heard, and related of Jesus."[55]

A critical approach to history determined not only the status of the data, but how the data were treated. Methodologically, as critic Loisy independently studied a history that precedes the faith and dogma that are coordinate with it. Inversely, the

Roman procedure first examined dogma in its fully expanded form, and only then followed up the different stages through which it had passed.

Data and method in turn interacted in determining the problematic. Because Loisy began with the history as he reconstructed it, in lieu of a dogmatic position from which to reconstruct history, he admitted contradictions within the tradition. With the sacraments, for example, he saw discontinuities between contemporary Church practices and the primitive Church history. Continuity could only be retrieved, he thought, through reformulation of the "theological postulate" to accommodate a process of historical development. Reformulation of the "ecclesiastical postulate" followed as a natural corollary.

Hopefully, this summary account has served to render more explicit some of the links between the paradigm analysis as set forth initially, and some of the material of the intervening chapters. If conceptions of science and theology are taken as "paradigmatic", then incommensurability of world view engages paradigm infrastructure -- epistemological and metaphysical commitments. Incommensurability of data/ methods/ problems (and solutions) involves the "regulative" aspects of a paradigm. Language is constitutive of all levels, and as such has occupied center stage in the overall analysis.

In considering our central problem -- theological polarization -- incommensurability of world view will be examined first. The theological innovators felt that the profound changes which had followed in the wake of empirical science had created a different world, a changed intellectual climate. In this they represent a theological expression of a much broader collision of different "cultures". Historical investigation's claims, with its attendant notions of relativity and development -- claims that stood at the basis of the modernist understanding of the Church and their desire to adapt it to the modern world -- were intolerable from the point of view of a classicist mentality with its "eternal verities and universally valid laws."[56] To put this another way, historicism was almost as fanatically concerned with pure facts (and this constitutes one of its significant weak points) as neo-Thomism was preoccupied with pure truths -- "perhaps the reason why the confrontation between these two points of view continued for so long to be a pure antithesis."[57] As Bernard Scott concludes, "the Modernists were doomed to failure because they represented a mind-set that contained components which were both unintelligible and threatening to the classicists."[58]

The mention of "eternal verities" targets one of those threatened components. The organicist and idiographic modes of argumentation employed by Loisy and neo-Thomists respectively

142

held to different notions of truth — a factor certainly
contributory to their mutual antagonism. The initial quote at
the beginning of this chapter makes reference to "objective and
absolute certitude"; through a process of reification, ultimately
founded on the ahistorical stance of neo-Thomism, theological
statements were given an objectivity and absoluteness that
blurred any distinction between Truth and its formulation into
human expressions. There is a confusion here, an assimilation of
truth to Truth, an assimilation of theology to dogma. The quote
of Loisy's which began this section advances a contrasting
conception of truth, one that seeks to incorporate a sense of the
historicity of all human language. Yet the proper distinctions
do not appear to have been maintained here either; here dogma
seems to be dissolved into theology, Truth into truth. The
perennial truth that is at the core of dogmatic pronouncements is
rather radically relativized into a somewhat arbitrary expression
in Loisy's thought. The elements of continuity at a very
fundamental level are difficult to discern in the successive
stages of what Jesus taught and did, what the early Church
believed, and what this presently means for men and women formed
in the intellectual climate of modern science.

The lack of a "shared horizon of meaning", then, tended to
polarize the respective positions. Lacking a vision of
historicity and the concepts with which to translate it
theologically, neo-Thomists could only interpret attempts to
assess the historically relative character of human formulations
as leading to a complete relativity. To Billot, for instance,
such a notion as relative truth did not make sense — of such he
said, "you are joining words without sense, making an empty
noise, and you do not understand what you are saying."[59] On the
other hand, heavily influenced by a historicism heavily tinged
with an evolutionary naturalism, Loisy's own formulations did not
bear the weight of bridging the realm of history, with the
element of revisability which that built into human thought, and
a transcendent order with the elements of absoluteness and
immutability revealed in history. The second term threatened to
volatilize into pure symbolism, and indeed his appreciation of
religion eventually became more and more functional.

Billot's struggle to comprehend how Loisy could even join
words like "relative" and "truth" into a formulation which
purported to be meaningful, provides a convenient transition to
the linguistic aspect of paradigm incommensurability.[60] This
occurs most prominently in the use of a common vocabulary by
proponents of rival paradigms, but a vocabulary whose terms
receive different meanings within the framework of each
paradigm. Thus Loisy employed terms of common theological
parlance: "revelation", "dogma", "development", "Church",
"eucharist" — and so on. But the metaphorical networks in which
such terms were embedded imparted a very different signification

than that operative in the dominant theological paradigm. Since, on the one hand, Loisy's theological opponents failed to grasp what the exegete found problematic, and on the other their orientation was informed by a classicist mentality, inevitably a metaphorical rendering of development in terms of "child" and "mature adult" was read with a different meaning by them. When the exegete used the traditional language, often he understood it in a more historical, psychological, and ultimately ethical manner. "Development" may serve as an illustration of the first of these, "revelation" has connections with the second. The brief summary of Loisy's commentary on Jn. 13, 1-20 as a functional interpretation of the eucharist, as fostering unity among people in agapaic love exemplifies the last category.

If neo-Thomists failed to understand Loisy's use of the received theological language when he employed it, or why he felt such a different use necessary, they failed utterly to comprehend how he could regard it as dispensible. A case in point would be the scholastic understanding of the sacraments in the categories of Aristotelian philosophy. For the exegete, the formulas of sacramental theology, like the greater number of dogmatic definitions, were formulated in response to positions deemed erroneous. Inevitably, such formulations, conceived under the pressure of circumstance, must admit of progress to achieve a fuller and more balanced formulation. In Loisy's mind, the conceptualization necessary to meet the needs of a given time may be dispensed with, as very different circumstances arise. The Aristotelian language of form and matter, "artificially applied to the sacraments", could therefore be set aside in the attempt to communicate their meaning to contemporary Christians formed by modern culture. By contrast, to the neo-Thomist mentality such terminology was not in any way "artificially applied", but rather necessary to preserve orthodox meaning. To dismiss it as no longer applicable to changed circumstances would be tantamount to excising theorems from Euclidean geometry -- the logical coherence of the system is undermined. Just as the Christological definitions of the councils were deemed valid and binding, necessary for the preservation of the proper distinction between Christ's divinity and humanity, transubstantiation was considered normative for the preservation of the real presence in the eucharist. Its inclusion in the list of concepts declared "unthinkable" by "the innovators" in the quote at this chapter's beginning is telling.

Loisy's dislike of scholastic precision, coupled with his awareness of the historical relativity of human conceptions, led him to affirm the impossibility of elucidating religious mysteries except by analogous conceptions. From such an awareness, their revisability followed. However, if Loisy's critics failed to grasp his point here, the exegete's own appreciation of the issues is not problem free. As J.-B. Hogan,

the liberal French Sulpician, noted to Loisy, there was a real
danger in "the very indefiniteness" of these analogous
expressions. They would engender confusion, vague beliefs, and a
disorganized religion. "Without neat conceptions and precise
affirmations Christianity will survive . . . with little
practical effect upon the mass of Christians."[61]

Another component of the linguistic environment is the
nontraditional vocabulary utilized by the innovators. Categories
imported from the current language of science and history were
often accompanied by the objectionable connotations which they
had picked up from the Protestant and rationalist milieux in
which they had developed. The innovators themselves were not
unaware of the difficulty, as Loisy's care to dissociate his work
from liberal Protestant, Kantian, and rationalist positions
attests. This did not prevent the difficulty from being seized
upon by critics, as the texts give ample evidence. On the other
hand, the traditional scholastic categories as understood by the
neo-Thomists were not without their own insufficiencies after the
long period of scholastic decline and the latent distortions of
their crypto-rationalism. Thus, one may judge that the verbal
fundamentalism of the conservatives and the scientific and
critical language of the modernists lacked common medium for
discussion. In consequence,

> The Church saw Loisy as leaving nothing
> outside of history and thereby destroying
> transcendence; Loisy saw the Church as
> confusing what is genuinely permanent and
> transcendent within its temperally [sic]
> conditioned attempts to grasp and formulate
> it.[62]

Thomas O'Dea provides the convenient summary:

> Looking at the modernist crisis after more
> than half a century, one gets the uneasy
> feeling that both sides thought they had the
> 'metalanguage' for handling the vast complex
> -- Loisy in history, Pius in scholastic
> theology, or even commonsense language. With
> such a complete failure to comprehend the
> complexity of knowing, it is little wonder
> that events assumed a tragic cast.
> Conservatism placed its adherents in the
> embarrassing situation of insisting upon a
> fundamentalist literalness in the gospel as
> history and thereby losing the sense of what
> is meant by history. Modernism advocated
> demythologization before there was any
> language (or any sense of the need for a

language) to sort out the elements in the complex assertions of faith as they had come into existence.[63]

Lastly, the competing paradigms evoked different conceptions of what major theological problems were and different criteria for what could be acceptable solutions. In Kuhn's analysis, this problem incommensurability also engages methods and data. In speaking of the historically conditioned nature of problems Edward Schillebeeckx has observed, "Every period of history has its own problem. If the problem is changed, the resulting question cannot be answered, at least directly, with the earlier answer. What is more, the earlier question cannot be asked outside its own problem without at least partially changing the meaning of it."[64] The fundamental theological problem for the modernists was that of historicity. Earlier answers, arrived at within an ahistorical scholastic framework, could not meet the resulting questions. The received answers to the institution of Church and sacraments were no longer cogent for Loisy. In his posing of those questions the meaning was not the same as the scholastic rendering. Specifically, in relation to the eucharist, the problems for Loisy centered on ascertaining the meaning of the Last Supper for Jesus as distinguishable from that which the early Church attached to it, of discerning the elements of continuity that would relate these different meanings to the later tradition, and finally of translating the traditionally received teaching into a radically changed intellectual environment. He felt compelled by "the facts" to admit discontinuity in the meaning which the Last Supper had for Jesus (his imminent death and the coming of the kingdom), the significance its continuance had for the early Church (commemoration of the salvific death of Jesus as the highest expression of his loving service for his followers, a commemoration which brings about the continued presence of Christ within the community through the consecrated bread), and the meaning it is able to have for the contemporary Catholic. In face of "the facts" taken as starting point, a logical theory of development failed to provide an adequate solution. Continuity had to be sought in an overall process of development, not in identity among successive stages. Espousing a theological paradigm which possessed theology with a normative status vis-à-vis other disciplines, which on the basis of an ahistorical attitude employed Scripture in a manner commensurate with that attitude, the official theologians did not, could not have the same set of problems. Against Loisy they reiterated the understanding which the orthodox theology drew from Trent, an understanding which it held to be congruent with that of Jesus himself (as exemplified in claims as to the essential historicity of the discourse on the bread of life).

The challenge that Loisy's understanding of the sacraments

146

posed to the church was in the very nature of the case one that was more than merely institutional. For the self-understanding of the Church under its "orthodox"[65] theological paradigm rendered any challenge to its legitimacy a questioning of more than merely human authority. In the theology of the late 19th century, supported by the teaching of Vatican I, the Church assumed miraculous dimensions. More than a merely natural society, it was considered a supernatural society, manifesting in its historical existence a unity, a universality, a holiness, and an apostolicity that revealed miraculous proportions -- in short, its very existence indicating the divine origin of its message. Bridging the gap between the divine and the human, the Church is frequently described in the contemporary neo-scholastic theology by the hyphenated phrase humano-divina, representing the juridical identification of the human society with the divine.[66]

> The Church was the continuation of the Incarnation, the uniting of the human and divine on earth. Who hears the church, hears Christ. The same obedience due to Christ is also due to the 'legates of God.' An attack on the authority of the church is an attack on Christ himself. The communicatio idiomatum that applied between the two natures of Christ is now applied between Christ as the head of the church, his body.[67]

To attack the Church is to attack Christ himself. Through their espousal of critical methods of biblical study, through their handling of the data of the tradition, through their attempts to reformulate the understanding of church doctrine and ecclesiastical development, the modernists were indeed perceived to attack the authority of the Church. And given the understanding and function of authority within the dominant paradigm, this was very much the case. As if this were not enough, the innovators' Christology was perceived as an attack on Christ himself. But, as the above quote points out, the two were not unconnected in the Church's reaction to the modernist crisis.

In a general way, the differences in viewpoint may be summarized by saying that, if Loisy and other modernists appear to have given an exaggerated emphasis to the immanence of God and to the empirical data of revelation, their overemphasis must be seen as a reaction to the one-sided concentration on the transcendence of God and on rational thought in the theology of the period. From the vantage point of that theology the fruits of the modernist tentative were pernicious. In its summation of the modernist position, Pascendi reflected: "Certainly this suffices to show superabundantly by how many roads Modernism leads to the annihilation of all religion. The first step in this direction was taken by Protestantism; the second is made by Modernism; the next will plunge headlong into atheism."[68] To which George Tyrrell's observation forms an interesting (an incommensurable) reply: "When the Encyclical tries to show the Modernist that he is no Catholic, it mostly succeeds in showing him that he is no Scholastic -- which he knew."[69]

Notes to Chapter Four

[1]J. Brugerette, Le Prêtre français et la societé contemporaine, quoted in Pierre Fernessole, Pie X, (Paris: P. Lethielleux, 1953), pp. 162-163.

[2]Mémoires I, p. 176.

[3]Jules Jacques, L'Heure H, quoted by Maisie Ward, Insurrection verses Resurrection, p. 1.

[4]For example, Abbé Sédelot's comment on L'Evangile et l'Eglise: "c'est du renanisme, et du renanisme plus vague encore que celui de Renan." Quoted in Poulat, La crise moderniste, p. 128. Interestingly in 1908 Loisy acceded to the chair of the History of Religions at the Collège de France, once occupied by Renan. In referring to his birthdate, 28 February 1857, Loisy once observed, "34 years, to the day, after Renan", Loisy to Petre, 12 August 1931. Quoted by Petre, p. 124.

[5]Wherlé to Blondel, 15 March 1904. Maurice Blondel-Joannès Wherlé: correspondance 2 vols., (Paris: Aubier Montaigne, 1969), 1: 245.

[6]Mémoires I, p. 449.

[7]GC, p. 166.

[8]Ibid., p. 231.

[9]Ibid, pp. 232-233.

[10]Ibid., pp. 246-247; 235-239.

[11]Ibid., p. 249.

[12]Cf. Cardinal Perraud's reaction to L'Evangile et l'Eglise. Houtin, Q bib XX, pp. 91-92.

[13]APL, pp. 220-221.

[14]Ibid., pp. 255-256.

[15]Ibid., p. 224. This distinction has been interpreted as tantamount to a "double truth" theory -- "true" for faith in its way, and "true" for history in another. For Wernz, if that is to involve contradiction between the truths, then that is not Loisy's position. One can speak of a "double truth" in Loisy's

thought, however, "if that means only that the theological truth will be a deeper and harmonious appreciation of the religious facts whose surface alone appears to history." Wernz, p. 260. As part of paradigmatic "infrastructure", and as it bears upon the issue of mutual intelligibility between Loisy and critics, the conception of truth will be taken up again later in this chapter.

[16]See chapter 2, note 139.

[17]APL, p. 227.

[18]"These opinions are in agreement with the knowledge which they had, at that time, of Christian origins, that is to say, far removed from those professed by contemporary historians, even Catholic ones." Ibid., p. 223.

[19]As early as 1881; see Introduction.

[20]Duel, p. 105. This was the tack Edouard Le Roy was later to take in his article, "Qu'est-ce qu'un dogme?" (1905).

[21]Chapter II of Etudes évangéliques on Jn. 6 had appeared earlier in Revue d'histoire et de littérature religieuses 5 (1900): 416-451 and 6 (1900): 480-502. The last chapter (V) on Jn. 13, 1-20 had not previously been published.

[22]"Certainly, Jesus never directed these words at a Jewish audience; he never spoke of the eucharist, a year before his death, as an institution currently in force; but it is the evangelist who speaks through the mouth of Christ and who informs us how the eucharist was understood in the Christian milieu in which he lived." Alfred Loisy, Etudes évangeliques, (Paris: Alphonse Picard et fils, éditeurs, 1902), p. 279. The position of the official theology was much to the contrary. Cf., for example, the decree of the Pontifical Biblical Commission on the authorship and historical truth of the fourth gospel, dated 29 May 1907. Rome and the Study of Scripture, (St. Meinrad, Indiana: Abbey Press, 1964), pp. 119-120.

[23]Etudes évangéliques, p. 293.

[24]Ibid., p. 329.

[25]Alfred Loisy, Le Quatrième évangile, (Paris: Alphonse Picard et fils, éditeurs, 1903), p. 115.

[26]APL, p. 161.

[27]Ibid., p. 181.

[28]Ibid., p. 227.

[29]GC, pp. 262-263. Cf. APL, p. 224.

[30]APL, pp. 244-245.

[31]Bouvier, p. 44.

[32]Le Camus, Lettre 1901, p. 2.

[33]Bouvier, pp. 48 and 49.

[34]Gayraud, L'Univers, 10 Jan. 1903.

[35]Ibid.

[36]Gayraud, L'Univers, 24 Oct. 1903.

[37]Gayraud, L'Univers, 1 Dec. 1903.

[38]"It is humanity which seeks, but it is God who prompts it; it is humanity which sees, but it is God who enlightens it. Revelation is realized in humanity, but it is the work of God in it, with it and through it. The efficient cause of revelation is supernatural in its object, because this cause and this object is God himself, but God acts in humanity, and he is known by humanity." APL, pp. 197-198.

[39]GC, p. 171.

[40]Le Camus, Fausse exégèse, mauvaise théologie, p. 100. The bishop acknowledges that "it is not easy to find in the Gospel the conclusive texts which prove the immediate institution of certain of them." But, he avows that "whatever M. Loisy thinks, for our principal sacraments, the teaching of the Church rests on the gospel testimonies." pp. 99 and 100.

[41]Ibid., p. 96.

[42]Gayraud, L'Univers, 24 Oct. 1903.

[43]Gayraud, L'Univers, 10 Jan. 1903.

[44]Bouvier, p. 39.

[45]Le Camus, p. 98.

[46]Bouvier's contribution to the syllabus has been noted earlier.

[47]All citations from Lamentabili will be taken from the text in Vincent A. Yzermans, ed., All Things in Christ: Encyclicals and Selected Documents of Saint Pius X, (Westminster, Maryland: The Newman Press, 1954), pp. 223-228.

151

48Loisy, Simples réflexions, pp. 97-98.

49Also censured were: "The Sacraments had their origin in the fact that the Apostles and their successors, swayed and moved by circumstances and events, interpreted some idea and intention of Christ." (#40), and "The Sacraments are intended merely to recall to man's mind the ever-beneficent presence of the Creator." (#41). Propositions 42 through 51 touched individual sacraments.

50The Encyclical of His Holiness Pius X on the Doctrine of the Modernists, p. 67.

51Ibid., pp. 65-66.

52GC, p. 217.

53APL, pp. 56-57.

54W.J. Wernz, "Loisy's 'Modernist' Writings", The Downside Review 92 (1974), p. 39.

55Le Camus, Vraie et fausse exégèse, p. 17.

56Cf. Lonergan, Method in Theology, p. 301.

57T. Mark Schoof, O.P., A Survey of Catholic Theology, 1800-1970. Translated by N.D. Smith. (New York: Paulist Newman Press, 1970), p. 185.

58Scott's introduction to GC, p. xxxi.

59Quoted in Sanks, p. 116.

60In Ricoeur's terms, noted in chapter 2, this is a move from the horizon of reality surrounding the speech situation, to the context of the linguistic environment of the actual words.

61Bibliothèque Nationale, Papiers Loisy XXI No. 15654 F. 382 John Hogan to Alfred Loisy, April 8, 1898. Cited in Christopher J. Kauffman's manuscript on the history of the Sulpicians in the U.S., to be published in 1987.

62 O'Dea, The Catholic Crisis, p. 74.

63Ibid., p. 170.

64Edward Schillebeeckx, The Understanding of Faith, (London: Sheed and Ward, 1974), p. 79.

[65]In David Tracy's sense of that. See his Blessed Rage for Order, (New York: The Seabury Press, 1975), pp. 24-25

[66]Sanks, pp. 109-113.

[67]Ibid., pp. 110-111.

[68]Judge, p. 87.

[69]Quoted in Schoof, p. 186.

Conclusion

> The intellectual frame of a man's thought
> displays itself less in the detailed results
> he enunciates than in the questions he asks
> and the assumptions that underlie his
> theorizing.[1]

The syllabus _Lamentabili_ and the encyclical _Pascendi_
promulgated the Church's rejection of the modernist attempt at
reform. In the polarization of positions that had taken place,
Rome could do no other, for the modernist reformulation
constituted a threat to certain essential structures of
Catholicism. The polarization of positions and their
incommensurability certainly contributed to the severity of the
measures taken -- the description of the innovators and their
motives in _Pascendi_ is not overly kind, and a section of the
encyclical was devoted to institutionalizing social control
measures to ensure modernism's extinction. An Oath against
Modernism, imposed in September of 1910, may be said to have
finished the work largely accomplished in the two documents
issued three years previously. The integralist reaction brought
its own type of extremity, and for decades any liberal tentatives
were regarded with suspicion.

It has been argued that "the reality of the disagreement"
served strongly to polarize Loisy and neo-Thomist critics, but
this is a reality which was to a significant degree constituted
by language. The "difficulty of the interlocutors in
understanding and being understood"[2] is importantly an artifact
of divergent systems of discourse. A language constitutes an
internal system of rules that act as principles of inclusion and
exclusion, that permit some questions to be asked and answers to
be formulated, while ruling others "unthinkable"/ (unsayable).[3]
The underlying argument has maintained that the dominant
metaphors utilized by Loisy and his theological critics inform
their very understanding of what is problematic; that their
respective metaphorical networks inform their mutual
understanding (misunderstanding); that these networks are
reflective of "root metaphors", and ultimately dominant tropes
which figure and prefigure discourse and interact to enhance/
inhibit ability to communicate meaningfully.

Schillebeeckx has argued that when problems that are central
to a period undergo a shift, new questions cannot be satisfied
with earlier answers. Even if the form of the question remains
relatively unchanged, it is no longer the same question. If its
terms are traditional, they are also new. For Loisy, the
progress of science had posed the problem of God in new terms,
the progress of history had likewise impacted the problem of

Christ and that of the Church. It was that triple problem which imposed the necessity of a new apologetic, of a reformulation of the traditional answers in terms cogent to a culture both scientifically minded and historically conscious. The resulting question, then, became one of development -- of developmental continuity. It concerned "seeing how the Gospel, which announced the proximate coming of the kingdom of God, produced the Christian religion and the Catholic Church."[4] For the exegete, "the facts" which emerged through application of critical methods demanded an account adequate to them. To the historian's "hypotheses" advanced to render the best possible account of those facts, the tradition could oppose -- to his mind -- neither "certainties" nor "probabilities". "It opposes nothing to them, and for a good reason: it has never envisaged the problems which criticism has raised, and those who today advance the tradition as opposed to criticism have the air of not suspecting them yet."[5]

Of course, incommensurability runs two ways: if Loisy can complain that scholastics are blind to the problems entertained by a critical exegesis, his critics could in turn charge him with a dismissal of their concerns. Loisy found it easy to target their approach to the gospels as biographies, to impugn their methodology. His scholastic adversaries occasionally find it expedient to raise the name of an exegete of more moderate stamp -- such as Lagrange -- whose criticism is to remind Loisy that the issues raised run deeper than methodological divergences.

It would appear that the very ability to perceive what is problematic is linked to methodological commitment. For neo-Thomism the starting point is the dogmatic thesis that is given in the tradition, e.g., the Tridentine decrees on the institution of the sacraments. The role of the theologian is to gather from the scattered data of Scripture, the Fathers, the councils and other sources of the tradition the dogmatic truths which are found there, and to organize them systematically. Theology is to be characterized by a fruitful fusion of the positive method, whose aim is to demonstrate the apostolic origin of Catholic dogma; and the speculative, which is to effect the rational synthesis of the dogmas whose apostolic origin has been demonstrated. Theology, then, is to proceed deductively, from revealed first principles to conclusions which follow logically and with the requisite degree of certainty from the premises. Methodologically, the unity of the tradition is a given: the sources are to be taken as speaking in accord with it -- any evidence to the contrary being categorized as a deficiency of language. The orthodox sense was meant; at that time the requisite language was yet lacking to articulate it properly.

For Loisy, on the other hand, one begins with "the facts" of the historical record, and constructs hypotheses -- on the analogy of the hard sciences -- to best account for those facts.

156

For the exegete, development becomes a scientific hypothesis, derived from consideration of empirical data, and subject to confirmation from that same source. When the unitary nature of the tradition is not assumed, it was found not to exist -- at least not in the sense that the dominant theology held. It was found by that theology only because it was put there. Critical method, then, is scientific, inductive; it consists in part in removing the prejudices, the theological a priori which do not allow the data to emerge with clarity. Autonomy of criticism is essential to the scientific nature of that enterprise. Loisy could not understand how, to be truly critical, criticism could be anything else. To Le Camus he replied in Autour d'un petit livre: "To begin, Monseigneur, I frankly declare that I do not understand your exegetical position. I do not see how a Catholic critic would be less free than a Protestant critic and an unbeliever in the examination of questions of authenticity or in the historical commentary of Scripture."[6] To Le Camus there is "true exegesis" and there is "false" -- just as for Bouvier there is criticism -- and there is criticism. Their metaphorical networks evoke a limit language which orients exegesis within boundaries, charts dangerous shoals and indicates safe waters, guides it through the labyrinths of critical scholarship.

Loisy was not concerned to provide a philosophical analysis of historical method as such, but to pragmatically solve what he saw as compelling difficulties within the dominant presentation of Catholicism. Thus his methodology remains largely implicit in his work, emerging more explicitly (though hardly systematically) in his response to opponents. This being the case, Bouvier was led to reconstruct the exegete's "methodological principles". A mere summary listing of them is sufficient to indicate his perception of their procedure and effect: 1. To get rid of inconvenient texts, either by contesting their authenticity from Jesus, or supposing them altered by subsequent retouching; 2. To explain the texts without taking account of their received interpretation in the Church; 3. To interpret the Sacred Books as an historian, scholar, or philologist, with the pretension of escaping all properly theological preoccupation; 4. To conserve the traditional terminology while modifying its meaning, under the pretext of harmonizing Catholic thought with the progress of science; 5. To accept information nearly exclusively from heterodox authors, while neglecting the teaching of Catholic doctors, both historical and contemporary.[7] Of course this list reflects polemical presentation more than representation, but even in that light is indicative.

The first of Bouvier's attributed procedures engages the status of the data. The terms of comparison of their respective positions -- authentic biography/ history versus faith testimony -- has been explicated sufficiently. Here it will be enough to note the perceived effect of that disparity, from Le Camus' viewpoint:

> Once our Synoptics thus placed under
> suspicion by the successive touching-up which
> they have undergone, and Saint John
> transformed into a symbolic composition born
> with the second and third Christian
> generation, the field remains entirely open
> for outlining the history of the successive
> creation of dogmas in the early Church.
> Periods of formation are easy to establish,
> and Christian revelation remains the
> progressive and entirely natural consequence
> of the simple religious impetus given by
> Jesus to the soul of several Galilean
> rustics.[8]

This brings us full circle back to problem perception. For
Loisy "the facts" do not permit an affirmation of "substantial
identity" among the successive stages of the tradition. Jesus is
influenced by the eschatological tenor of his environment. The
Last Supper is for him connected with the coming kingdom. It was
not intended to take its place in a sevenfold sacramental system,
to be perpetuated in a Church hierarchically established and
designed to endure for an indefinite temporal period. In that
primitive Church, only as eucharist assumed the proportions of
sacrifice did its presiders acquire the role of priests, properly
so understood. A pious custom such as anointing of the sick,
gradually became institutionalized to a point where it became
endowed with sacramental status. And the very organizational
structure of the Church itself has developed in accord with the
needs of the time. A set of historical circumstances has
produced its monarchical nature, not an explicit intention of
Jesus "before leaving earth". (Therefore, in a more democratic
political environment, the organizational structure of the Church
would, in principle, be reformable to better conform to those
changed circumstances.) The solution, then, is to admit the
existence of substantial difference in the historical tradition.
In other words, to admit a process of development of a type that
requires reform of the theological postulate. There has been
progress in fundamental religious ideas; continuity must be
sought in the overall process, not in a comparison of the ideas
with one another. That developmental solution, metaphorized
organically, entails reform of the ecclesiastical postulate in
consequence: dogmatic language which no longer communicates with
people formed by modern culture may be dispensed with, in favor
of more adequate formulations; the very number of the sacraments
themselves may undergo modification by authoritative
ecclesiastical decision; the monarchical structure of the
Church's hierarchy could admit of alteration.

Sufficient texts have been retrieved from Loisy's critics to demonstrate that, failing to grasp the proportions of the exegete's problem, they could hardly entertain such solutions. Indeed, one is strongly impressed that Loisy's exegesis is itself regarded as the fundamental problem. It seemed to Le Camus, for one, that Loisy "arrived at the theological conception constituting his system, very much less through taste for dogmatic speculation than swept along by the difficulties which his exegesis, daring and entirely outside the tradition, revealed to him as insoluble in the Holy Books. Could he not resolve them in another way?"[9] The Bishop seems to think he could: by relinquishing the "false exegesis" which got him into those difficulties in the first place -- in short, through acquisition of proper method, of "correct" evaluation of the status of the data, by a conception of the science of exegesis that is consonant with the orthodox theology of the Church.

This amounts to establishing the legitimacy of the principle of theological control considered more abstractly in the initial paradigm analysis: the theology/ science, faith/ reason relation which was considered to constitute the heart of the application of that analysis to theology. Incommensurability of problems (and solutions) is reflective of an incommensurable conception of what theology as a "science" is/ does.

When Loisy and other theological innovators employed words such as "revelation", "dogma", "development", they did so with a meaning much different from that intended by the dominant theology. More fundamentally, when they spoke of "science" and "theology", again while using the same words they were not speaking the same language. To reiterate, science for the neo-Thomist evoked an Aristotelian, deductive enterprise, a matter of establishing first principles and reasoning to the appropriate conclusions. As a "conclusion theology" neo-Thomism presented objective, coherent, permanently valid statements of transcendent facts, whose certainty was guaranteed by the revealed status of its first principles and the logical rigor and clarity of its procedure. (Symptomatically, Daly observes that one of this theology's major problems was to defend the obscuritas of faith.[10]) Loisy, on the other hand, took an empirical, inductive model of science as his norm, formulated "hypotheses" to account for the data, and accented the role of intuition over cognition in religious knowing. From the point of view of his theological opponents, the latter was regarded as weakmindedness, the role assigned to history as leading to a relativism and ultimately, to an undermining of the objective order of truth.

The very logic of the neo-Thomist conception of theology as an Aristotelian science of faith involved a normative relation to other disciplines. Revelation as assertion, faith as intellectual assent, required a subordinate role for the exercise of reason: "natural" sciences must accede to theology as a supernatural science. History is merely the contingent set of circumstances which form the backdrop to the appearance of perennially valid truths. As has emerged at a number of points, the role accorded history by Loisy was quite divergent. Critical method required an autonomy for history vis-à-vis theology, presented as a distinction/ relation between fact and faith. In part due to the refractory nature of the areas involved to clear definition, in part an artifact of his professed impatience with philosophical work, and perhaps also due to a recognition of the consequences of being too clear, Loisy regulates the faith/ history relation via bridging notions, or metaphorically. The historical is the "root" of the dogmatic; the latter is the "living" development of the former.

Thus the issue of language -- and particularly of metaphorical language -- emerges yet again. It permeates the whole area of problem formulation and solution, of exegetical method and data of the tradition, informs the very conception of theology and science, and the faith/ history relation that involves. Admittedly, eucharist, sacraments more generally, the organizational structure of the Church have developed -- but the crucial question is, developed how? Language orients more towards what was said, less towards what was said. The neo-Thomists reviewed spoke a metaphorical language of geometrical axioms and logical deduction; of integral "deposit" -- precious, jewel-like, to be guarded and perhaps crafted. Loisy preferred an organic vocabulary of seed and plants, roots and fruits, child and adult. Admittedly there is some overlap: his critics occasionally employ the same metaphors, but utilized in a very different sense, enmeshed in the static networks which for them preserved the proper meaning. Loisy's organic terminology lacked necessary correctives, appeared too narrow, led to erroneous -- indeed heretical -- conclusions. The same general orientation emerges in the conception of theology and its status: that can be metaphorized hierarchically: (master)/ "servant"; (lord)/ "vassal" (Gayraud). Or it can be represented geographically: river banks which constrain the water's course; or in a different mode, the clipped wings of a bird (Le Camus). The limits, however specified, are necessary and salutary, lest the believer be led astray on "dangerous routes" (Bouvier), or lose sight of the shore and undergo shipwreck (Le Camus). The point of Ricoeur's analysis was to challenge the conception of metaphor as merely rhetorical ornament; enmeshed in larger networks metaphors are constitutive of a reality. As Dulles points out, when taken for granted and not subjected to serious questioning the root metaphors which lie at the base of theological constellations can be productive of serious disagreement. Perhaps it was Tyrrell who posed the dilemma most sharply: "Ultimately the question resolves itself into this: Does thought grow architecturally or biologically?"[11] Both Loisy and the critics surveyed evidence distinct preferences for one category of metaphorical networks or the other, which are adopted as controlling. A _via media_ did not materialize as practicable, nor did a third alternative emerge then.

Metaphors are "tensive": if, on one level, they are logically absurd (the Gospel is a "root"); on another, they are productive of new meaning. If a metaphor (or a network of them) can be said to constitute a gestalt, that viewpoint is constituted through selectivity: some of the metaphorical connotations are "positive" -- they are illuminative of the area or object to be understood. Since they are informative they are incorporated into the "pattern". Others are not related, forming the negative analogy. A third set of categories may not stand in any clear relation; when it is not yet known if they are positive or negative, they form a sort of neutral analogy. As metaphors undergo development -- through their interaction with other metaphors in a network, with other networks in a text -- or with different texts by the same or other authors -- the "texture" of the gestalt they constitute may be altered. The "neutral analogy" may be configured differently, affecting the meaning which the metaphor communicates. From the standpoint of the larger conceptual framework of this study, one would expect that what are constituted as "positive", "negative", or "neutral" analogies are not paradigm independent. The metaphorical "gestalt" is related to the larger frame of reference constituted by the paradigm. The way in which Loisy tended to read his own metaphors, highlighting some of their implications while leaving others recessive (cf. Turvasi's comment [12]), and the way his metaphors were read by critics support this expectation.

Organicism, however, serves not only as a broad term to indicate metaphorical preference with Loisy, but also to refer to a mode of argumentation, one by its very nature likely to clash with the formist mode characteristic of neo-Thomism. It has been argued that, construed in terms of Hayden White's conceptualization, the dominant theology emplotted history in a "romantic" mode, joined that with an idiographic mode of representation and conservative ideological position. Deep structurally, the historical field was prefigured via the trope of metaphor. Its idiography led to a focus on the uniqueness of agents, agencies, and acts which comprised the "events" to be explained, and to a relative neglect of the historical environment in which these events occur. This is reflected in its theory of development, in which supernaturally revealed truths underwent a process of logical explication while being little affected by the historical context in which they appeared or were subsequently shared. As revealer of divine truths and founder of the Church as their repository, Jesus Christ is presented in the high Christological terms of the fourth gospel,

161

its narrative taken as historically accurate. As the continuation of the Incarnation, the Church itself is both human and divine, the uniting of the human and the divine on earth, unique among institutions as befits the uniqueness of the deposit with which it has been entrusted. A conservative ideology which conceived historical evolution as the progressive elaboration of the institutional structure which currently prevails is also reflected in this theology's developmental theory. As Le Camus observed, without great effort the monarchical form of the Church could be recognized as having issued from Jesus Christ, Peter's primacy as having been operative from the very beginning. The monarchical form of the Church is therefore a structural given, divinely instituted for the salutary exercise of a sovereign authority. Certainly in the course of centuries it has undergone progressive elaboration and may continue to do so. But the structural principle itself is not susceptible to historical mutation.

Applying White's framework to Loisy, it was argued that his position rested on a comic mode of emplotment (for which historicism has an elective affinity), an organicist mode of argumentation, with an ideological orientation somewhat radical in its implication. The deep structural trope identified was that of synecdoche. The concern is always with the whole over the parts: the comic provisional reconciliation of forces reflected in a developmental process in which parts undergo modification so that the equilibrium of the living Church might be preserved; the organicist view in which the tendency characteristic of the whole is reflected in successive forms which each manifest or express the developmental process. That process itself admits of qualitative change, and emphasis falls on depiction of the integrative course of development more than on delineation of its various elements. Both Jesus and the Church are firmly set in their historical environment, and as such are subject to the effects of transformations in that context. Loisy felt compelled to account for discontinuities in the tradition, and to provide resources for the Church to adapt to the transformed circumstances of a modern, scientific culture. In White's rendering, a radical orientation is concerned to bring about an altered state of affairs now, a sense of crisis to be met with revolutionary means that is reflected in modernism generally.

Tropologically, the neo-Thomist configuration is undergirded by metaphor. On a prefigurative level this has an affinity with the correspondence theory of truth espoused by idiography. The implications of this are expressed in the following comment by Daly:

> The neo-scholastic system was constructed on
> the conviction that God's existence can be

demonstrated by speculative reason through
the principle of causality; that the
essential characteristics of the divine
nature can be discerned by the same means,
through the medium of the doctrine of the
analogy of being; that the possibility of
revelation has first to be vindicated by pure
reason and its actual occurrence demonstrated
by historical investigation; that the content
of revelation is expressed, not symbolically,
but analogically; and that this content is
guaranteed as authentically divine in origin
by empirically verifiable facts. Not merely
did this system stand or fall as a whole; it
was fatally vulnerable to any suggestion that
causality does not operate in the same manner
in the transcendent as in the historical
realm.[13]

Now the point is that metaphor tropologically grounds such a
conception of causality, with its more general apprehension of
the world as "one term of a Metaphor, the other and dominant term
of which, that by which the world is given its meaning and
identity, is conceived to exist in another world."[14] Idiography
is grounded on similarity, and that is precisely the mark of
metaphor. On a preconscious level, metaphor provides a
plausibility structure in which such consciously held theological
commitments "make sense", are felt to be cogent, are sensed to
fit the very nature of things. At a precritical level this mode
of linguistically prefiguring the field legitimated the
scholastic superimposition of the dominant term of the metaphor
-- the supernatural -- on the mundane term.[15] Prefiguring the
field in a different -- and divergent -- way, modernists
experienced the scholastic rendering of this relationship as an
extrinsic one.[16]

For Loisy in particular, organicism is tropologically
grounded in synecdoche. The metaphorical networks rendering his
conception of development stress whole over part, process over
elements, in a way that regards the "essence" of Christianity as
integrative rather than reductive (versus Harnack). It is the
fulness and totality of Christianity's life which provides the
continuity amidst the manifest qualitative changes present in the
various stages of that life. From a neo-Thomist perspective that
implied letting go of the dominant term of the metaphor, a
substitution of symbol for analogy, a Kantian failure of nerve
which confined the apprehension of causality to the mundane
sphere and lapsed into an agnosticism with regard to the
supernatural. The "whole" no longer encompassed an objective,
transcendent order, and instead fell into an immanentism confined
to historical phenomena. Loisy's continued assertions regarding

163

the object of faith, while insisting on the inability of historical fact to prove that object, seemed in reality to relinquish the object itself. From the standpoint of a conception which linked supernatural and natural orders metaphorically, Loisy's metaphorical rendering of their relation in organic terms was experienced as being far from satisfactory.

There is an additional complicating factor in Loisy's presentation: the strong possibility of an ironic perspective. Jack Forstman has rendered the terms of that orientation rather succinctly: "The author who states what he sees with unmitigated seriousness and who, at the same time, smiles at his own vision, at himself in the construction of that vision, is ironic."[17] In light of that characterization, Loisy's rendering of the Abbé Icard's response to his work at the Institut catholique in the early 1890s is suggestive. He recounts,

> My articles were carried to him to read, and their bearing elucidated to him. . . . To one who tried to get him to recognize the moderation of my language, the aged superior replied that a smile could change the entire sense and purport of a phrase. Moreover, he said, he knew my smile was irreverent, and that students who entered my class room lost all their respect for Holy Scripture. I am convinced, that if my smile could have been printed at the same time with my text, it would be recognized today as much less directed at the Bible than at its interpreters, and that its irreverence was not for the Holy Spirit but for the Catholic apologists. However that may be, Abbé Icard decided to remove his pupils from this pernicious influence.[18]

The illocutionary force with which words are spoken can be less adequately conveyed in writing through the more austere conventions of punctuation. Loisy's smile could indeed not be printed with the text of L'Evangile et l'Eglise -- but there are strong indications that its presence came soon to be suspected, and that what on one level was a penetrating critique of Harnack, on another struck with equal force at the received Catholicism. Loisy's content is not always easy to specify, given a factor such as the nature of his terminology. If anything, judgments based on his style are harder to verify. Daly has referred to L'Evangile et l'Eglise as "a book which mystified many . . . and which still fascinates both by the elegance of its style and by a dexterity which verges on sleight-of-hand. The reader has a persistent feeling of 'now you see it, now you don't'."[19] This characterization can be taken as an indication of the presence of

164

irony, for the presence of a perspective at the same time presented and negated, the "second thoughts" that are raised by the structure of the language.

Brief as they were, the extracts from the antimodernist syllabus and encyclical quoted in the previous chapter indicate the uncompromising nature of authoritative reaction. A reading of Pascendi's provisions for measures of social control underscores the impression conveyed by its rhetoric. By 1907 positions had polarized to the extent that moderism had become the problem -- its solution was extinction. This study has looked at that polarization mainly at its crisis point: the publication of L'Evangile et l'Eglise and its more immediate aftermath. It has sought to understand modernist - neo-Thomist polarization as a theological species of Kuhnian incommensurability. Conceiving their intellectual commitments paradigmatically, it has been argued that Loisy and proponents of the dominant theology did not address the same problems, disagreed on what were admissable as appropriate solutions because they differed in their respective methods, and in what they allowed as data and how they regarded it. More fundamentally, they were committed to incommensurable notions of theology and science and constituted their interrelations divergently. Most fundamentally, one must invoke Kuhn's incommensurability of world views to elicit their polarization regarding religious knowledge and ontological conceptions. All of this attests that those positions were incommensurable, targets major points where they were incommensurable. A further intent is to account for something of how incommensurability occurred. In this, language was examined as a significantly operative factor. The "tensive" character of metaphor, its creation of meaning as a gestalt, informs the way problems are read, their proposed solutions expressed. Linguistic systems are apparently paradigm dependent (from the reverse point of view, paradigm constitutive). Even where proponents of rival paradigms share the same linguistic terms, they do not necessarily share the same meanings. Language "says" different things in different paradigms (and is not able to say others in consequence). The tensive character of metaphor has implications for how they are understood by those who share a paradigm and those who do not. The positive, neutral, and negative analogies created in the metaphoric process are in part paradigm dependent and surface in the process of their understanding. The tensive character of metaphor points to language as constitutive of reality, and it is here that a transition to world view can be made. Pepper has argued that there are several major types of "world hypotheses" which are grounded in root metaphors. The conception of the way the world is and what passes for knowledge of its elements and relationships is rooted linguistically. White carries this a step farther, to a precritical ground, in which dominant tropes prefigure the field of investigation. Language is "iconic" -- it evokes rather than mirrors. And the reality evoked by different tropes may be sufficiently discontinuous as to inhibit mutual understanding at very basic levels. The incommensurability detectable in correspondence versus coherence theories of truth at level of argument, for example, are rooted in linguistic deep structures. In White's terms, Billot's apprehension of "relative truth" as nonsense is grounded in a depth structure of metaphor. The linguistic aspect of incommensurability, then, permeates all levels of the theological paradigms in question, and arguably contributes importantly to an understanding of their interaction and polarization at all these levels.

At the outset, it was said that the intent here would not be to generate a general model of theological interaction, but rather to construct a framework which would be illuminative of a particular episode of such interaction. A few comments are in order on this.

Although Kuhn draws on theology as a discipline which in significant respects parallels the characteristics of normal science, the nature of its progress sets it with the humanities and not with the hard sciences. He targets three factors that are operative in this distinction: hegemony, problem insulation, and educational initiation. The absence of competing schools, the ability to engage problems because they appear soluble rather than socially pressing, and a textbook tradition instead of recourse to a field's classics are held to be characteristic of science properly so-called, and to influence the type of progress it manifests. For historically contingent reasons, however, neo-Thomism appears to approximate these conditions to a degree that renders application of Kuhn's framework fruitful.

A further factor invoked by Kuhn, however, is that of authority: if non-professional authority can arbitrate paradigm debates, then the outcomes of such may be revolutionary, but not scientifically revolutionary. It was observed earlier that historical contingency on this score might engage science -- that in the examples chosen by Kuhn extra-scientific authority plays a smaller role than it does currently. Arguably, the difference between science and theology here is less one of kind than one of degree. Nonetheless, this does point to a need to supplement the analysis presented here. This has proceeded on the level of paradigm content and linguistic expression. The notion of paradigm does make reference to groups of practitioners -- conceptual frameworks are proposed by individuals embedded in larger associational networks. And the authority variable raises questions regarding available avenues of influence and structures of social control.[20] The analysis largely brackets these structural dimensions, which would have to be taken into account in investigating the broader dynamics of interaction between Loisy and representatives of the dominant theology.[21] Any analysis of paradigms, then, whether in science or theology, could usefully investigate the structure of practitioner networks. Influence and control structures would be especially crucial for investigation of theologies, particularly in Roman Catholicism.

The three factors advanced by Kuhn, which neo-Thomism appears to approximate raise the issue of temporal limits. Is the conceptual framework constructed in the course of this study limited to the modernist crisis? I would suggest that it can transcend the period of this particular theological episode to shed light on Catholic theology right up through Vatican II. In Blessed Rage for Order, David Tracy has identified several theological models.[22] Without detailing those here, let me simply note his identification of the Vatican I model for theology with his "orthodox" model. Neo-Thomism would thus be encompassed by that, while modernism falls under the rubric of his model of "liberal" theology. While modernism as a movement was countered by authoritative intervention, the questions it raised did not simply disappear. Its central problem, that of historicity, endured, and eventually engaged a group of Catholic theologians who became identified with the movement known as the "nouvelle théologie". Gaining momentum in the 1940s it tried to deal with history through a creative renovation of neo-Thomism itself. Tracy places it under the model he terms "neo-orthodox". Despite its name, he argues that the model has closer ties with its "liberal" predecessor than with the "orthodox" conception of theology. "There seems every good reason to agree with the judgment of Wilhelm Pauck that neo-orthodoxy is not really a radically new alternative model for theology, but rather is a moment -- to be sure, a critical one -- in the larger liberal theological tradition."[23] This indicates that the theological hegemony maintained by neo-Thomism throughout the period renders that portion of the paradigm analysis ongoingly operative, while the potential for adapting the paradigm conceptualization of modernism as exponent of a liberal theology to the nouvelle théologie is a strong possibility. Although checked in 1950 by the encyclical Humani Generis, a number of the partisans of this attempt at theological renewal participated in Vatican II. The analysis of the Council's Constitution on Divine Revelation by Nicholas Lash[24] surfaces issues that engaged Loisy and his critics. Though the terms in which they are posed had themselves undergone development, and the resources for addressing them had likewise evolved, the contours of the opposing viewpoints are still discernible. Suitably adapted, this framework arguably has utility for interpreting 20th century Catholic theology.

Notes to Conclusion

[1]Stephen Toulmin, _Foresight and Understanding_, (New York: Harper and Row, 1963), pp. 94-95.

[2]Cf. Poulat, _La crise moderniste_, p. 112.

[3]Cf. in chapter 3: the introductory quote, and Billot's comment on "relative truth", respectively.

[4]APL, p. xxv.

[5]Ibid., pp. 36-37.

[6]Ibid., pp. 63-64.

[7]Bouvier, pp. 55, 59, 61, 65, 68-69 respectively.

[8]Le Camus, _Fausse exégèse, mauvaise théologie_, p. 65. By contrast, if the authenticity of the rendering of Jesus in the gospels is upheld, the position taken by "false exegesis" collapses. "The badly disguised reason that [Loisy] has closed his eyes to the evidence, is, as I have observed already, that if one of the apostles had the idea of Jesus presented by the fourth gospel, the entire system of the successive creation of dogma by the Christian consciousness collapses, and it is necessary to return to what Catholic theology commonly teaches: dogma is clarified from age to age, it is not made. This is hard for him who hoped to produce by his thesis a renewal of the life in the Church; but let him be consoled, the Church will not live any less, and theology will still be able to cope with the attacks of rationalism, even without recourse to the peace signed with it on the evolutionist terrain." pp. 64-65.

[9]Ibid., p. 65.

[10]Daly, p. 15.

[11]George Tyrrell, _Through Scylla and Charybdis_, (London: Longmans, Green, and Co., 1907), p. 153.

[12]Chapter 3: note 47.

[13]Daly, p. 18.

[14]See chapter 3, note 34.

[15]Recall Mazzella's _De Deo Creante_.

[16]Cf. Blondel's characterization of "extrinsicism" in "History and Dogma" in Dru and Trethowan, eds., The Letter on Apologetics and History and Dogma, London: Harvill Press, 1964.

[17]Jack Forstman, A Romantic Triangle: Schleiermacher and Early German Romanticism, (Missoula, Montana: Scholar's Press, 1977), p. 3. Cf. p. 14.

[18]Duel, p. 127.

[19]Daly, p. 55. Of Loisy's style in general, he writes: "Gallic clarity is there; but it is a deceptive clarity, achieved by a frequent shifting of perspective which robs us of a central point of reference." Ibid.

[20]Jurgen Habermas has pointed out that language functions as a medium of domination and social power. The ideological component in White's conceptualization, for example, undermines any notion of language as an innocent instrument in the hands of unbiased authors and interpreters. Linguistic concerns, then, are intimately linked to institutions of power and domination. For amplification of language as a potential "carrier" of domination see Georges De Schrijver, "Hermeneutics and Tradition" in Leonard Swidler and Piet Fransen, eds., Authority in the Church and the Schillebeeckx Case, New York: The Crossroad Publishing Company, 1982.

[21]In "Paradigm and Structure in Theological Communities" I did take these factors into account in analyzing the modernist movement.

[22]See Tracy, chapter 2 for description of these models.

[23]Ibid., p. 27. For substantive connections see Schoof, pp. 93-118.

[24]Change in Focus, Part I.

Bibliography

Aubert, Roger. "Aux origines de la réaction antimoderniste: deux documents inédits". Ephemerides theologiae lovanienses 37 (1961): 557-578.

_____ et al. The Church in a Secularized Society. New York: Paulist Press, 1978.

Aubry, J.-B. Essai sur la méthode des études ecclésiastiques en France 2 vols. Lille: Desclée, De Brouwer et Cie, s.d.

Barmann, Lawrence. Baron Friedrich von Hügel and the Modernist Crisis in England. Cambridge: Cambridge University Press, 1972.

Barnes, Barry. T.S. Kuhn and Social Science. New York: Columbia University Press, 1982.

Bedoyere, Michael de la. The Life of Baron von Hügel. London: J.M. Dent & Sons, Ltd., 1951.

Bellamy, J. La théologie catholique au XIXe siècle. Paris: Gabriel Beauchesne et Cie, 1904.

Berger, Peter and Luckmann, Thomas. The Social Construction of Reality. Garden City, New York: Anchor Books, 1967.

Berger, Peter. The Sacred Canopy. Garden City, New York: Anchor Books, 1969.

Bernstein, Richard. Beyond Objectivism and Relativism. Philadelphia: University of Pennsylvania, 1983.

Black, Max. Models and Metaphors. Ithaca, New York: Cornell University Press, 1962.

Blondel, Maurice. Lettres philosophiques. Paris: Aubier, 1961.

_____. Correspondance: Blondel-Wherlé 2 vols. Paris: Aubier Montaigne, 1969.

Booth, Wayne. A Rhetoric of Irony. Chicago: University of Chicago Press, 1974.

Bouvier, Pierre. L'exégèse de M. Loisy 2nd ed. Paris: Victor Retaux, 1904.

Brucker, Joseph, S.J. "Le condemnation du livre L'Evangile et l'Eglise". Etudes 94 (1903): 495-511.

Burke, Roland. "Loisy's Faith: Landshift in Catholic Thought". The Journal of Religion 60 (1980): 138-164.

Byrnes, Robert F. Antisemitism in Modern France. New York: Howard Fertig, 1969.

Chadwick, Owen. From Bossuet to Newman. Cambridge: Cambridge University Press, 1957.

Coward, Rosalind and Ellis, John. Language and Materialism. London: Routledge and Kegan Paul, 1977.

Daly, Gabriel, O.S.A. Transcendence and Immanence. Oxford: Clarendon Press, 1980.

Dawson, Joseph L. "Billot's Analysis of the Act of Faith". S.T.L. thesis, St. Mary's Seminary (Baltimore), 1951.

de Man, Paul. Allegories of Reading. New Haven: Yale University Press, 1979.

Detweiler, Robert. Story, Sign, and Self. Philadelphia: Fortress Press, 1978.

Dru, Alexander and Trethowan, Illtyd, eds. Maurice Blondel. The Letter on Apologetics and History and Dogma. London: Harvill, 1964.

Dudon, Paul. "Origines françaises du décret Lamentabili (1903-1907)". Bulletin de litterature ecclésiastique 32 (1931): 73-96.

Dulles, Avery, S.J. Models of Revelation. New York: Doubleday and Company, Inc., 1983.

The Encyclical of His Holiness Pope Pius X on the Doctrines of the Modernists. Translated by Thomas E. Judge. n.p.

L'Episcopat français: depuis le Concordat jusqu'à la Séparation (1802-1905). Paris: Librairie des Saints-Péres, 1907.

Fernessole, Pierre. Pie X. Paris: P. Lethielleux, 1953.

Feyerabend, Paul. Against Method. London: Verso, 1980.

Forstman, Jack. A Romantic Triangle: Schleiermacher and Early German Romanticism. Missoula, Montana: Scholar's Press, 1977.

Frye, Northrop. Anatomy of Criticism. Princeton: Princeton University Press, 1973.

Gager, John C. Kingdom and Community: The Social World of Early Christianity. Englewood Cliffs, New Jersey: Prentice-Hall, Inc., 1975.

Gaigalas, Vytas V. Ernest Renan and His French Catholic Critics. North Quincy, Mass.: The Christopher Publishing House, 1972.

Gayraud, Hippolyte. Questions du jour. Paris: Bloud et Barrel, libraires-éditeurs, 1897.

_____. "L'Evangile et l'Eglise". L'Univers, 31 Dec. 1902; 2, 4, 9 and 10 Jan. 1903.

_____. L'Univers, 24 Oct.; 16 and 30 Nov.; 1, 2, 28 Dec. 1903

_____. "L'Interprétation du loisysme". Revue du clergé français XXXVII (1903): 195-198.

Gerhart, Mary and Russell, Allen. Metaphoric Process. Fort Worth: Texas Christian University Press, 1984.

Gutting, Gary, ed. Paradigms and Revolutions. Notre Dame: University of Notre Dame Press, 1980.

Harnack, Adolf von. What is Christianity? Translated by Thomas B. Saunders. New York: Harper and Row, Publishers, 1957.

Hartley, Thomas. Thomism During the Modernist Era. Toronto: University of St. Michael's College, 1971.

Hawkes, Terence. Structuralism and Semiotics. Berkeley: University of California Press, 1977.

Heaney, John. The Modernist Crisis: von Hügel. Washington: Corpus Books, 1968.

Hennesey, James, S.J. American Catholics. New York: Oxford University Press, 1981.

Hennings, F.W.J. The Life and Times of Emile Zola. New York: Charles Scribner's Sons, 1977.

Hocedez, Edgar, S.J. Histoire de la théologie au XIXe siècle 3 vols. Paris: Desclée de Brouwer, 1947-1952.

Houtin, Albert. La Question biblique au XXe siècle. Paris: Librairie E. Nourry, 1906.

Hügel, Friedrich von. "Loisy". The Encyclopedia Britannica 11th ed., vol. 16, New York: Encyclopedia Britannica, Inc., 1911.

Iggers, Georg G. The German Conception of History. Middletown, Conn.: Wesleyan University Press, 1983.

Johnson, Mark, ed. Philosophical Perspectives on Metaphor. Minneapolis: University of Minnesota Press, 1981.

Kierkegaard, Soren. The Concept of Irony. Translated by Lee M. Capel. Bloomington: Indiana University Press, 1968.

Krige, John. Science, Revolution and Discontinuity. New Jersey: Humanities Press, 1980.

Kuhn, Thomas S. The Structure of Scientific Revolutions. Chicago: University of Chicago Press, 1962. 2nd edition 1970.

_____. The Essential Tension. Chicago: University of Chicago Press, 1977.

La Capra, Dominick. Rethinking Intellectual History: Texts, Context, Language. Ithaca: Cornell University Press, 1983.

Lakatos, Imre and Musgrave, Alan, eds. Criticism and the Growth of Knowledge. Cambridge: Cambridge University Press, 1970.

Lakoff, George and Johnson, Mark. Metaphors We Live By. Chicago: University of Chicago Press, 1970.

Lash, Nicholas. Change in Focus. London: Sheed and Ward, 1973.

_____. Newman on Development. Shepherdstown, West Virginia: Patmos Press, 1975.

Lebreton, Jules. Le Père Léonce de Grandmaison. Paris: Gabriel Beauchesne et ses fils, 1932.

Le Camus, Emile-Paul. Lettre de Monseigneur l'Evêque de la Rochelle et Saintes réglant la réorganisation des études ecclésiastiques dans son grand séminaire de la Rochelle. La Rochelle: Imprimerie Rochelaise, 1901.

_____. Lettre sur la formation ecclésiastique de ses séminaristes. Paris: H. Oudin, éditeur, 1902.

_____. Vraie et fausse exégèse. Paris: Librairie H. Oudin, 1903.

_____. Fausse exégèse, mauvaise théologie. Paris: Librairie H. Oudin, 1904.

Lecanuet, Edouard. Les signes avant-coureurs de la séparation. Paris: Félix Alcan, 1930.

Lilley, A. Leslie. Modernism: A Record and Review. New York: Charles Scribner's Sons, 1908.

Loisy, Alfred [A. Firmin]. "Le développement chrétien d'apres le cardinal Newman". Revue du clergé français XVII (1898): 5-20.

_____ [A. Firmin]. "La théorie individualiste de la religion". Revue du clergé français XVII (1899): 202-215.

_____ [A. Firmin]. "La définition de la religion". Revue du clergé français XVIII (1899): 193-209.

_____ [A. Firmin]. "L'idée de la révélation". Revue du clergé français XXI (1900): 250-271.

_____ [A. Firmin]. "Les preuves et l'économie de la révélation". Revue du clergé français XXII (1900): 126-153.

_____ [A. Firmin]. "La religion d'Israël". Revue du clergé français XXIV (1900): 337-363.

_____. L'Evangile et l'Eglise 1902. ET: The Gospel and the Church. Translated by Christopher Home. Philadelphia: Fortress Press, 1976.

_____. Etudes evangéliques. Paris: Alphonse Picard et fils, éditeurs, 1902.

_____. Autour d'un petit livre. Paris: Alphonse Picard et fils, éditeurs, 1903.

_____. Le Quatrième évangile. Paris: Alphonse Picard et fils, éditeurs, 1903.

_____. Simples réflexions sur le décret du saint-office "Lamentabili sane exitu" et sur l'encyclique "Pascendi dominici gregis". 2nd ed. Ceffonds: chez l'auteur, 1908.

_____. Choses passées 1913. ET: My Duel with the Vatican. Translated by Richard W. Boynton. New York: Greenwood Press, Publishers, 1968.

_____. Mémoires pour servir à l'histoire religieuse de notre temps 3 vols. Paris: Emile Nourry, éditeur, 1930-1931.

175

Lonergan, Bernard. Method in Theology. New York: Herder and Herder, 1972.

_____. A Second Collection. Philadelphia: The Westminster Press, 1974.

Loome, Thomas. Liberal Catholicism, Reform Catholicism, Modernism. Mainz: Matthias-Grünwald-Verlag, 1979.

Mandelbaum, Maurice. History, Man, & Reason. Baltimore: The Johns Hopkins University Press, 1977.

Mc Avoy, Thomas, C.S.C. The Great Crisis in American Catholic History, 1895-1900. Chicago: Henry Regnery Company, 1957.

Mc Cool, Gerald, S.J. Catholic Thought in the Nineteenth Century. New York: The Seabury Press, 1977.

Mc Knight, Edgar. Meaning in Texts. Philadelphia: Fortress Press, 1978.

Miall, David S., ed. Metaphor: Problems and Perspectives. New Jersey: Humanities Press, 1982.

Mignot, E.I. Lettres sur les études ecclésiastiques. Paris: Librairie Victor Lecoffre, 1908.

Moran, Valentine, S.J. "Loisy's Theological Development". Theological Studies 40 (1979): 411-452.

Morris, Wesley. Friday's Footprint. Columbus: Ohio State University Press, 1979.

Mulkay, Michael. Science and the Sociology of Knowledge. London: George Allen and Unwin, 1979.

Newton-Smith, W.H. The Rationality of Science. London: RKP, 1981.

O'Dea, Thomas. The Catholic Crisis. Boston: Beacon Press, 1968.

Ortony, Andrew, ed. Metaphor and Thought. Cambridge: Cambridge University Press, 1979.

Patte, Daniel. What is Structural Exegesis? Philadelphia: Fortress Press, 1976.

Pepper, Stephen. World Hypotheses. Berkeley: University of California Press, 1970.

Perrier, Joseph. The Revival of Scholastic Theology in the Nineteenth Century. New York: Columbia University Press, 1909.

Petre, Maude. Alfred Loisy, His Religious Significance. Cambridge: Cambridge University Press, 1944.

Phillips, Derek L. Wittgenstein and Scientific Knowledge. London: The Macmillan Press, 1977.

Polayni, Michael. The Tacit Dimension. Garden City, New York: Anchor Books, 1967.

Poulat, Emile, ed. Alfred Loisy, sa vie son oeuvre. Paris: Editions du centre national de la recherche scientifique, 1960.

_____. Histoire, dogme et critique dans la crise moderniste. Tournai: Casterman, 1979.

Provencher, Normand, O.M.I. "The Origin and Development of Loisy's Modernism". Science et Esprit XXXII (1980): 316-330.

Ricoeur, Paul. "From Existentialism to a Phenomenology of Language". Philosophy Today 17 (1973): 88-97.

_____. "Creativity in Language" Philosophy Today 17 (1973): 97-111.

_____. Interpretation Theory. Fort Worth: Texas Christian University Press, 1976.

_____. The Rule of Metaphor. Translated by Robert Czerny et al. Toronto: University of Toronto Press, 1979.

Ritzer, George. Sociology: A Multiple Paradigm Science. Boston: Allyn and Bacon, Inc., 1980.

Rome and the Study of Scripture. St. Meinrad, Indiana: Abbey Press, 1964.

Sabatier, A. The Vitality of Christian Dogmas. Translated by Mrs. E. Christen. London: Adam and Charles Black, 1898.

Sabatier, Paul. Modernism. London: T. Fischer Unwin, 1908.

Sanks, T. Howland. Authority in the Church: A Study in Changing Paradigms. Missoula, Montana: Scholar's Press, 1974.

Scheffler, Israel. Science and Subjectivity 2nd ed. Indianapolis: Hackett Publishing Company, 1982.

Schillebeeckx, Edward, O.P. The Understanding of Faith. London: Sheed and Ward, 1974.

Schoof, T. Mark, O.P. A Survey of Catholic Theology, 1800-1970. Translated by N.D. Smith. New York: Paulist Newman Press, 1970.

Schwartz, Barry. Vertical Classification. Chicago: University of Chicago Press, 1981.

Scott, Bernard. "Adolf von Harnack and Alfred Loisy: A Debate on the Historical Methodology of Christian Origins". Ph.D. dissertation, Vanderbilt University, 1971.

Silkstone, Thomas. Religion, Symbolism and Meaning. Oxford: Cassirer, 1968.

Suppe, Frederick. The Structure of Scientific Theories. 2nd ed. Urbana: University of Illinois Press, 1979.

Swidler, Leonard and Fransen, Piet, eds. Authority in the Church and the Schillebeeckx Case. New York: Crossroads Publishing Company, 1982.

Talar, Charles J.T. "Paradigm and Structure in Theological Communities: A Sociological Reading of the Modernist Crisis". Ph.D. dissertation, Catholic University of America, 1979.

Toulmin, Stephen. Foresight and Understanding. New York: Harper and Row, 1963.

_____. Human Understanding. Princeton: Princeton University Press, 1972.

_____ and Goodfield, June. The Discovery of Time. Chicago: University of Chicago Press, 1982.

Tracy, David. Blessed Rage for Order. New York: The Seabury Press, 1975.

Turvasi, Francesco. The Condemnation of Alfred Loisy and the Historical Method. Roma: Edizioni di Storia e Litteratura, 1979.

Tyrrell, George. Through Scylla and Charybdis. London: Longmans, Green, and Co., 1907.

_____. Medievalism. New York: Longmans, Green & Co., 1909.

Van Riet, Georges. Thomistic Epistemology 2 vols. Translated by Gabriel Franks, O.S.B. St. Louis: B. Herder Book Co., 1963-1965.

178

Vidler, Alec. The Modernist Movement in the Roman Church. Cambridge: Cambridge University Press, 1934.

_____. 20th Century Defenders of the Faith. London: SCM Press, Ltd., 1965.

_____. A Variety of Catholic Modernists. Cambridge: Cambridge University Press, 1970.

Walgrave, J.-H., O.P. Newman the Theologian. Translated by A.V. Littledale. New York: Sheed and Ward, 1960.

Ward, Maisie. Insurrection verses Resurrection. New York: Sheed & Ward, 1937.

Wernz, William J. The 'Modernist' Writings of Alfred Loisy: An Analysis". Ph.D. dissertation, University of Iowa, 1971.

_____. "Loisy's 'Modernist' Writings". The Downside Review 92 (1974): 25-45.

White, Hayden, ed. The Uses of History. Detroit: Wayne State University Press, 1968.

_____. Metahistory. Baltimore: The Johns Hopkins University Press, 1973.

_____. Tropics of Discourse. Baltimore: The Johns Hopkins University Press, 1978.

Williams, W.J. Newman, Pascal, Loisy and the Catholic Church. London: Francis Griffiths, 1906.

Yzermans, Vincent A., ed. All Things in Christ: Encyclicals and Selected Documents of Saint Pius X. Westminster, Maryland: The Newman Press, 1954.

L'Evangile et l'Eglise, 3, 4, 6, 8, 45, 51, 53, 59, 60, 72, 106,
  107, 112, 113, 126, 128, 130, 164, 165
L'exégèse de M. Loisy, 6, 63

faith, 22, 40n., 49, 50, 57, 58, 60, 75-76, 104, 105, 130,
  159-160
  and history, 52, 128-129, 131-132, 136, 138, 140-141, 160
  and reason, 26-27, 28, 29, 159
Fausse exégèse, mauvaise théologie, 6, 59, 62, 136
Feyerabend, Paul, 35, 36, 43n.
Fonsegrive, George, 5, 7
Forstman, Jack, 164
Frye, Northrop, 95, 99, 117n.

Gayraud, Hyppolite, 4, 5, 13n., 23, 40n., 53-54, 57, 59, 63,
  82n., 83n., 99, 113, 114, 123n., 133, 135, 160
      criticism of L'Evangile et l'Eglise, 54-56
      criticism of Autour d'un petit livre, 60-62
de Grandmaison, Léonce, 4

Habermas, Jurgen, 169
von Harnack, Adolf, 3, 4, 51, 53, 54, 65, 72, 102-103, 107,
  108-109, 113, 123n., 124n., 163, 164
Hartley, Thomas, 39n.
historicism, 104-108, 134, 140, 142, 143
Hogan, Jean-Baptiste, 144-145
Houtin, Albert, 5, 107
von Hügel, Friedrich, 7, 8, 14n., 33, 34, 47, 59, 81n.
Humani Generis, 167

Icard, Henri, 164
ideology, 95-97, 100, 106, 117-118n., 162
Iggers, Georg, 121
incommensurability, 9, 10, 20, 33-37, 43n., 44n., 45, 66-67,
  76-77, 91-92, 98, 112-115, 118n., 125, 133, 135, 137, 142, 143,
  146, 155-156, 165, 166
Institut catholique (Paris), 1, 2, 3, 46, 164
                        (Toulouse), 53
irony, 45, 96, 101, 107-115, 123n., 164-165

Kauffman, Christopher, 152n.
Kierkegaard, Soren, 115
Kleutgen, Joseph, 28
Kuhn, Thomas, 9, 17-21, 24-28, 32, 33-37, 65, 67, 88n., 91, 92,
  118n., 146, 166

Laberthonnière, Lucien, 32
La Capra, Dominick, 123n.
Lagrange, Marie-Joseph, 156
Lamentabili Sane Exitu, 6, 15n., 126, 137-138, 139, 152n., 155
Lash, Nicholas, 47, 167

Le Camus, Emile—Paul, 4, 5, 6, 59, 66, 67, 69-70, 83n., 99, 113,
  135, 136, 141, 151n., 157-158, 159, 160, 162, 168n.
    criticism of L'Evangile et l'Eglise, 57-58
    criticism of Autour d'un petit livre, 62-63
Le Roy, Edouard, 150n.
Letourneau, George, 6, 8, 14n., 63
Loisy, Alfred
  early career, 1-3
  livre inédit, 46, 51, 53
  "Firmin" articles of, 3, 12n., 45, 46-51, 59, 107, 108, 126, 129
  characterization of L'Evangile et l'Eglise, 106, 107
  on institution of the sacraments, 126-129, 131-132, 142, 158
  reaction to Lamentabili, 15n., 137
  reaction to Pascendi, 7
  criticism of scholasticism, 31
  "loisysme", 6
Lonergan, Bernard, 17, 29, 33, 34, 36

Maignen, Charles, 4, 5, 12n.
de Man, Paul, 119-120n.
Mandelbaum, Maurice, 104
Mannheim, Karl, 96
Marlé, René, 12n.
Masterman, Margaret, 37, 41n., 46
Mazzella, Camillo, 101
McCool, Gerald, 22, 26, 39n.
metaphor, 8, 33, 35, 37, 49, 54, 55, 57, 58, 60, 62, 64-65, 72,
  75, 76, 101, 102, 103, 107, 108, 155, 160-163, 165, 166
    metaphorical networks, 9, 71-73, 133, 143, 155, 157, 161, 163
    root metaphors, 9, 65, 71, 73, 76, 91, 101, 155, 160
    and polysemy, 67-70
Mignot, Eudoxe-Irénéé, 4, 7, 32, 43n., 59, 81n.
modernism, 6, 7-8, 26, 28, 36, 42n., 74, 112, 138-139, 147-148,
  162, 167
    as theological paradigm, 30-33
Moran, Valentine, 12n.
Morris, Wesley, 116n.
Mulkay, Michael, 38n.

neo-Thomism, 21-25, 31, 33, 34, 36, 39n., 53-54, 66, 101-102,
  107, 111, 112, 119n., 142, 146, 156, 159, 161, 162-163, 166, 167
    relation to other disciplines, 23-24, 27-28
    as dominant theological paradigm, 26-30
Newman, John Henry, 45, 47, 50, 58, 74, 78n., 110, 111, 112, 136
nouvelle théologie, 167

oath against modernism, 155
O'Dea, Thomas, 145

paradigm, 17, 18-20, 26-28, 31-32, 65-66, 119n., 137, 142, 144,
  161, 165

Vatican II, 167
La Vérité française, 4, 12n.
Vidler, Alec, 14n.
Vigouroux, Fulcran, 2, 11n., 14n.
Vollot, Abbé, 31
Vraie et fausse exégèse, 4, 56

Wehrlé, Joannès, 126
Wernz, William J., 3, 50, 66, 89n., 121-122n., 149-150n.
White, Hayden, 9, 76, 77, 99, 113, 115, 122n., 161, 162, 165, 166
  tropological analysis of historical narrative, 91-92, 94-98
  tropological analysis of neo-Thomism, 98-102
  tropological analysis of Loisy's work, 102-112
Whorf, Benjamin, 93
world view, 8, 9, 17, 29, 33, 34, 66, 74, 76, 142, 165